Rural Entrepreneurship
Growth and Potentials

M. SOUNDARAPANDIAN

KANISHKA PUBLISHERS, DISTRIBUTORS
NEW DELHI-110 002

Preface

The development of an economy depends much upon persons who are motivated to achieve something tangible by shouldering responsibilities and are willing to take risk. These persons are known as entrepreneurs. Developed nations are flooded with the success stories of entrepreneurs. The need for developing entrepreneurial skills was also felt by the third world countries engaged in fuller utilisation of resources—human and natural—abundantly available in these countries. In India, after implementation of New Economic Policy, the rural industries are facing the stiff competition in marketing their products. It is the right time to analyse the factors influencing the sustainable rural entrepreneurship in India.

The objective of this book is to provide a picture about the growth and potentials of rural entrepreneurship in India. After implementation of economic reforms in India and the impact of the policies and programmes on small scale industries have been analysed in detail in this book. A few case studies on rural entrepreneurship, institutional support, role of cooperatives and voluntary organisations are also discussed in first four chapters. The feasibility on entrepreneurial promotion of selected rural industries viz., bakery industry, poultry industry, handmade paper industry and village oil industry, have also described in the last part of this book. The book is very useful to the researchers and students studying Rural Developments, Rural Industrialisation, Rural Economics etc.

I am thankful to the researchers Mr. K. Selva Prakash, Mr. V. Muthiah, Mr. B. Gunasekaran, Mr. K. Alagarsamy for their help in completing the field work for the studies related to rural entrepreneurship in Dindigul District of Tamilnadu.

I am grateful to Dr. N. Thillainayagam, Professor and Head, Department of Rural Industries and Management, Gandhigram Rural Institute, Gandhigram, for his encouragement and support. The support of my wife Mrs. S. Indhumathy and my children Diwakaran and Vidya, helped me to complete this work. My typist, Mrs. B. Dhanalakshmi have always been cooperative and neat in their execution of work. Finally, my sincere thanks to the Kanishka Publishers, Distributors, for their acceptance in publishing the book.

M. Soundarapandian

1

Rural Entrepreneurship Growth and Potentials

The labour force in India is increasing at 2.5 per cent per annum but employment is increasing only by 2.2 per cent per annum. Agriculture is not able to provide gainful employment to the surplus rural labour. Development planners are, therefore, turning towards non-farm employment generation. Employment potential of cottage and rural small industries, size and composition of family and hired labour, differential contribution of men and women to the household employment among the workers, wage-rates and intensity of employment are some of critical issues that need to be analysed to comprehend the employment and income aspects of rural industries.

In the preparation of every Five Year Plan, and formulation of industrial policy, the Government has repeatedly expressed that employment and income generation for the rural poor as its policy objective and underlined the need to promote the rural, small and labour intensive industry. Approach paper to the Eighth Five Year Plan 1990-95 observed that the numerous State interventions reservations, fiscal discrimination favouring small industry, subsidies, promotional measures during the last three decades have been half-hearted and ineffective.

Many studies in South India found that the cost of

employment generation has been formed to be low in brick manufacturing, handloom industry, grain processing and oil-seed processing. Rural service enterprises such as bicycle repairing, agricultural implements' servicing, tailoring, type cart operation for local transport were formed to enjoy more employment potential. With minimum investment outlays, they are able to generate productive, gainful and sustaining work opportunities which have helped in reducing the incidence of poverty among rural poor. A study has been conducted in Dindigul district of Tamilnadu analyse the rural entrepreneurship growth and potentials of rural industries.

The specific objectives of the study are:

(i) To assess the employment and income generation of the rural industries in Dindigul district;
(ii) to examine the availability and utilisation of local raw materials and skills and the market potentials for the rural entrepreneurship development in Tamilnadu;
(iii) to review the problems faced by the rural entrepreneurs in promoting the rural industries; and
(iv) to suggest the concrete measures for raising the income and employment potentials of rural entrepreneurs.

Primary data as well as secondary data are used for the present study. Secondary data are collected from the office records of Khadi and Village Industries Commission, District Industries Centre, National Small Industries Corporation and various books and journals.

Dindigul district has been purposively selected for the present study. Four sample blocks were selected on the basis of the criteria of large number of industries covering blocks. The sample blocks are: Attur, Batalagundu, Dindigul and, Nillakottai.

After selecting the study blocks, the respondents are selected on the basis of stratified random sampling technique. The sample of 10 entrepreneurs in each category of the rural industries was selected in these four blocks. A total of 70 sample entrepreneurs were interviewed with a pretested questionnaire.

Studies on Rural Entrepreneurship

The review of past studies relating to the development of rural industries are presented in the second chapter. The chapter is divided into three sections. The first section deals with the rural industrialisation—problems and prospects in India. The studies on small, cottage and village industries are presented in the second section. The last section explains the income and employment potential of rural industries in India.

Harisingh (1968) defined the concept "Rural Industrialisation" as idea behind rural industrialisation was to spread the industries to small urban centres and rural areas. It was envisaged that the small assembly units in urban centres might be linked with the units in rural areas manufacturing parts and components of those units. On the other hand, the small units and artisans in rural areas might have facility for service in workshops set up in small towns. At later stage, this idea was modified and the stress was laid on diversification as well as balanced rural economy. This idea later came to be known as 'Cooperative Agro Based Economy'. Lately, the idea of rural industrialisation has been expanded to include full scale development of modern mechanised small scale and medium industries.

Krishangarbhas block of Alwar district of Rajasthan was adopted by Rajasthan Consultancy Organisation (RAJCON) in 1984 (Sharma, 1994). It is an organisation promoted by All India Financial Institutions, state agencies and banks to act as a catalyst for industrial development in Rajasthan state and to provide consultancy support to tiny and small scale industries. A case study concluded that in terms of physical achievement, there is no doubt that with a minimum investment, the programme has been able to generate self-employment to a large number of people. But in many cases, ventures ran into crisis and a few of them were closed also. To make them self-sustaining in the long-run without any external intervention is a challenge before RAJCON.

A study was conducted in Pollachi Taluk of Coimbatore district in order to analyse the investment and, employment patterns in the coir industry (Isabella Rani and Krishnamoorthy, 1993). It reveals that the labour share to the total cost accounted for 10.39 per cent. Further from the gross income and net income, it can be seen that the curling units enjoy more profit than the fibre units which implies that the vertical integration is more profitable than with a single operation unit. The results indicate the potential for increasing the turnover by using more and more of raw materials namely, coconut husks. Similarly there exists potentiality for increasing the labour and wage-rate. The total labour force for different units work out to 14.32 labour days per unit per day in the case of defibering units without conveyers, 7.3 labour days per units in the case of defibering units with conveyers and 17.35 labour days per unit in the case of curling units. The units also provide employment for both men and women.

The output can be increased by increasing labour inputs indicating a positive relationship between value added per worker and output of the units. There is a larger scope for providing more effective employment in terms of income to those engaged in rural industries (Jagadish Prasad and Rajendra Prasad, 1984).

Papalo (1982) derived that in pottery, mat-making, bed-making, lampshade-making, wiremeshing, handloom and food products-making, an increase in capital is associated with an increase in output as well as in employment. In carpentry, blacksmith, and leather products-making, an increase in capital lead to an increase in output.

A study conducted by Papalo (1983) in the Giri Institute of Development Studies, Lucknow on rural industries showed that the increase in employment is not associated with the increase in value added per worker in most of the industries. In fact, a large number of workers entering these industries will mean the increase in the underemployment and decline in income generation per worker in the given technological market and organisation situation.

The findings of the study show how macro economic policies after even the micro industrial enterprises in rural areas. Some industries and sectors grew after the policy change while others succumbed to the vicissitudes of open economic policy but some remained unaffected. The trade liberalisation has increased the competition from foreign products and there is sufficient evidence to believe that it has been detrimental to certain industries. Some sectors virtually collapsed due to competition from foreign countries (Ebel Wickramamayake, 1994).

An empirical study was conducted, based on the primary data, from a sample of 208 small scale chemical units in Gujarat for the year 1986 through 1990. The findings suggest no unique relationship among structure, conduct and performance. However, each of middle age, partnership form of organisation and location in Baroda/Ahmedabad district has, in general, proved a beneficial structural feature from the point of view of performance (G.S. Gupta and A.K.P. Rathi, 1996).

Sugar industry, which is the second largest among the processing industries, faces one of the major handicaps in terms of fluctuating area and production of sugarcane from time to time. Such fluctuations have often resulted in a kind of phenomenon of aggregate supply of sugarcane exceeding the aggregate demand in one year and falling short of demand in the following year. Such an uncertain state of affairs is neither conducive to the sound growth of sugar industry nor to the prosperity of cane growers (D.K. Grover and S.S. Grewal, 1992).

Giriappa (1996) has analysed the employment as well as income potential from fish as well as cashew, apple processing. He also mentioned that India is among the five major producers of at least a dozen agricultural commodities in the world. These include sugar, tea, tobacco, spices, fruits and vegetables, cotton, jute, milk and milk products, rice and wheat. Yet, it's contribution to the international trade in farm products is less than 0.5 per cent. Even in domestic market, the agro-processing is not a strong economic activity. It is estimated that 5 per cent increase in the processing of agricultural commodities can help in generating 65 million jobs for the rural people. This apart, branded farm products can bring more value to the economy.

A study on bee-keeping found that bee-keeping augments rural income through honey production and enriches agro-horticultural crops by pollination services. Income by way of increased crop-yield due to bee pollination is much higher than the value of honey. Bee-keeping as a rural non-traditional industry had been taken up by the KVIC since 1954. The new bee-keeping industry has generated employment and subsidiary income to bee-keepers and protected the beneficiary insects from destruction by honey hunters. It is an ideal activity for development as subsidiary occupation in apiculture providing supplementary income to a large number of rural, hilly and tribal population (Karnel Taori and Pulak Chakravarthy, 1994).

The study of Hina Sidhu (1995) shows that in Mehsana the small scale industries (SSIs) are playing an important role in employment generation. The employment per SSI unit has increased over the years which is contrary to the trend at national level. Therefore, while making any change in the industrial policy, the Government should give adequate weight to the fact that the SSIs play an important role in employment generation and decentralisation of industries in the country. As such the items produced by the small and cottage industries in the rural and backward areas should be reserved for the SSI sector and adequate arrangements should be made for quality checks of raw materials and products. The Government should also ensure the sale of certain items through competition sales agencies in the urban areas.

A study was conducted to analyse the role of incentives in the growth of small scale industries in terms of the number of units, fixed capital and employment in Chittor district of Andhra Pradesh. The results show that the subsidy schemes in the district have produced a positive effect on the growth of small scale units, fixed capital and employment in small scale units. But the benefits of growth failed to spread evenly among the blocks and among the entrepreneurs. It is time to provide the 15 per cent central subsidy to all blocks and development of infrastructure in the less developed blocks to diversify the industrial activity (L. Reddeppa and K. Manidaraswarmy, 1992).

Despite that relatively their direct labour absorbing impact has been small, in countries, with much unemployment or under-employment and with small capacity to produce and limited foreign exchange to import capital goods, the development and use of intermediate technology will permit the absorption of more labour through advanced methods, while still permitting substantial increase in productivity (Carl Riskin, 1980).

According to Udaya Baskara Reddy (1988) maximum number of units in urban areas employ 2-4 persons (54.3%), which signifies that household industries cannot absorb more number of persons per unit. The average number of persons per unit is only 1.7 and 2.2 for rural and urban areas respectively and the combined average per unit is 1.8.

Jaiwal (1982), in his article, narrated that the cost of employment in rural industries is very low as compared to the cost of employment in large and small industries. While Rs. one lakh to Rs. 1.5 lakh is required for employing one person under large scale industry and about Rs. 15,000 to Rs. 50,000 in small scale industry, only Rs. 500 to Rs. 5,000 is required under village industries.

The study was conducted in North Arcot district in different types of rural industries which revealed that these industries require low capital investment with a maximum of Rs. 1,243 in stone carving and a minimum of Rs. 118 in lime-making (Ramasamy and Chandrasekaran, 1984).

Grover and Dak (1986) carried out their study in three districts of Haryana and concluded that in spite of various efforts for the promotion of rural industries, they have not made satisfactory progress, because rural industries were associated with caste structure and traditional techniques. Personal as well as institutional factors have tended to affect the technology system and modernisation of rural industries.

The results of the study provided micro level evidences in support of using dairy enterprise as a measure tool for anti-poverty programme. The additional productive employment generated through the activity of dairying among the beneficiaries was 166, 169 and 171 man days for small and marginal farmers and the landless respectively, accounting for 43.45 to 53.27 per cent more labour employment, compared to the non-beneficiaries. The study further revealed that the adoption of dairy enterprise raised the income levels of the beneficiaries by Rs. 2,527, Rs. 2,606 and Rs. 2,210 for small and marginal farmers and the landless respectively, which were higher by 35 to 40 per cent than the non-beneficiary households. However, the benefits seemed to attract the upper castes rather than the tribals who did not respond well to the dairy schemes (H.N. Atiludhi, 1995).

The study found that rural industry was the principal source of employment for all categories of workers, irrespective of the size of landholdings and sex. Even during the peak agricultural season, rural industry provided as much as 54 per cent of the household employment for the worker families. However, the magnitude of seasonal variation in rural industry employment has been lesser among male workers than among female workers. Rural industry provided 84 per cent of the family income in cottage industries and 96 per cent in rural small industry entrepreneurs. The proportion of family wage incomes in total household income is among the cottage industry entrepreneurs. Among the hired worker households, cottage industry wage income has accounted for over 64 per cent wage income of families. Rural industry incomes have had a positive effect in reducing the magnitude of income inequality among entrepreneurs as well as worker households (P. Purushotham and J.M. Rao, 1993).

Choudhary (1995) conducted a study in Madhya Pradesh to find out the role of crop and dairy enterprises in income generation and sustainable rural employment and labour utilisation. The study found that dairy enterprise generates better economic returning in farming situations of agriculture combined with dairy enterprise specially with large dairy herd size due to minimum cost of milk producing, using surplus farm family human labour and by-product. The study further indicates that male labour power is mainly responsible for the viability of the dairy enterprise. The percentage of female labour engaged in both the categories is more than that of male labour.

A study indicates that annual earnings of non-agricultural labourers were higher than those of agricultural labourers though the scope for migration of rural agricultural labourers was limited due to certain obligation to their employees (big farmers) and other factors linked with them (V.N. Singh and A.M. Jaulkar, 1993).

Over time the coir industry has evclved as the second most important source of labour absorption in Kerala. These industries have been predominantly characterised by low productivity, traditional technologies, low level of skills and low wage earnings. The situation has been further aggravated in recent years in the state due to decline in the world demand for coir and its products and shortage of raw materials besides competition with mechanised brown fibre processing in the neighbouring states. Thus, coir industries in the eighties presented a rather dramatic instance of adverse market conditions, stagnant productivity, rise in wages and reduced output and employment (T.M. Thomas Isac. *et al.*, 1992).

Another study analyses the impact of livestock on the income of 72 landless agricultural labour households selected from 12 villages in two zones of Karaikal region of Pondicherry. It revealed that in the total annual household income of Rs. 6,716 and Rs. 7,120 in Zone I and Zone II respectively, the contribution of livestock was 7.74 per cent and 10.50 per cent. The regression analysis revealed that the number of days of employment and investment on livestock had significant impact on the household income. The results of the study reinforces the rationale of including livestock development as an integral part of our poverty alleviation and employment generation programmes (P. Mohamed Dasir *et al.*, 1995).

Rajagopal (1995) has succeeded in substantiating as to how the special programmes failed in generating income to the beneficiaries due to lack of proper marketing management. One noteworthy observation is that processing of various agricultural products within the purview of rural areas itself is a good resource for income generation for rural poor and the District Supply and Marketing Societies (DSMS) should properly be organised to solve the practical problems in rural business activities.

On an average, two persons per family worked in the dairy enterprise. The average number of days they worked in dairying was 70 and 90 in the case of male and female adults respectively during the year. The total income earned by the dairy farmers during the reference year came to Rs. 1,63,015 or Rs. 8,151 per dairy farmer or about Rs. 679 per month. Further, if computed wages of family labour are also excluded from the total expenditure, then the sample farmers earned a large surplus. The study shows that the dairy enterprise is profitable (R.D. Khodaskar, 1995).

Rajkishor Meher (1995) observed that due to lack of proper organisational efforts, this traditional cottage industry of Orissa is losing its attractive occupational status notwithstanding the high demand potential of tie and dye handloom fabrics among a large section of affluent consumers in the country and abroad. Owing to unorganised nature of the industry the weavers in general earn a very preparious living from this age-old caste based occupation. Although the nature of work requires the involvement of all the adult members and children of household irrespective of age and sex and one loom in general provides full time employment to 2.01 persons an average the amount of average income earned by a weaver household is sometimes lower than an unskilled, daily wage earner.

A case study of employment potential in brick kilns reveals that about 90 per cent are employed for a period of 120 to 150 man days during a year. The study demonstrates that the rural industry has a great promise in alleviating the rural unemployment problem (Pandey and Shantisarpur, 1984).

In Madhya Pradesh, the employment growth in rural industries has increased and there has been a marginal shift of working force from agriculture to rural industries and other occupation (A.C. Minocho, 1983).

In the case of household industries conflict between employment and technology did not arise as much as it did in the case of non-household industries. In fact the practice of adopting increasingly capital intensive production function either consciously for prestige reasons or unconsciously as a consequence of direct Government controls, proved detrimental to the growth process under condition of an unlimited supply of labour (R.R. Doshi, 1984).

Employment generation in India by Khadi and Village Industries (KVI) is significant and majority of the labour force is employed in this sector. The employment composition of KVIC changed significantly in KVIs rose from 9.65 lakh persons in 1956 to 37.69 lakh persons in 1985. The employment in favour of village industries, the share of Khadi sector in the total KVIs employment has declined from 68 per cent in 1956 to 34 per cent by 1985 (Rama and S. Ramakrishana, 1987).

Chikara (1989) found that a considerable level of employment was generated and the highest increase was observed in processing of cereals and pulses followed by furniture, lime-stone, Khadi industry, carpentry, blacksmithy and cottage match box. This reflects that the Khadi and Village Industries Commission (KVIC) has great potential for generating through financing rural cottage industries.

Based on the above review of the past studies presented in this section, the present study had been conducted in the Dindigul district of Tamilnadu.

Rural Entrepreneurship in India

Ever since the inception of planning for economic development in India, great emphasis has been laid on the development of the small scale industries (SSI) sector. In fact, the SSI sector has been expected to play a crucial role in the industrial development of the country. Indeed, the growth of industries in this sector has been a dominant feature of our economic development since independence. It is estimated that this sector accounts for about 40 per cent of the total industrial output and contributes about 35 per cent of the total direct exports. So far as employment is concerned it comes next only to agriculture.

The objectives of the development of village and small industries are as following:

- *(i)* to assist in the growth and widespread dispersal of industries;
- *(ii)* to increase the levels of earnings of artisans;
- *(iii)* to sustain and create avenues of self-employment;
- *(iv)* to ensure regular supply of goods and services through use of local skills and resources;
- *(v)* to develop entrepreneurship in combination with improved methods of production through appropriate training and package of incentives; and
- *(vi)* to preserve craftsmanship and art heritage of the country.

The Governments (Central and States) have taken a number of measures to solve the age-old problems of these industries, such as lack of credit facilities, outmoded methods and techniques, absence of organised marketing, unsatisfactory arrangements for the supply of raw materials and competition from large-scale units.

The Central Government has set up a number of agencies to foster the development of the Village and Small Industries (VSI). These include the National Small Industries Corporation (NSIC), the Small-Scale Industries Board (SSIB), the Khadi and Village Industries Commission (KVIC), the All-India Handicrafts Board, the All-India Handloom Board, the Coir Board and the Silk Board.

Apart from these, credit facilities are made available to these industries through a number of institutions. Industrial estates and rural industrial projects have been set up, and industrial co-operatives have been organised. State Directorates of Industries and other agencies are responsible for their development in the States.

Table 1.1

Performance of Village Industries in India

Sl. No.	*Year*	*Production Rs.*	*Sales Rs.*	*Employment (Person) (Lakhs)*	*Earning Rs.*
1.	1983-84	72,260	NA	NA	NA
2.	1984-85	80,706	NA	37.89	NA
3.	1985-86	92,902	1,00,877	39.08	NA
4.	1986-87	1,09,864	1,20,880	40.70	NA
5.	1987-88	1,26,088	1,39,151	41.80	NA
6.	1988-89	1,44,337	1,59,813	42.87	NA
7.	1989-90	1,70,560	1,89,547	48.57	NA
8.	1990-91	1,99,407	2,22,896	50.16	NA
9.	1991-92	2,26,416	2,52,636	50.16	NA
10.	1992-93	2,96,435	2,78,114	52.50	53,500
11.	1993-94	2,84,797	3,02,458	53.28	96,170
12.	1994-95	3,36,942	3,43,650	53.46	1,03,618
13.	1995-96	3,46,025	3,80,779	56.72	1,11,264
14.	1996-97	3,78,647	4,27,389	58.17	1,20,649
	Total	28,65,389	29,18,190	625.36	5,15,203

Source: KVIC, Annual Reports, 1983-84 to 1996-97.

A number of measures have been taken up by the Governments to protect the village industries and to promote its growth. They are:

(i) Reservation of products;
(ii) Infrastructural and institutional support;
(iii) Machinery on hire purchase;
(iv) Marketing Assistance;
(v) Financial Assistance;
(vi) Training;
(vii) Supply of raw materials; and
(viii) Promotion of Ancillarisation etc.

The performance and growth of village industries are analysed by four important indicators, namely, production, sales, employment and earnings. The overall performance of village industries in India are exhibited in Table 1.1.

The categorywise production level of rural industries for the period from 1992-93 to 1996-97 is given in Table 1.2.

Table 1.2 reveals that the production value of rural industries during the study period (1992-93 to 1996-97) was increased from Rs. 2,96,435.22 lakh in 1992-93 to Rs. 3,78,647.93 lakh in 1996-97. Among these Agro food based industries has been contributed for 37.39 per cent of total value of production of Rs. 6,14,253.30 lakh.

Rural industries in India are facing increasing difficulties in selling their products due to growing competition from their sister concerns, recession, etc. Besides, there are well established large industries which produce the same products and compete with the same products, as they have their own selling network and sophisticated techniques.

The erratic availability of raw materials and their rising prices present formidable difficulties in adhering to the schedules of production and maintaining the production cost ultimately they create serious problems at the sales stage. Small units, which fare well in normal times, hardly do anything to cultivate and develop their sales systematically. As a result of it, they suffer and shiver even with the slightest depression. The attitude of the rural industrial entrepreneur towards selling his own products is a crucial factor in the success and growth of his enterprise.

Table 1.2

Production Level of Rural Industry in India

(Rupees in lakhs)

Sl. No.	Year	Mineral-based Industry Rs.	Forest-based Industry Rs.	Agro and Food-based Industry Rs.	Polymer and Chemical-based Industry Rs.	Engineering-based Industry Rs.	Textile-based Industry Rs.	Service-based Industry Rs.	Total Rs.
1.	1992-93	31,480.09	14,447.67	98,995.63	48,739.72	94,967.81	5,158.25	2,646.06	2,96,435.22
2.	1993-94	34,868.30	16,451.49	1,07,476.46	57,812.52	56,870.01	6,124.50	3,194.45	2,84,797.73
3.	1994-95	38,987.70	22,832.86	1,28,637.53	66,717.63	67,876.64	7,312.92	4,586.51	3,36,942.79
4.	1995-96	42,551.58	22,212.57	1,31,581.29	67,888.96	68,261.23	8,592.69	4,937.07	3,46,025.39
5.	1996-97	53,625.67	23,628.87	1,47,562.39	69,875.75	69,379.34	9,228.79	5,347.12	3,78,647.93
	Total	2,01,513.13	1,01,573.46	6,14,253.30	3,11,034.58	3,57,346.03	3,647.14	20,711.21	16,42,849.00
	Percentage	12.27	6.18	37.39	18.93	21.75	2.22	1.26	100.00

Source: KVIC Annual Reports, 1992-93 to 1996-97.

Table 1.3

Sales Value of Rural Industry in India

Sl. No.	Year	Mineral-based Industry Rs.	Forest-based Industry Rs.	Agro and Food-based Industry Rs.	Polymer and Chemical-based Industry Rs.	Engineering-based Industry Rs.	Textile-based Industry Rs.	Total Rs.
1.	1992-93	38,142.18	17,560.13	1,12,474.64	58,099.32	47,068.57	4,769.42	2,78,114.26
2.	1993-94	42,242.23	22,529.35	1,02,775.07	74,143.57	55,332.28	5,436.29	3,02,458.79
3.	1994-95	47,356.54	27,632.45	1,23,623.14	79,242.86	59,420.37	6,375.36	3,43,650.72
4.	1995-96	51,423.36	26,723.32	1,46,790.86	83,102.65	63,466.15	9,272.86	3,80,779.20
5.	1996-97	56,348.47	28,634.72	1,75,921.92	88,214.62	68,344.18	9,925.36	4,27,389.25
	Total	2,35,782.78	1,23,079.97	6,61,585.63	3,82,803.62	2,93,631.55	35,779.29	17,32,392.24
	Percentage	13.16	7.10	38.19	22.09	17.00	2.07	100.00

Source: KVIC Annual Reports, 1992-93 to 1996-97.

Sales value of rural industries has raised in very year and it has shown better performance of rural industries during the study period. There was a normal growth from 1992-93 to 1995-96, but higher growth was observed from the year in 1996-97.

Total sale value of rural industries was Rs. 17,32,392.24 lakh during the study period. Among this values agro and food-based industries alone constituted Rs. 6,61,585.63 lakh and it has shown 38.19 per cent of total sales of rural industries. Agro and food-based industries placed first in their sales contribution to rural industries.

Polymer and chemical-based industries also contributed largely by their sales value. It has contributed Rs. 3,82,803.02 lakh or 22.09 per cent of sales. Further, 17 per cent of sales contributed by engineering-based industries and 13.61 per cent of sales contributed by mineral-based industries during the study period.

Forest and Textile industries contribution to sales was very less when compared to other type of industries. These industries achieved only Rs. 1,23,079.97 lakh and Rs. 35,779.29 lakh respectively. Their contribution was only 7.10 per cent and 2.07 per cent respectively.

The major aim of development policy in India is to provide employment to its millions of unemployed where pressure on land is high. India's economy is agricultural oriented, but the rapid rise in its population with consequent pressure on land has led the planners to lay greater emphasis on decentralised industrial development. The core of the problem in countries like India is surplus agricultural labour and obsolescence of traditional village industries, giving rise to a large number of unemployment labour. The employment provided by the village industries is depicted in Table 1.4.

Rural industries has generated employment to 47.97 lakh persons in the year 1996-97 as against 37.21 lakh persons in the year 1992-93. The performance of employment generation has been continuously increasing over a period of five years. Agro and food-based industries has generated large amount of employment opportunities to rural people. It has contributed 47.72 per cent of employment generation in rural industries.

Table 1.4

Employment of Rural Industry in India

(Persons in lakhs)

Sl. No.	Year	Mineral-based Industry	Forest-based Industry	Agro and Food-based Industry	Polymer and Chemical-based Industry	Engineering-based Industry	Textile-based Industry	Service-based Industry	Total
1.	1992-93	5.10	2.73	18.43	5.90	4.24	0.62	0.19	37.21
2.	1993-94	5.81	2.93	19.56	6.33	4.10	0.64	0.22	39.59
3.	1994-95	6.21	3.04	19.79	6.22	4.53	0.52	0.62	40.93
4.	1995-96	6.48	3.17	20.06	6.83	4.77	0.38	0.81	42.50
5.	1996-97	7.72	4.13	21.52	7.51	5.63	0.48	0.98	47.97
	Total	31.32	16.00	99.36	32.79	23.27	2.64	2.82	208.20
	Percentage	15.04	7.70	47.72	15.75	11.17	1.27	1.35	100.00

Source: KVIC Annual Reports, 1992-93 to 1996-97.

Table 1.5

Earnings of Rural Industry in India

(Rupees in lakhs)

Sl. No.	Year	Mineral-based Industry Rs.	Forest-based Industry Rs.	Agro and Food-based Industry Rs.	Polymer and Chemical-based Industry Rs.	Engineering-based Industry Rs.	Textile-based Industry Rs.	Service-based Industry Rs.	Total Rs.
1.	1992-93	13,239.23	5,757.24	30,219.42	15,916.02	14,763.87	1,795.60	1,808.72	83,500.10
2.	1993-94	15,399.31	6,630.47	33,511.27	20,044.35	16,145.52	2,179.92	2,259.21	96,170.05
3.	1994-95	17,278.42	7,143.53	35,205.36	20,092.86	18,236.41	2,736.86	2,925.36	1,03,618.80
4.	1995-96	18,405.03	7,358.67	38,473.27	20,976.34	19,283.36	3,275.73	3,491.87	1,11,264.27
5.	1996-97	19,524.22	7,725.27	42,561.38	21,862.76	21,326.26	3,724.33	3,925.76	1,20,649.98
	Total	83,846.21	34,615.18	1,79,970.70	98,892.33	89,755.42	13,712.44	14,410.92	5,15,203.20
	Percentage	16.27	6.72	34.93	19.19	17.42	2.66	2.80	100.00

Source: KVIC Annual Reports, 1992-93 to 1996-97.

Table 1.5 indicates the earnings of rural industries in India during the study period. In the year 1996-97 earning of rural industries was estimated at Rs. 1,20,649.98 lakh as against Rs. 83,500.10 lakh in the year 1992-93 and it has shown the earning performance of rural industries rose to 7.21 per cent between the year 1992-93 to 1996-97. The performance of earning indicated an increasing tendency. Earnings of rural industries is estimated at 2 per cent. The total earnings of rural industries has been estimated at Rs. 5,15,203.20 lakh between the years 1992-93 to 1996-97. Agro-based industries alone has achieved Rs. 1,79,970.70 lakh in terms of earnings and it has contributed highly to total earnings of rural industries.

Rural Entrepreneurship in Tamilnadu

The share of Tamilnadu in all India production of Khadi and Village Industries has been significant. It holds the first place in khadi, cottage match, polymer industries, non-edible oils, soap and bee-keeping. In the state, the responsibility for the development of khadi and village industries is vested with the Khadi and Village Industries Board (KVIB). The board implements its programmes through its own units.

The board is concerned with 14 other village industries also. Till 1973-94, these were run mainly through the Board's own units and also by forming industrial cooperatives. From 1974-75, greater emphasis is laid on the promotion of individual artisans. On 31st March 1984, there were 2,901 industrial cooperatives and 200 departmental production units, besides 33,844 individual units with a total investment of Rs. 17.96 crore that provided employment to 5.50 lakh persons producing Rs. 90,000 crore worth of products through these industries. Palm gur and the ghani oil enterprises, accounting together for 60 per cent of aggregate production. The carpentry, blacksmith and village leather industry account for another 18 per cent of the total production. Village pottery, hand pounding of cereals and pulses, non-edible oils and soap contribute another 11 per cent. The board helps in the introduction of improved technology, new design and training programmes.

The rural industries projects, sponsored by the government of India in 1969-70, aims at the development of industrially backward villages and towns, besides creating additional employment in rural areas which suffers from under-employment, and unemployment. In order to encourage the growth of private units, the project provides loans at low rates of interest to prospective entrepreneurs. By 1975-76, the project covered the industrially backward districts of Salem, Tirunelveli, Ramanathapuram, Chengalpattu and Dharmapuri.

Table 1.6

Performance of Village Industries in Tamilnadu

(Rs. and Persons in Lakhs)

Sl. No.	*Year*	*Production Rs.*	*Sales Rs.*	*Employment (Persons)*	*Earning Rs.*
1.	1992-93	35,691.06	36,623.48	9.16	14,414.07
2.	1993-94	38,669.56	40,031.74	9.49	15,716.16
3.	1994-95	21,510.44	42,836.74	10.57	16,769.21
4.	1995-96	44,421.72	44,983.67	10.20	18,538.33
5.	1996-97	52,390.48	52,792.42	11.82	21,728.73
	Total	1,92,683.33	2,17,268.13	51.24	87,166.50

Source: Annual Report of KVIC, Mumbai.

The main problem of these industries is that of low productivity and they could sustain only when the demand is generated by projecting the projects as socially desirable. As the Nayadamma Committee has pointed out, these industries have to face stiff and unfair competition from large scale organised units. The committee recommended establishment of marketing corporation to look into the problems of marketing.

The volume of production in rural industries in Tamilnadu is given in Table 1.7. The Table reveales that the production value of rural industries was Rs. 435.75 lakh in 1996-97 as against Rs. 199.33 lakh in the year 1992-93. Agro and food-based industries had contributed to the extent of Rs. 90,438.20 lakh in terms of production value. It had shown 46.94 per cent to total production value of rural industries. Service-based industries contribution to production value of rural industries

Table 1.7

Production Value of Rural Industries in Tamilnadu

(Rs. in Lakhs)

Sl. No.	Type of Rural Industries	1992-93 Rs.	1993-94 Rs.	1994-95 Rs.	1995-96 Rs.	1996-97 Rs.	Total Rs.	Percentage
1.	Mineral-based industries	2,761.85	2,887.76	3,021.62	3,394.56	3,785.69	15,851.48	8.22
2.	Forest-based Industries	1,739.47	1,932.05	2,134.07	2,607.03	3,125.46	11,538.08	5.99
3.	Agro & Food-based Industries	17,702.14	19,694.45	2,275.14	23,340.33	27,426.14	90,438.20	46.94
4.	Polymer & Chemical-based Industries	5,904.21	5,833.15	6,285.17	6,893.61	7,563.62	32,479.76	16.85
5.	Engineering & Non-conventional-based Industries	5,290.48	5,938.50	5,032.76	5,150.81	7,124.96	28,537.51	14.81
6.	Textile-based Industries	2,093.58	2,127.95	2,436.45	2,660.95	2,928.86	12,247.79	6.36
7.	Service-based Industry	199.33	255.70	325.23	374.50	435.75	1,590.51	0.83
	Total	35,691.06	38,669.56	21,510.44	44,421.79	52,390.48	1,92,683.33	100.00

Source: K.V.I.C. Annual Reports, 1992-93 to 1996-97.

was very less between the year 1992-93 to 1996-97. It had contributed Rs. 1,590.51 lakh only.

During the year 1994-95 the rural industrial production value was very less when compared to 1992-94. The achievement of production value of rural industries increased significantly. Agro-based industry was placed first in the production value and service-based industry was least in the production value. The polymer and chemical-based industries and engineering and non-conventional-based industries were contributed 16.85 per cent and 14.81 per cent respectively to production value of rural industries.

The Table 1.8 indicates that the false value of rural industries in the year 1996-97 was Rs. 52,792.42 lakh as against Rs. 36,622.48 lakh in the year 1992-93. The growth of value of sales has been increased over the period.

Agro and food-based industries had achieved Rs. 28,623.85 lakh in the year 1996-97 as against Rs. 19,432.25 lakh in the year 1992-93. The contribution of agro and food-based industries was 54.48 per cent to the total sales of rural industries. Polymer and chemical-based industries had achieved Rs. 33,906.91 lakh to total sales value of rural industries between the year 1992-93 to 1996-97.

In Tamilnadu engineering and non-conventional industries had achieved Rs. 2,48,338.88 lakh to total sales value of rural industries between the year 1992-93 to 1996-97 and Mineral-based industries had achieved Rs. 17,484.64 lakh. It's contribution was 8.05 per cent to total sales value. Textile-based and forest-based industry had contributed 4.62 per cent and 5.82 respectively.

Table 1.9 reveals that Agro and Food-based industries had generated more employment during the study period. It had generated 35.53 lakh persons employment opportunities during the period 1992-93 to 1996-97. It's contribution was estimated of 69.34 per cent of total employment generated through Rural Industries in Tamilnadu. Polymer and chemical-based industries had generated 5.71 lakh persons employment in Tamilnadu during the study period.

Table 1.10 indicates that in 1992-93 the earning performance of rural industries in Tamilnadu was Rs. 14,414.07

Table 1.8

Sales Value of Rural Industry in Tamilnadu

(Rs. in Lakhs)

Sl. No.	*Type of Rural Industries*	*1992-93* Rs.	*1993-94* Rs.	*1994-95* Rs.	*1995-96* Rs.	*1996-97* Rs.	*Total* Rs.	*Percentage* Rs.
1.	Mineral-based Industries	2,959.35	3,036.42	3,562.36	3,700.65	4,225.86	17,484.64	8.05
2.	Forest-based Industries	1,845.97	2,046.97	2,625.86	2,910.35	3,205.07	1,263.22	5.82
3.	Agro & Food-based Industries	19,432.35	22,051.91	23,361.18	24,896.93	28,623.85	1,18,366.22	54.48
4.	Polymer & Chemical-based Industries	6,087.07	6,414.12	6,524.37	6,906.16	7,975.19	33,906.91	15.60
5.	Engineering & Non-conventional-based Industries	4,724.98	4,858.52	4,928.02	4,199.79	6,126.85	24,838.28	11.43
6.	Textile-based Industries	1,573.76	1,623.80	1,834.95	2,369.79	2,635.68	10,037.98	4.62
	Total	36,623.48	40,031.74	42,836.74	44,983.67	52,792.42	2,17,268.13	100.00

Source: K.V.I.C. Annual Reports, 1992-93 to 1996-97.

Table 1.9

Rural Industry in Tamilnadu—Employment

(Persons in Lakhs)

Sl. No.	*Type of Rural Industries*	*1992-93*	*1993-94*	*1994-95*	*1995-96*	*1996-97*	*Total*	*Percentage*
1.	Mineral-based Industries	1.07	1.09	1.16	1.20	0.42	4.94	9.642
2.	Forest-based Industries	0.29	0.31	0.32	0.31	0.39	1.62	3.16
3.	Agro & Food-based Industries	6.54	6.84	7.01	7.06	8.08	35.53	69.34
4.	Polymer & Chemical-based Industries	0.84	0.80	1.00	1.02	2.05	5.71	4.96
5.	Engineering & Non-conventional-based Industries	0.28	0.31	0.92	0.40	0.63	2.54	4.96
6.	Textile-based Industries	0.12	0.12	0.04	0.06	0.07	0.41	0.80
7.	Service-based Industries	0.02	0.02	0.12	0.15	0.18	0.49	0.96
	Total	9.16	9.49	10.57	10.20	11.82	51.24	100.00

Source: Annual Reports, 1992-93 to 1996-97, K.V.I.C.

Table 1.10

Earnings Value of Rural Industry in Tamilnadu

(Rs. in Lakhs)

Sl. No.	*Type of Rural Industries*	*1992-93 Rs.*	*1993-94 Rs.*	*1994-95 Rs.*	*1995-96 Rs.*	*1996-97 Rs.*	*Total Rs.*	*Percentage*
1.	Mineral-based Industries	1,408.29	1,561.88	1,324.76	1,488.13	1,675.18	7,458.24	8.56
2.	Forest-based Industries	516.89	551.89	565.81	640.40	856.65	3,131.64	3.59
3.	Agro & Food-based Industries	8,779.64	9,522.69	10,407.78	11,617.10	13,929.18	54,256.39	62.24
4.	Polymer & Chemical based-Industries	1,419.89	1,588.43	1,632.24	1,773.41	1,827.81	8,241.78	9.46
5.	Engineering & Non-Conventional-based Industries	1,646.01	1,742.44	1,758.87	1,786.35	1,895.76	8,829.43	10.13
6.	Textile-based Industries	493.85	557.27	765.38	826.99	1,026.36	3,669.85	4.21
7.	Service-based Industries	149.50	191.56	314.37	405.95	517.79	1,579.17	1.81
	Total	14,414.07	15,716.16	15,769.21	18,538.33	21,728.73	87,166.50	100.00
	Percentage	16.54	18.03	19.24	21.27	24.92		

Source: Annual Reports, 1992-93 to 1996-97, K.V.I.C.

lakh only. But it had raised to Rs. 21,728.73 lakh in the year 1996-97.

Agro and Food-based industries alone achieved Rs. 54,256.39 lakh as earnings. It was the higher earning industries among the types of industries. Engineering and non-conventional-based industries had contributed 10.13 per cent total earnings. Textile-based industries and forest-based industries had contributed 4.21 per cent and 3.59 per cent respectively.

Rural Entrepreneurship in Dindigul District—Growth and Potentials

The study district—Dindigul is popular for the leather industry and lock industry. It has the vast potentials for the generation of employment and income through the rural industries. The growth of registered rural industries in Dindigul district is presented in Table 1.11.

Table 1.11

Rural Industries in Dindigul District

Sl. No.	*Types of Industries*	*1992-93*	*1996-97*	*1997-98*	*Growth*	*Per-cent-age*
1.	Food & Agro-based Industries	632	980	1,002	370	36.92
2.	Forest-based Industries	125	251	258	133	51.55
3.	Leather Industries	215	452	479	264	55.11
4.	Textile-based Industries	1,102	1,510	1,623	521	32.10
5.	Chemical-based Industries	137	490	951	814	85.60
6.	Engineering-based Industries	1,032	1,824	1,895	863	45.54
7.	Electrical & Electronics	127	332	347	220	63.40
8.	Construction Items	95	185	185	90	48.64
9.	Other Industries	197	640	1,269	1,072	84.48
	Total	3,662	7,859	8,009	4,347	54.28

Source: District Industries Centre, Dindigul, 1999.

The Table 1.11 reveals that the number of registered rural industries had increased from 3,662 units in 1992-93 to 8,009 units in 1997-98. During the six years period, the growth of the village industries was 54.28 per cent. The chemical based (85.60%) and electrical and electronics industries (63.40%) dominated in the development performance in Dindigul district for the past six years. Due to the government policy and other unfavorable business conditions, the textile-based industries 32.10%) and food and agro-based industries (36.92%) had the slow growth during the study period.

A sample of 70 rural entrepreneurs in four sample blocks were interviewed and the findings of the survey are presented in this section.

Socio-economic Status of Sample Entrepreneurs

In order to analysis performance of entrepreneurs in developing rural industries, the socio-economic background such as age, community, education , etc., could be identified. The age-wise classification of sample entrepreneurs is presented in Table 1.12.

It is clear that 30 per cent of the sample respondents are belonging to the category of age between 26 to 35 years. It is inferred that most of the entrepreneurs are youngster in the study district. Communitywise classification of sample entrepreneurs are given in Table 1.13.

The table reveals that 87.14 per cent of the entrepreneurs are belonging to backward community (57.14%) and most backward community (30.00%). Only a meager portion of the entrepreneurs are belonging to the scheduled castes. The weaker section and the depressed class peoples are not involved in the business and enterprises.

Education and training are the important factors influencing the development of rural entrepreneurs. The Educationwise classification of sample entrepreneurs is presented in Table 1.14.

From the Table 1.14, it is clear that 41.43 per cent of the entrepreneurs got the secondary school level education and 35.71 per cent got primary level education. Only 11.43 per cent of the respondents got degree level education and 11.43 per cent are illiterate sample entrepreneurs. It is inferred that

Table 1.12

Age-wise Classification of Entrepreneurs

Category	*Mineral-based Industry*	*Forest-based Industry*	*Agro and food-based Industry*	*Polymer and Chemical-based Industry*	*Engineering and Non-conventional Energy*	*Textile Industry*	*Service Industry*	*Total*
Below-25	2	1	—	1	2	2	2	11 (15.71)
26-35	3	4	2	3	4	2	3	21 (30.00)
36-45	4	3	3	2	3	2	3	20 (28.57)
46-55	1	2	3	3	1	3	1	14 (20.00)
56 above	—	—	2	1	—	1	—	4
Total (100.00)	10	10	10	10	10	10	10	70 (100.00)

Note: Figures within parenthesis denotes percentages.

Source: Computed from primary data.

Table 1.13

Community-wise Classification of Sample Entrepreneurs

Category	*Mineral-based Industry*	*Forest-based Industry*	*Agro and Food-based Industry*	*Polymer and Chemical-based Industry*	*Engineering and Non-conventional Energy*	*Textile Industry*	*Service Industry*	*Total*
BC	6	5	6	7	3	8	8	40 (57.14)
MBC	3	4	3	3	3	2	2	21 (30.00)
SC	1	1	1	—	4	—	2	9 (12.86)
Total	10	10	10	10	10	10	10	70 (100.00)

Note: Figures within parenthesis denotes percentages.
Source: Computed from primary data.

Table 1.14
Education Level of Sample Entrepreneurs

Category	*Mineral-based Industry*	*Forest-based Industry*	*Agro and Food-based Industry*	*Polymer and Chemical-based Industry*	*Engineering and Non-conventional Energy*	*Textile Industry*	*Service Industry*	*Total*
Illiterate	2	1	2	3	—	—	—	8 (11.43)
Primary	4	5	5	2	3	4	2	25 (35.71)
Secondary	3	4	2	4	5	5	6	29 (41.43)
Degree	1	—	1	1	2	1	2	8 (11.43)
Total	10	10	10	10	10	10	10	70 (100.00)

Note: Figures within parenthesis denotes percentages.
Source: Computed from primary data.

nearly 90 per cent sample educated entrepreneurs could be used for the development of rural industries with skill developing training programmes.

Production

The locally available raw materials has been generally used for the production of village industries products. The sources of raw materials are: Private, Government and cooperative.

Table 1.15
Source of Raw Materials

Category	*Private*	*Government*	*Co-operative*	*Total*
Mineral-based Industry	10	—	—	10
Forest-based Industry	9	—	1	10
Agro and Food-based Industry	9	—	1	10
Polymer and Chemical-based Industry	7	—	3	10
Engineer and Non-conventional Energy	9	—	1	10
Textile Industry	3	1	6	10
Service Industry	10	—	—	10
Total	57 (81.42)	1 (01.43)	12 (17.11)	70 (100.00)

Note : Figures within parenthesis denotes percentage.
Source: Computed from primary data.

The sample entrepreneurs are purchasing raw materials mainly from private traders. Only 1.43 per cent of the respondents are getting raw materials from government. The cooperative provided raw materials only to 17.11 per cent of the rural entrepreneurs of Dindigul district. It is clear that the role of government and cooperative sector in supplying raw materials are very poor. The private source of raw materials influenced the higher cost of production due to the higher price of raw materials. The government may take necessary steps in supplying raw materials at reasonable rate to the rural entrepreneurs.

The production technique adopted in rural industries of Dindigul district is exhibited in Table 1.16.

Table 1.16

Production Techniques Adopted in Rural Industries

Category	*Traditional*	*Modern*	*Total*
Mineral-based Industry	4	6	10
Forest-based Industry	3	7	10
Agro and Food-based Industry	3	7	10
Polymer & Chemical-based Industry	3	7	10
Engineering and Non-conventional Energy	8	2	10
Textile Industry	5	5	10
Service Industry	5	5	10
Total	31 (44.29)	39 (55.71)	70 (100.00)

Note: Figures within parenthesis denotes percentage.
Source: Computed from primary data.

The Table 1.16 reveals that the sample rural entrepreneurs in Dindigul district are equally adopting the traditional as well as modern technology in producing rural industries products. The Engineering Non-conventional energy industry are mostly using the traditional methods. Till now, the modern techniques are mostly used in other industries which are utilising the machineries with power. In order to improve the technique of production the awareness and training programmes may be effectively implemented in rural areas.

The average cost of production per sample rural industry in Dindigul district was Rs. 22,006.03. The categorywise classification of cost of production are presented in Table 1.17.

It is clear that at an average, 46.28 per cent of the total cost incurred for the purchase of raw materials. The labour cost was only 24.83 per cent of the total cost. The remaining 29 per cent are the cost for interest on borrowing, depreciation and other costs.

Table 1.17

Average Cost of Production

Category	*Raw Material* Rs.	*Labour Cost* Rs.	*Interest on Borrowing* Rs.	*Depre-ciation* Rs.	*Other Costs* Rs.	*Produc-tion Cost* Rs.
Mineral-based Industry	1,86,521 (37.06)	1,18,088 (23.46)	1,42,497 (28.31)	8,159 (01.62)	48,019 (09.54)	5,03,284 (100.00)
Forest-based Industry	75,102 (31.84)	85,945 (36.44)	42,222 (17.90)	10,814 (04.58)	21,820 (09.25)	2,35,903 (100.00)
Agro and Food-based Industry	1,69,859 (74.47)	60,511 (26.53)	46,839 (20.54)	18,178 (07.97)	32,696 (14.34)	3,28,083 (100.00)
Polymer and Chemical-based Industry	97,124 (27.45)	1,51,031 (42.69)	53,906 (15.24)	14,993 (04.24)	36,728 (10.38)	3,53,782 (100.00)
Engineering and Non-conventional Energy	1,09,897 (44.65)	60,581 (24.61)	42,932 (17.44)	12,995 (05.28)	19,737 (08.02)	2,46,142 (100.00)
Textile Industry	2,72,723 (81.40)	29,870 (08.92)	11,666 (03.48)	9,809 (02.93)	10,972 (03.27)	3,35,040 (100.00)
Service Industry	1,07,167 (54.02)	40,346 (20.34)	18,229 (09.19)	18,810 (09.48)	13,817 (06.97)	1,98,369 (100.00)
Total	10,18,393 (46.28)	5,46,372 (24.83)	3,58,291 (16.28)	93,758 (04.26)	1,83,789 (08.35)	22,00,603 (100.00)

Note: Figures within parenthesis denotes percentages.

Source: Computed from primary data.

The polymer chemical-based industry spent a higher amount of cost for labour changes (42.69%). But the other category of industry spent only 1/4 of the total cost for labour charges. It is inferred that the Forest-based industry and polymer chemical-based industry are providing more employment and higher amount of labour cost. These types of industries may be encouraged for providing employment opportunity in rural sectors of Dindigul district.

Investment

Rural industries are capital light and is suitable to the country like India where capital is deficient. It helps in mobilising capital. An essentially agrarian economy, people have a tendency to keep their money idle rather than investing in large scale industries. Since the rural industries are located close to the areas where people stay, mobilisation of rural savings is easy. These industries are run with local labour and locally available materials. Thus, they help in the proper utilisation of local resources. The investment pattern in the sample rural industries in Dindigul district is presented in Table 1.18.

Table 1.18

Investment Pattern in Rural Industry

Category	*Working Capital*	*Fixed Capital*	*Total Investment*	*Working/Fixed Capital*
Mineral-based Industry	2,17,500	2,12,139	4,29,639	1.03
	(50.62)	(49.38)	(100.00)	
Forest-based Industry	89,655	50,426	1,40,081	1.78
	(64.00)	(36.00)	(100.00)	
Agro and Food-based	1,61,560	80,502	2,42,062	2.01
Industry	(66.74)	(33.26)	(100.00)	
Polymer & Chemical-	1,03,430	53,750	1,57,180	1.92
based Industry	(65.80)	(34.20)	(100.00)	
Engineering and Non-	59.540	26.250	85.790	2.30
conventional Energy	(69.40)	(30.60)	(100.00)	
Textile Industry	1,74,650	2,59,400	4,34,050	0.67
	(40.24)	(59.76)	(100.00)	
Service Industry	63,870	22,462	86,332	2.84
	(73.98)	(26.02)	(100.00)	
Total	8,70,205	7,04,929	15,75,134	1.23
	(55.25)	(44.75)	(100.00)	

Note: Figures within parenthesis denotes percentages.
Source: Computed from primary data.

Table 1.18 reveals that the maximum limit of the investment was Rs. 4.29 lakhs in Mineral-based industries and Rs. 4.34 lakh in Textile industries. The minimum limit of investment was Rs. 0.86 lakh in service industry, Rs. 0.86 lakhs in Engineering and Non-conventional energy industries. Of the total investment, more than 50 per cent (55.25%) of investment was used as working capital in rural industries. The textile industries required the highest percentage (59.76%) of investment for fixed capital. The source of investment in rural industries is exhibited in Table 1.19.

Table 1.19

Sources of Investment in Rural Industries

Category	*Own Funds*	*Borrowing*		*Total*
		Informal Institution	*Formal Institution*	*Investment*
	Rs.	Rs.	Rs.	Rs.
Mineral-based Industry	1,66,855	90,999	1,71,785	4,29,639
	(38.84)	(21.18)	(39.98)	(100.00)
Forest-based Industry	59,688	25,759	54,634	1,40,081
	(42.61)	(18.39)	(39.00)	(100.0)
Agro and Food-based Industry	1,05,291	47,061	89,710	2,42,062
	(43.50)	(19.44)	(37.06)	(100.0)
Polymer and Chemical-based Industry	58,121	42,396	56,663	1,57,180
	(36.98)	(26.97)	(35.05)	(100.00)
Engineering and Non-conventional Energy	37,241	18,473	30,076	85,790
	(43.41)	(21.53)	(35.06)	(100.0)
Textile Industry	91,764	1,45,078	1,97,208	4,34,050
	(21.14)	(33.42)	(45.43)	(100.0)
Service Industry	65,459	321	20,552	86,332
	(75.82)	(0.37)	(23.81)	(100.0)
Total	5,84,419	3,70,087	6,20,628	15,75,134
	(37.10)	(23.50)	(39.40)	(100.0)

Note: Figures within parenthesis denotes percentages.
Source: Computed from primary data.

It is clear that the rural entrepreneurs invest capital from own funds was only 37.1 per cent of capital. The remaining 62.9 per cent of capital was borrowed capital from informal institutions like money-lenders and chit funds and formal institutions like banks cooperatives etc. The percentage of borrowing from informal institutions and formal institutions was 23.5 per cent and 39.40 per cent respectively. It is inferred that nearly 40 per cent of capital funds are invested from formal institutions like Banks and Cooperative societies.

Income and Employment Potentials

Rural industries are quick yielding in nature. In other words, their gestation period is very much less when compared to their large scale counterparts. These industries are labour-intensive and provide innumerable employment opportunities. A given investment in rural industries can provide 10 to 15 times more employment than the industries have special significance in rural areas of India which face the inverse problem of seasonal unemployment. Faced with the problems of seasonal unemployment and low wages, Indian economy is characterised by the migration of labour from rural areas to urban areas. There is no need for sophisticated technology and any person with some basic training would be able to run village industries.

Table 1.20 explained the composition of labour in sample rural industries. The average number of labourers employed in sample rural industries are: 47 workers in mineral-based industries, 35 workers in forest-based industries, 36 workers in agro and food-based industries, 38 workers in polymer & chemical-based industry, 27 workers in engineering and non-conventional energy industries, 42 workers in textile industry and 16 workers in service industry.

A highest level of employment was provided by the mineral-based industries and textile industries in Dindigul district of Tamilnadu. But the service industries are providing only meagre employment for 16 persons and the female labour did not get any employment opportunities in these industries.

Table 1.20
Composition Labour in Rural Industries

(Unit average)

Category	*Family Labour*			*Hired Labour*			*Total Labour*			*% F.L in TL*	*% Fa.L in TL*
	M	*F*	*T*	*M*	*F*	*T*	*M*	*F*	*T*		
Mineral-based Industry	13	12	25	9	13	22	22	25	47	53.19	53.19
Forest-based Industry	11	13	24	6	5	11	17	18	35	51.43	68.57
Agro and Food-based Industry	14	12	26	6	4	10	20	16	36	44.44	74.22
Polymer & Chemical-based Industry	12	13	25	5	8	13	17	21	38	55.26	65.79
Engineering and Non-conventional Energy	13	6	19	4	4	8	17	10	27	37.03	70.37
Textile Industry	13	9	22	6	14	20	19	23	42	54.76	52.38
Service Industry	14	—	14	2	—	2	16	—	16	00.00	87.50
Total	90	65	155	38	48	86	128	113	241	46.89	64.32

Source: Computed from primary data.

Note: M—Male, F—Female, T—Total.
Fa.L—Family Labour, F.L—Female Labour.

Hence, 87.5 per cent of the family labourers are engaged in the service industries.

Nearly 50 per cent of family labourers are engaged in the mineral-based industries and Textile industries. All other industries such as Forest-based, Agro-based, Polymer & Chemical-based, Engineering and Non-conventional energy industries are utilising a large amount of (more than 50%) family labours. The details of composition of family and hired labour in rural small industries are exhibited in Table 1.21.

Table 1.21
Composition of Family and Hired Labour (No. of Workers) in Rural Small Industries

	Investments
A. Family Labour	
(i) Male No.	91
(ii) Female No.	65
(iii) Total No.	156
B. Hired Labour	
(i) Male No.	32
(ii) Female No.	48
(iii) Total No.	80
C. Total	
(i) Male No.	132
(ii) Female No.	113
(iii) Grand Total No.	245
D. 1. Total Family Labour as % of total labour	63.67
2. Male Family Labour as % of total labour	37.14
3. Female Family Labour as % of total labour	26.54
4. Total Hired Labour as % of total labour	32.65
5. Male Hired Labour as % of total labour	13.10
6. Female Hired Labour as % of total labour	19.60
7. Male Labour as % of total labour	53.87
8. Female Labour as % of total labour	46.12

Source: Computed from primary data.

The unit average of hired labourers in the sample rural industries are: 22 persons (25.58%) in mineral-based industries, 20 persons (23.26%) in textile industries, 11 persons (12.79%) in forest-based industries, 10 persons (11.62%) in agro and food-based industry, 13 persons (15.11%) in Polymer and chemical-based industry, 8 persons (9.3%) in Engineering and Non-conventional energy and 2 persons (2.33%) in service industries. It is inferred that most of the hired labour (unit average) were having the regular work (71%) and the seasonal nature was only 29 per cent of the hired labour in the sample rural industries of Dindigul district. These figures are presented in

Table 1.22. The status of previous occupation of workers are given in Table 1.23.

Table 1.22
Regular and Seasonal Character of Hired Labour (Unit Average)

Category	*Regular*		*Seasonal*		*Total*		*Grand Total*
	M	*F*	*M*	*F*	*M*	*F*	
Mineral-based Industry	7	8	2	5	9	13	22 (25.58)
Forest-based Industry	5	4	1	1	6	5	11 (12.79)
Agro and Food-based Industry	5	4	1	0	6	4	10 (11.62)
Polymer & Chemical-based Industry	5	5	0	3	5	8	13 (15.11)
Engineering and Non-conventional Energy	4	0	0	4	4	4	8 (09.30)
Textile Industry	4	8	2	6	6	14	20 (23.26)
Service Industry	2	0	0	0	2	0	2 (02.33)
Total	32	29	6	19	38	48	86
	(71)		(29)		(44)		(56)

Source: Computed from primary Data.

Note: Figures within parenthesis denotes percentage.

Table 1.23 reveals that the previous employment status of workers of rural industries in the study district were mostly self-employed (64.32%) persons and only 29.05 per cent of the workers were daily wage employment workers. The seasonal workers and contract workers were only 4.15 per cent and 2.49 per cent respectively. It is clear that previously self-employed persons are employed in the rural industries after losing the previous employment due to many reasons and bottlenecks for the development of rural entrepreneurs.

Table 1.23

Status of Previous Occupation of Workers in Rural Industries

Category	*Self Employment*	*Contract Workers*	*Daily Wage Employment Worker*	*Seasonal*	*Total*
Mineral-based Industry	25 (53.19)	6 (12.77)	10 (21.28)	6 (12.77)	47 (100.00)
Forest-based Industry	24 (68.57)	—	11 (31.43)	—	35 (100.00)
Agro and Food-based Industry	26 (72.22)	—	10 (27.78)	—	36 (100.00)
Polymer & Chemical-based Industry	25 (65.79)	—	10 (26.32)	3 (07.89)	38 (100.00)
Engineer and Non-conventional Energy	19 (70.37)	—	7 (25.93)	1 (3.70)	27 (100.00)
Textile Industry	22 (52.38)	—	20 (47.62)	—	42 (100.00)
Service Industry	14 (87.50)	—	2 (12.50)	—	16 (100.00)
Total	155 (64.32)	6 (02.49)	70 (29.05)	10 (04.15)	241 (100.00)

Source: Computed from primary data.

Note: Figures within parenthesis denotes percentage.

The average earning per unit in the Dindigul district includes the profit for the entrepreneurs and the wages as family member workers in the village industries. The total share of earnings covered the 62.84 per cent of profit and 37.16 per cent of wages. The share of profit was higher in the cases of textiles industries, service industries and polymer & chemical-based industries in Dindigul district.

The share of wages as family member workers was higher in the case of mineral-based industries, forest-based industries, Agro and Food-based industries in the study district. The unit average of earnings per year was higher in mineral-based industries (Rs. 1,49,318) and in Textile industries (Rs. 62,416).

But it was lower in the Engineering and Non-conventional energy industry (Rs. 13,050), Agro and Food-based industry (Rs. 15,366) and Forest-based industry (Rs. 15,614) in the study district. It is inferred that the mineral-based industries like lime-stone, stone crushing,. fuel brightening and bricks industries and the textile industries like embroidery, tailoring, handloom and powerloom are most profitable rural industries in Dindigul district.

Problems for Rural Entrepreneurship

The sample of seventy rural entrepreneurs revealed some problems in the development of rural industries in Dindigul district of Tamilnadu. The problems are summarised in this section.

1. Rural industries except agro-based have to depend on raw materials from outside and such type of procurement influence the wastage of time and cost in transport. Non-availability of raw materials or prohibitive cost of these industries has weakened the liability of rural industries. Nearly 80 per cent of the raw materials are purchased from the private concerns in the study district.

2. These industrial units may encounter problems of marketing due to lack of marketing information, marketing channel and transport cost. Problems also arise and account of lack of standardisation besides marketing on conventional products. There is also practically no marketing research or study of market potentials.

3. It is evident from the research that only small proportion of the credit has reached the rural entrepreneurs. It is clear that the consultancy unit of the District Industries Centre (DIC) hesitates to attend to the problems of small industries in rural areas. Credit was given under importance by entrusting the task of providing it to commercial banks and cooperatives. But the Government failed to provide infrastructure, education and awareness about the people regarding utilisation of credit. The benefits of subsidy and concessional interest rate extent to rural artisans were nullified by delay in sanctioning of credit, cost of loan by way of grease money, etc.

4. Many rural industries suffer due to laçk of skilled labour. Most of the units located in the rural areas find it extremely difficult to get suitable labour. With the work experience in small units, skilled workers tend to turn to large scale units, attracted by their higher emoluments.

5. Low technology-base has been one of the major constraints in the growth of rural industries. In this study, 44.29 per cent of the sample respondents use the traditional method of production techniques in rural industries.

6. Rural industrial activity continuous to be poorly organised. This is in spite of specialised organisation network established exclusively of each industry. Lack of adequate managerial expertise, resource and member confidence continue to plague these institutions.

Suggestions for Promotion of Rural Entrepreneurship

The present study suggested the following measures for the development of rural industries.

1. Setting up of raw material bank for materials and intermediate component of good quality from the open market on behalf of the institutions. It would then store them in central places. This measure would ensure a smooth supply of raw materials of rural industries.

2. Fairs and exhibition should be conducted periodically so as to enable the rural industries to market their products through these means. Government may arrange for commercial advertisement at concesional rates. Efforts should be made to organise small industries common associations. This will help to follow a common programme relating to advertisement.

3. Full time employment can also be generated in organized sector, if the agricultural based processing units are started in rural areas. Government may set up processing units in the village itself thereby save both producing farmer and provide employment to surplus labour from the farm sector. The migration to urban sectors may be reduced.

4. For energy, the agricultural wastes, biogas, biomass and solar energy may be used. Though the cost may be higher in the initial period in the long run, it is sustainable. Subsidies

may be given for units using non-conventional sources of energy.

5. Dr. J.C. Kumarappa suggested that the multi-purpose cooperative societies can supply raw materials, stock the finished goods and help in distributing all village industries products especially those connected with food processing, textiles and other primary needs. They should be ever watchful of the interests of the villagers.

Conclusion

At present, the Government of Tamilnadu is establishing the 'Farmers Market' in each and every districts of Tamilnadu. The government aims to provide the reasonable prices to the consumers and profit to the farmers of Tamilnadu. Similarly, it is concluded that in order to marketing the rural industries products, a common complex in every block, or at least in every district should be established by the Government/District Industries centre. Such solutions to the marketing problems of rural industries products would generate the large amount of income and employment potentials in the rural areas.

References

1. Bepin Behari, *Rural Industrialisation in India,* Vikas Publication House, New Delhi, 1976.
2. Gandhi, M.K., *Village Swaraj,* Navajeevan Publishing House, Ahmedabad, 1962.
3. Gandhi, M.K., *Khadi, Why and How?* Navajeevan Publishing House, Ahmedabad, 1955.
4. Kumarappa, J.C., *Economy of Permanence,* Sarva Seva Sangh Prakashan, Varanashi, 1997.
5. Kumarappa, J.C., *The Gandhian Economy and Other Essays,* All India Village Industries Association, Wardha, 1949.
6. Mishra, R.P., *Rural Industrialization in Third World Countries,* Sterling Publishers Private Limited, New Delhi, 1985.
7. Mohanlal, *Rural Industrialisation and Regional Development,* Deep and Deep Publication, New Delhi, 1987, 142.
8. Pai Panadiker, V.A. Arun Sud, *Rural Industrialisation,* Oxford, IBH Publishing Co. Pvt. Ltd., New Delhi, 1986.
9. Rao, R.V., *Rural Industrialisation in India,* Concept Publishing Company, New Delhi, 1978.

10. Rizwanul Islam, *Rural Industrialisation and Employment in Asia*, ILO—ARTEP, New Delhi, 1986, p. 6.
11. Sen, K.K., *Rural Industrialisation in India*, Sultan Chand & Sons, New Delhi, 1995.
12. Shetty, M.C., *Small Scale and Household Industries in a Developing Economy*, Asia Publishing House, 1963.
13. Soundarapandian, M., *Rural Industries in India*, Mohit Publications, New Delhi, 1999.
14. Soundarapandian, M., *Women Entrepreneurship—Issues and Strategies*, Kanishka Publishers, Distributors, New Delhi, 1999.
15. Soundarapandian, M., "Women Cooperation and Rural Enterprise Development", S.N. Tripathy (ed.), *Cooperatives for Rural Development*, Discovery Publishing House, New Delhi, 1998, pp. 125-41.
16. Suri. K.B., *Small Scale Enterprises in Industrial Development*, Sage Publications India, Ltd., New Delhi, 1987, pp. 125-41.

Journals

17. Anandharajakumar, P. (1997), "Small Industries and Sustainable Rural Development", *Kisan World*, October, 1997.
18. Chhabra, N.N., "Rural Industries are on the March", *Kurukshetra*, Vol. XLVI, No. 5, February, 1998.
19. Dikshit, B.D., "Financing of Small Scale Industries: Some Thrust Areas", *State Bank of India Monthly Review*, Vol. XXVIII, No. 3, March, 1989.
20. Francis, O.H., "Animal Husbandry Schemes—Vast Scope on the Horizon," *State Bank of India Monthly Review*, Vol. XXXVI, No. 9, pp. 477-93.
21. Johari, D.C., "Prospects of Poultry Industry in India", *Poultry Guide*, Vol. XXXII, No. 1-2 January-February, 1995.
22. Krishna Kumar, "Future of Rural Industrialization", *Khadi Gramodyog*, Vol. XXXVII, No. 4, January, 1991.
23. Kulkarni, P.R., "Employment Generation—SSI Sectors", *Southern Economists*, Vol. 36, Nos. 23 & 24, p. 22.
24. Malik, S.K., & Malik, R.N., "Employment and Income Prospects in Blanket Manufacturing Cottage Industry", *Kurukshetra*, Vol. XLVL, No. 5, February, 1998.
25. Mahanth, K., "Rural Industrialization in India—Policy, Programmes and Prospects", *Journal of Rural Development*, Vol. 7, No. 2, March, 1988, p. 216.
26. Mohinder Singh, "Nehru and Rural Development", *Khadi Gramodyog*, Vol. XXXVI, No. 2, November, 1989.

27. Raghava Rao, M.V., "Industries in Villages: Role of KVIC, *Khadhi Gramodyog*, Vol. XXXVI, No. 2, November, 1989.
28. Ramasamy, D., "Khadi and Village Industries the Role of Technology", *Khadi Gramodyog*, Vol. XXXVI, No. 1, October 1989.
29. Ramesha, L., "Rural Micro Enterprises", *State Bank of India Monthly Review*, Vol. XXXVI, April, 1997.
30. Roy, N.K., "Relevance of Village Industry as Enumerated by J.C. Kumarappa", *Khadhi Gramodyog*, Vol. XXXVI, No. 6, March, 1991.
31. Satya Sundaram, S., "Relevance of Gandhian Economics", *Southern Economist*, Vol. 36, No. 8, August, 1997, pp. 13-19.
32. Sathyanarauana, T., "Role of Planning and Marketing in Rural Industries", *Kurukshetra*, Vol. 33, No. a, June, 1985 p. 24.
33. Shinha, V.C., "A Case for Rural Industrialisation", *Kuruskhetra*, Vol. XLVI, No. 5, February, 1998.
34. Smita Mehrosre, "Village Industries in Rajasthan", *Khadhi Gramodyog*, Vol. XXXIV, No. II, August, 1988.
35. Soundarapandian, M., "Development of Rural Industries: Issues and Strategies", *Kurukshetra*, Vol. 48, No. 2, November, 1999, pp. 2-7.
36. Soundarapandian, M., and Shiny Phillip, "Wage Disparities in Coir Industry", *Khadi Gramodyog*, Vol. XXXI, No. 10, July, 1998, pp. 394-98.
37. Soundarapandian, M., "ISB Sector under IRDP: A Case Study", *Khadi Gramodyog*, Vol. XXXX, No. 9, June, 1994, pp. 584-88.

Reports

38. *Annual Reports of KVIC*, 1982 to 1998, Mumbai.
39. *Report of the Village and Small Scale Industries Committee*, 1955 (Karve Committee).

APPENDIX—I

Share of Schedules Castes and Scheduled Tribes in the Overall Employment Under KVI in 1997-98

Sl. No.	*Industry*	*Total Employment*	*Scheduled Caste*	*Scheduled Tribes*
1.	Cottage Pottery	5.27	0.61	0.62
2.	Lime Mfg.	2.97	1.12	0.07
3.	Match & Agarbatti	0.38	0.23	0.06
4.	Handmade Paper	0.15	0.01	0.06
5.	Shellac	*	*	*
6.	Cane* Bamboo	2.40	0.79	0.26
7.	Katha	0.11	*	*
8.	Gum Resins	0.04	*	*
9.	Bee-keeping	2.41	0.19	0.22
10.	Ghani Oil	0.81	0.01	0.01
11.	Gur & Khandsari	2.46	0.28	0.08
12.	Palmgur	8.52	2.21	0.44
13.	P.C.P.I	2.53	0.27	0.13
14.	Collection of Medicinal Plants	0.30	0.09	0.14
15.	Fruit Processing & Preservation	0.34	0.01	0.01
16.	Fibre	3.24	1.00	0.38
17.	Cottage Soap	1.48	0.26	0.87
18.	Cottage Soap	5.16	3.91	0.21
19.	Bio-Gas	0.58	*	*
20.	Polymer	0.07	*	*
21.	Carpentry & Blacksmithy	3.46	0.25	0.31
22.	Household Aluminium Utensils	0.08	*	*
23.	Electronics	0.05	*	*
24.	Brass, Copper & Bell Metal	0.03	*	*
25.	Polyvastra	0.46	0.09	0.03
26.	Other Textiles	0.48	0.03	0.02
27.	Service Industry	0.47	0.02	*
	Total	42.49	10.38	3.36

* Less than 500 (Employment)

Source: Annual Report, KVIC, 1998-99.

APPENDIX—II

Performance of the Five Top Industries in Terms of Employment

Sl. No.	*Industry*	*1996-97*	*1997-98*	*% Share in Total V.I*
1.	Palmgur	8.52	8.52	20
2.	Pottery	5.66	5.27	12
3.	Leather	5.36	5.16	12
4.	Carpentry & Blacksmithy	4.26	3.46	8
5.	Fibre	3.08	3.24	8
	Total	26.89	25.65	60

Source: Annual Report, KVIC, 1998-99.

APPENDIX—III

Performance of Top Six States

Sl. No	*States*	*Production (Rs. in crores)*	*% Share in Total VI. Production*	*Employment (lakh persons) Production*	*% Share in Total V. I. Employment*
1.	Maharashtra	669.34	17	3.83	9
2.	U.P.	587.35	15	5.04	12
3.	Tamilnadu	458.51	12	10.29	24
4.	Rajasthan	366.72	9	3.15	7
5.	Karnataka	249.40	6	1.88	4
6.	Andhra Pradesh	224.22	6	3.24	8
	Total	2,555.54	66	27.43	65

Source: Annual Report, KVIC, 1998-99.

APPENDIX—IV

Progress of Village Industries

Sl. No.	*Item*	*1957-58*	*1967-68*	*1977-78*	*1987-88*	*1997-98*
1.	Production	14.50	74.56	192.54	1,260.88	3,895.21
2.	Growth Rate		18%	10%	21%	12%

(Contd.)

Sl. No.	Item	1957-58	1967-68	1977-78	1987-88	1997-98
3.	Sales	4.72	61.71	190.29	1,391.51	4,319.38
4.	Employment	5.64	7.70	14.94	27.66	42.49
5.	Earnings	3.71	11.43	50.10	353.52	1,275.58
6.	Net Disbursement (Budgetary)	5.09	21.86	53.67	313.26	933.92
7.	Villages Covered	0.15	0.24		1.50	2.50
8.	Number of V.I	10	22	22	26	116

Source: Annual Report, KVIC, 1998-99.

APPENDIX—V

Summary of Performance of Village Industries—1995-96

Sl. No.	States and Union Territories	Production	Sales	Employment	Earnings
I	**STATE**				
1.	Andhra Pradesh	22,421.79	22,861.41	3.24	9,193.14
2.	Arunachal Pradesh	76.62	79.67	0.01	32.09
3.	Assam	33,702.47	3,157.56	0.95	1,041.12
4.	Bihar	15,748.59	14,291.16	1.24	3,087.32
5.	Goa	803.52	1,037.72	0.05	333.06
6.	Gujarat	13,711.68	11,588.91	0.54	3,231.65
7.	Haryana	5,850.62	6,483.41	0.40	1,381.16
8.	Himachal Pradesh	6,097.36	6,690.85	0.66	2,317.12
9.	Jammu and Kashmir	7,348.04	7,962.51	0.70	2,337.30
10.	Karnataka	24,940.20	25,395.08	1.88	6,563.14
11.	Kerala	15,184.91	16,351.98	2.18	4,619.62
12.	Madhya Pradesh	12,650.02	13,719.08	0.95	5,106.69
13.	Maharashtra	66,933.34	83,615.21	3.83	19,160.47
14.	Manipur	2,951.97	3,112.62	0.42	949.01
15.	Meghalaya	1,411.82	1,755.84	0.13	874.85
16.	Mizoram	2,085.46	1,962.73	0.12	514.52
17.	Nagaland	1,907.83	2,135.16	0.19	1,046.21
18.	Orissa	6,910.98	7,104.34	2.07	2,551.09

(Contd.)

Sl. No.	*States and Union Territories*	*Production*	*Sales*	*Employ-ment*	*Earnings*
19.	Punjab	17,101.30	19,247.09	0.95	4,834.71
20.	Rajasthan	36,672.29	54,566.62	3.15	15,356.46
21.	Sikkim	265.21	259.96	0.05	82.57
22.	Tamilnadu	45,850.97	45,968.62	10.29	19,797.45
23.	Tripura	1,226.89	1,274.41	0.27	459.78
24.	Uttar Pradesh	58,735.29	61,329.42	5.04	17,016.00
25.	West Bengal	15,151.53	15,802.29	2.95	4,086.82
	Total I	3,85,740.70	4,27,773.65	42.26	1,25,973.35
II.	**UNION TERRITORIES**				
1.	Andaman and Nicobar Islands	110.14	99.22	—	55.36
2.	Chandigarh	604.56	697.84	0.04	136.10
3.	Dadra and Nagar Haveli	—	—	—	—
4.	Daman and Diu	—	—	—	—
5.	Delhi	2,586.76	2,895.57	0.15	1,188.83
6.	Lakshadweep	9.79	6.00	—	1.54
7.	Pondicherry	469.06	465.26	0.04	202.50
	Total—I	3,780.31	4,163.89	0.23	1,584.33
	Total—II	3,89,521.01	4,31,937.54	42.49	1,27,557.68

Source: Annual Report, KVIC, 1998-99.

APPENDIX—VI

Village Industry—Eighth Five Year Plan (1992-97) Indicate Targets

Sl. No.	*Industry*	*Unit*	*Production*		*Employment lakh Person*		*Export (Rs. in crores)*	
			1991-92	*1996-97*	*1991-92*	*1996-97*	*1991-92*	*1996-97*
1.	Traditional Industries	Rs. Crores	20,916	41,432	26,432	328,24	10,331	30,015
2.	Khadi Industries	Mill. Mts.	114	160	14.61	16.50	—	—
3.	Village Industries	Rs. Crores	278	560	35.40	46.25	—	—
4.	Handloom Cloth	Mill. Mts.	5,000	7,000	106.00	117.00	450	1,000
		Rs. Crores	4,064	5,690	—	—	—	—
5.	Sericulture	Tonnes	13,535	21,400	54.60	65.00	600	1,000
	Raw Silk	Rs. Crores	996	1,590	—	—	—	—
6.	Handicrafts	Rs. Crores	13,260	29,620	48.25	77.65	9,215	27,915
7.	Coir Fibre	Lakhs tones	2.2	2.77	5.46	5.84	66	100
		Rs. Crores	168	121	—	—	—	—
	Total	Rs. Crores	60,483.2	1,11,426.77	528.64	656.48	20,662	60,030

Source: Economic Survey, 1997-98.

2

District Industries Centre for Rural Enterprise Development

Governments both Central and State have, in the past, taken a number of measures for the development of small and village industries, but the actual achievements have been far below the expectations. Also the focus of attention for industrial development was mainly on large cities and states capital to the neglect of district areas. In addition, multiplicity of institutions involved in small industries development and the job of promoting the industrial units on difficult task for small entrepreneurs. Hence, it was felt necessary to establish required facilities to village and small industries under one roof. Accordingly, the District Industries Centres (DICs) were established in May 1978 in order to cater to the needs of small units.

Each district has a DIC at its headquarters. And the main responsibility of DIC is to act as the chief coordinator or multi-functional agency in respect of various Government departments and other agencies. The prospective small entrepreneur would get all assistance from DIC for setting up and running industry in rural areas. Up to 1991 about 422 DICs have been set up throughout the country. These DICs have assisted more than 1.5 lakh units generating employment for more than 10.1 lakh persons. The metropolitan cities of Delhi, Bombay, Calcutta and Madras have been kept outside the purview of the DIC.

Under the Industrial Policy statement 1977, District Industries Centre (DIC) was established in Dindigul district of Tamilnadu in the year 1978-79. At the time of inception, there were only 677 registered small scale industries and 16 large and medium scale industries in the district. At present, there are 4,134 registered small scale industries and 153 large and medium scale industries. The DIC provides the facility for registration of the units and a number of incentives, concessions and subsidies to small scale industrial units in the industrially backward taluk of the Dindigul district. The present study attempts to analyse the performance of District Industries Centre in the promotion of small scale industries in Dindigul district during the period from 1992-93 to 1996-97. The various problems faced by the DIC in implementation of schemes and few suggestions are also reviewed in this study.

The specific objectives of the study are:

(i) to analyse the performance of DIC in the small enterprise development of Dindigul district;

(ii) to review the various problems faced by the implementors of the DIC's scheme in the study district; and

(iii) to suggest the concrete and suitable measures for the effective implementation of the schemes of DIC for small enterprise development.

Secondary data for the period from 1992-93 to 1996-97 were obtained from the various records available with the DIC of Dindigul district. A oral discussion was held with the General Manager and the various managers of the DIC of Dindigul district, in order to identify the problems of the DIC.

Performance of Provisional and Permanent Registration Scheme

The provisional registration is made on a prescribed form and is to enable a party to take steps to bring the unit into existence, and is valid for first six months, renewable for next six months. It enables entrepreneur to apply for a shed, plot, power connections, financial assistance and to obtain sales tax and excise duties certificates.

Table 2.1
Performance of Registration Scheme in Dindigul District

Sl. No.	*Performance*	*Provisional*		*Permanent*	
		Target	*Achievement*	*Target*	*Achievement*
1.	1991-92	1,300	1,300 (100)	500	501 (100.2)
2.	1992-93	2,000	1,763 (88.2)	700	676 (96.6)
3.	1993-94	2,160	1,943 (89.45)	780	733 (93.9)
4.	1994-95	2,160	2,168 (100.4)	935	743 (79.5)
5.	1995-96	1,632	1,648 (100.9)	970	1,161 (119.7)

Source: Annual Reports of DIC, Dindigul District.

The reasons for such shortfalls have been resulted mainly whenever there was protected duration between the application time and the time of approval, whenever the time span tended to be long there was tendency for number to fall subsequently resulting in shortfall.

Application for Permanent Registration scheme is to enable a unit be entitled for working capital requirements either in terms of material or in terms of cash. It is made in prescribed form one year after the commencement of commercial production and acquired provisional registration certificate and it enables a unit to obtain the incentives concessions as excise exemptions, income tax concessions, sales tax exemptions, power tariff concessions, price purchase preference for goods produced, availability of raw materials depending on the existing policy to avail permanent registration certificate, the following aspects of the unit is assessed.

- *(i)* Statutory and administrative clearances,
- *(ii)* Violation of locational restriction.
- *(iii)* The value of plant and machinery is within the limits prescribed.

(iv) If the unit is not owned, controlled or a subsidiary of any other industrial undertaking as per notification.

As may be visualised from Table 2.1 the decline in Dindigul district was in 1991-92, 1992-93, 1993-94 when it was 100.2 per cent 96.6 per cent and 93.9 per cent respectively, short of the targets laid by Director of Industries and Commerce for Dindigul district. This was mainly due to the fact that most of the units could not attain the required condition to qualify for permanent registration, thus clearance was delayed.

Performance of Cottage and Handicrafts Industry Registration Scheme

Cottage industries are those industries run within the residences of the artisans by family members without any hired labour, with the use of locally available raw materials, normally characterised by little capital investment. Mostly in rural areas, methods of production are traditional and carried down from generation to generation; and generally little power or no power at all is used.

Table 2.2

Cottage and Handicrafts Industries Registration Scheme

Sl. No.	*Performance*	*Cottage*		*Handicrafts*	
		Target	*Achievement*	*Target*	*Achievement*
1.	1991-92	320	321 (100.3)	220	202 (91.8)
2.	1992-93	340	344 (101.2)	340	320 (94.1)
3.	1993-94	340	340 (100)	340	341 (100.3)
4.	1994-95	340	345 (101.5)	340	340 (100)
5.	1995-96	340	341 (100.3)	350	350 (100)

Source: Annual Report of District Industries Centre of Dindigul District.

The major industrial activities in this scheme include pot making, cottage match making, ghani oil extraction; bee-keeping, bamboo cane works, basket-making, korai mat weaving, stone weaving items, clay folks.

The performance of the cottage industries registration scheme was quite satisfactory in Dindigul district where the DIC was still comparatively new and such new services of the artisans were motivated to come up for registration and more than 100 per cent achievement of targets was realised. Also contributing of the cottage industries registration; more number of entrepreneurs would come forward to start up small scale industries. If such delay like in granting of registration under could be avoided.

Handicrafts are those items that normally hand-made for purpose of providing beauty and are of aesthetic value, ability to produce such reveals the creative urge of the community, as a result of long practice and training.

Handicrafts products often vary in design and calls for great care, skill, dedication in their production. It is found from Table 2.2 that shortfalls in the target aimed at 94.1 per cent in Dindigul district in 1992-93 and being 91.8 per cent in 1991-92 and 100 per cent in 1995-96. This has been accounted to be the complacency of the officers whenever there was good performance in the previous years.

Self-Employment for Educated Unemployed Youth Scheme (SEEUY)

The scheme which aimed at providing self-employment opportunities to the educated unemployed youth. This scheme was started in 1983, and had the following important features. At present, the features have been liberalised.

1. Applicant must have passed tenth standard pass
2. Age limit between 18 and 35 years
3. Maximum loan amount was Rs. 25,000
4. Two or more could join together to start any business service or an industry.

The fixation of the target is subject to the availability of funds. In Dindigul district the trend fixation declined from

Table 2.3
Data on Self-Employment for Educated Unemployed Youth (SEEUY)

Sl. No.	*Performance Year*	*Target*	*Achievement*	*Target*	*Achievement*
1.	1991-92	325	330 (102)	3.50	3.50 (100)
2.	1992-93	400	408 (102)	4.73	4.73 (100)
3.	1993-94	400	400 (100)	5.20	5.20 (100)
4.	1994-95	450	400 (88.9)	5.20	5.20 (100)
5.	1995-96	450	450 (100)	36.42	36.42 (100)

Source: Annual Report of District Industries Centre of Dindigul District.

500 beneficiaries in 1992-93 to 350 beneficiaries in 1993-94. In 1991 only 80.2 per cent achievement was realised in Dindigul district and in all the five years it was 100 per cent or more achievement of the targets.

This kind of trend was largely as a result of selective popularity of the scheme in Dindigul. As most of the applicants were skilled in some trades and were thus more motivated to take up the opportunities.

State Capital Investments Subsidy Scheme

New SSIs started in industrially backward areas are eligible for this subsidy on fixed assets value at rate of 20 per cent of maximum or Rs. 20 lakh for not industrially backward areas and 15 per cent or Rs. 15 lakh for other areas. An additional of Rs. 5 lakh or 50 per cent of capital investment provided to those units employ a total of 30 per cent of total employment for regular workers of women.

In Dindigul district the performance of this scheme was satisfactory as the targets set by the Director of Industries and Commerce following the applications made by the District

Table 2.4

State Capital Investments Subsidy Scheme in Dindigul District

Sl. No.	*Performance Year*	*Target*	*Achievement*
1.	1991-92	3.50	3.50 (100)
2.	1992-93	4.73	4.73 (100)
3.	1993-94	5.20	5.20 (100)
4.	1994-95	5.20	5.20 (100)
5.	1995-96	36.42	36.42 (100)

Source: Annual Report of District Industries Centre of Dindigul District.

Industries Centre were all met, in the District over the five years from 1991-92 to 1995-96. The performance was 100 per cent and above, this was due to the popularity of this scheme among the entrepreneurs in the targeted areas.

Low Tension Power Tariff and Generator Subsidy Scheme

Low Tension Power Tariff subsidy is given at the rate of 40 per cent of the actual energy charges paid for the first year, 30 per cent for the second year and 20 per cent for the third year. To obtain the low tension power tariff subsidy scheme, an eligibility certificate should be obtained from the General Manager, District Industries Centre, within three months from the date of commencement of production of power connection whichever is later. This scheme helps the units to reduce their production cost consequently.

There was progressive growth in the target of the low tension power turn of subsidy scheme, plus the achievement of the same. In all the years, there was a 100 per cent achievement of the targets set in Dindigul. In 1995-96 there

Table 2.5
Performance of Low Tension Power-Tariff and Generator Subsidy Scheme

Sl. No.	*Performance Year*	*Low Tension Tariff Subsidy*		*Generator Subsidy*	
		Target	*Achievement*	*Target*	*Achievement*
1.	1991-92	1.40	1.40 (100)	NA	NA
2.	1992-93	3.50	3.50 (100)	1.46	1.46 (100)
3.	1993-94	3.93	3.93 (100)	1.98	2.00 (101)
4.	1994-95	4.73	4.73 (100)	2.00	2.00 (100)
5.	1995-96	15.32	15.32 (100)	1.00	1.09 (100)

Source: Annual report of District Industries Centre of Dindigul District.

was an increase of 224 per cent owing to the increased number of applicants. It is clear that in 1990-91 a total of Rs. 3.2 lakh was provided in the form of subsidy in Dindigul district to those units having consumption of 130 HP and below and increased to Rs. 15.32 lakh in 1995-96.

Generator subsidy scheme is given at the rate of 15 per cent of the cost of purchase subject to maximum of Rs. 5 lakh. This scheme is in effect from 22.5.1989.

To be eligible, the unit must meet the conditions that the equipment to be purchased must be brand new and from accredited manufacturers. The prior permission of Tamil Nadu Electricity Board should have been obtained for the installation of the new generator.

As per this scheme, the subsidy is disbursed through the General Manager, District Industries Centre within one year from the date of purchase of the generator-set, or installation of the generator-set, whichever is later.

During some years there were no applicants to this scheme like in 1991-92 in Dindigul District Industries Centre. This has been attribute to the fact that the most of the units operate below the installed capacities. Thus profit appropriation has been very long and it will be uneconomical running cost, thus they prefer to operate only when power connection is availed or else to for second-hand generators to which this scheme cannot be availed.

Interest Free Sales Tax Deferral and Waiver Scheme

Interest free sales tax deferral is established for a period of nine years for the units established in backward taluks and in the industrial estates and 5 years for other taluks to the extent of total investment made on the project. A scheme of sales tax waiver for 5 years to new industries started in the most backward taluks is simultaneously available.

The very objective of this scheme is to reduce the burden of taxation particularly during the early years of inception of an industrial unit to help the units to consolidate their financial position.

Table 2.6

Performance of Sales Tax Deferral Waiver Scheme in Dindigul District

Sl. No.	*Performance Year*	*Target*	*Achievement*
1.	1991-92	52.5	52.91 (100.4)
2.	1992-93	80.0	80.25 (100.3)
3.	1993-94	97.66	97.66 (100)
4.	1994-95	135.05	135.05 (100)
5.	1995-96	324.00	324.00 (100)

Source: Annual Reports of DIC, Dindigul District.

The performance of this scheme in Dindigul district was more satisfactory as the targets and achievements together maintained an upward trend from Rs. 52.5 lakh in 1991-92 with an achievement of Rs. 324 lakh. The popularity of this scheme is largely felt mainly due to the increasing competition from the large scale sector and the other small scale registered units. This scheme among others should be maintained in the light of increasing competition particularly to the newly started units.

Problems of the DIC in Dindigul District

1. *Poor Contact with the Beneficiaries*

As a result of long distance for the District Industries Centre and the entrepreneurs problems cropping are not promptly reported to the District Industries Centre; and whenever report is made, it is already too late for adequate measures to be taken.

2. *Inadequacy of Technical Staff*

In many technical areas, like production processes, material handling, many of the officers presently available with the District Industries Centre are not properly qualified to advice and counsel the entrepreneurs on many technical matters of production and management.

3. *Proliferation of Supporting Institutions*

The coordination of functioning of activities of the district industries centre is affected by the proliferation of supporting institutions which in many instance tend to perform similar functions.

4. *Shortage of Staff*

The number of field officers in the district industries centres is not adequate to visit all the taluks. For example, in Dindigul district four field officers are expected to visit and counsel beneficiaries and compile reports in all the seven taluks to cover ten taluks.

5. Delay in Sanctioning Approvals

The actual time span between the approval time by District Industries Centre for the various schemes and the final disbursement by the financial institutions, thus, resulting in demoralizing the applicants.

6. Training Opportunities

Many persons, particularly women, who on social considerations ignore the opportunities fearing the debt burden to their families; are reluctant to come to the District Industries Centre for loans and assistance even after the institution has offered them adequate training.

7. Restrictive Bank Credit

Many applications, submitted by the district industries centre, are not often honoured by the Bankers for fear of credit worthiness of the projects. So, frequently the district industries officers and managers are forced to intervene to convince the Bank officials of the viability of the intended project.

8. Inadequate Transport Facilities

Due to the vastness of areas under their work, the district industries centre find it difficult to send officers regularly in all the taluks to attend meetings, training programmes, seminars, field visits. The centres have currently two vehicles which are far from being adequate.

Recommendations

1. There is need to develop more infrastructural facilities particularly for communication for officers and credit and credit needs of the entrepreneurs, this will go a

long way to boost industrial development in the most backward and backward areas.

2. There is need to deploy more technical personnel who are technically qualified to man areas like production process, counseling and materials management techniques.
3. Since in Dindigul district the growth rate of small scale units has been rather slow yet there is increasing number of large scale and medium scale units, an ancillarcation committee may be constituted to find out how to make the two sectors of industry have beneficial co-existence.
4. The District Industries Centres should find out a more positive methods of motivation so that maximum number of participants may be obtained for the schemes and programmes, like institution of various awards for the successful entrepreneurs.
5. Since the number of staff presently available is inadequate to assist all the taluks to organize meetings, seminars, symposium regularly and compile reports of all the seven taluks in Dindigul district. It is a dire need of the hour to add more officers to the district industries centre.
6. There is need to strengthen the District Industries Centres to convert them into district entrepreneurs promotional agency, with support of three business associations, Government agencies and Banks, since the DIC is receiving the sympathy and the needs of the first generation entrepreneurs and other classes of micro-entrepreneurs than any other single agency in the district. It was also recommended by the Abdi-Hussain Committee report in February 1997.
7. Banks should be more attentive and concerned about their role in the promotion of the small scale industries. For this purpose, government should constitute a committee to monitor the extent of rejection of applications and delay of sanctions, and the possible reasons scrutinized and solutions be availed.

8. The lending rules and procedures for loaning and used credit extension to the small scale industries by the banks should be relaxed.
9. There should be standard record maintenance procedures by the District Industries Centres so that any comparative reference, study, could be made slightly easier. This would help where some uniform policies are envisaged.
10. There is need to motivate more female entrepreneurs to come up to take up business ventures, this calls for more seminars, motivation campaigns, meetings and symposiums in the district of Dindigul.
11. An equipped research labouration should be established under the District Industries Centre to enable small scale units to have easy access to the improved production technologies and processes, to enable quality upgradation and competitiveness of the small industries products.

References

1. C.B. Gupta and S.S. Khanka, *Entrepreneurial and Small Business Management*, Sultan Chand & Sons, 1996.
2. M.M. Verma, *Indian Economy—Development and Planning*, Forwarded Book Depot, 1993.
3. S.B. Srivastava, *A Practical Guide to Industrial Entrepreneur*, Sultan Chand & Co., 1992.
4. Government of India, Ministry of Industry, *Development of Small Scale Industries*, New Delhi, 1994.
5. Annual Reports of DIC, Dindigul District, Tamilnadu, 1990-91 to 1995-96.

3

Cooperatives for Rural Enterprise Development

Introduction

Co-operation is a democratic form of organisation and ordinarily co-operatives oppose political revolution because of the destruction which always accompanies it. The co-operative system, when once developed, can easily compete with and even out the capitalist system. Co-operation, in fact, is the true democratic answer to the existing evils of nepotism and favouritism, and is further the only way to obviate the pitfalls of dictatorship.

Co-operation is a joint or a collaborative behaviour that is directed towards some goals and in which there is common interest or hope of reward. Co-operation may be voluntary or involuntary, direct or indirect, formal or informal, but always there is a combination of efforts towards a specific end in which all the participants have a state, real or imagined. At its higher intellectual levels co-operation involves reciprocity of intent as well as jointness of behaviour, and it may even become an end in itself. There is no limit to potential range for co-operation; it is to be found in groups as small as the dyad and as large as leagues of sovereign states.

Five types of co-operation may usefully be distinguished, automatic, traditional, contractual, directed and spontaneous. Each can be found in all spheres of human society—political, religious, economic, cultural—and while it is important to distinguish the types from one another, it is equally important to emphasize that rarely, it ever, does any one of them exist in isolation.

Co-operation in simple term means some sort of joint action on the part of two or more persons associating themselves as social beings. V.L. Mehta has said: co-operation is only one aspect of vast movement which promotes voluntary association of individuals having common needs who combine towards the achievement of common economic needs.

Calvert, a Registrar of Co-operative Society has said, co-operation as a form of organisation wherein persons voluntarily associate together as human beings as the basis of equality for the promotion of the economic interest of themselves.

According to M.J. Herrick, Co-operation is the act of persons voluntarily united for utilising reciprocally their own forces, resources or both under their mutual arrangement to their common profit or loss. M.L. Darling has described co-operation as something more than a system. It is a spirit which appeals the heart and the mind. It is a Gospel of self-sufficiency and services.

Draft Fifth Plan observes, co-operation represents institutionalisation of the principle and impulse of mutual aid. It has the merit of combining freedom and opportunity for the small man with the benefit of large scale management and organisation. Thus, co-operation refers to an association of weak, poor and powerless masses who pool their resources for reaping those benefits which are open only to powerful and rich. It would not be co-operation, if persons working together for a common purpose, were not free partners; for example, the employment of a gang of laboureres by a contractor is not co-operation.

It is not for economic reasons alone that a machinery for co-operation is set up in undertakings. There is also a whole set of other arguments which stress the human aims of the undertaking, the need to improve the existing labour management relations, to ensure the development of the worker's individuality and to recognise his right to play an active part in organising production within the undertaking. Co-operatives eliminate distinction between employees and employers; and develop a sense of brotherhood among the members of a community or a vocation group.

Co-operatives can play the most important and successful role in the economic uplift of the weak and the poor, and in the large scale beneficial employment of the unemployed, both educated and uneducated. They give real freedom from poverty, disease and high prices and, instead, bestow an abundant life. These create an organisation of society, that places the advantage of even the best brains, at the service of the ordinary man. They will give the workers a sense of duty, responsibility and self-help, besides minimising corruption and uplifting their character, in general.

Co-operative Society

Co-operative Society is a voluntary organisation to which everyone is welcomed to join with equal rights and equal responsibilities. Its main motive is to provide services to its members and unlike private enterprise it does not work for earning profit. Report of the inquiry on Co-operative Enterprise in Europe states, "A co-operative enterprise is one which belongs to the people who use its services, the control of which rests equally with all its members and the gains of which are distributed in proportion to the use they make of its services".

According to C.R. Fray, "The co-operative association is an association of firms or households for business purposes—an economic institution through which economic activity is conducted in the pursuit of economic objectives."

Professor Paul Lambert, an authority on co-operation defines co-operative society as, "an enterprise formed and directed by an association of users, applying within itself the rules of democracy and directly intended to serve both its own members and the community as a whole".

The Indian Co-operative Societies Act, 1912, considers, "a co-operative society is a society which has its object the promotion of the economic interests of its members in accordance with co-operative principles". The industrial co-operative societies have been jointly setting up different types of co-operative organisations for providing common services. Industrial co-operative banks have been formed by them for the provisions of credit and banking facilities. Industrial associations have been formed at different levels for supply, sales and similar other activities; some of them also undertake organisational and developmental work. Supervising and guaranteeing unions also come in this category. The industrial co-operative societies are also setting up common facility workshops; e.g., co-operative spinning mills, co-operative wool processing plants and so on. The membership of some of these federal bodies is confined to co-operative societies only.

Co-operative Movement and Handloom Co-operative Societies

It is well known that handloom is an ancient industry in India, which has survived the storms of political and administrative changes that shock India. The Moghul invasion and later the Moghul Rule did no harm to the handloom industry. When later the East India Company came to India, they, however, looked upon with great jealousy the famous Dacca Muslin, of which it is said that several yards could be rolled into the palm of one's hand. When trading and shop-keeping soon evolved by a thousand trickery and chicanery into British Rule in India, the spinners and weavers of Dacca came in for a great deal of attention.

History tells us of the horrowing story of Dacca that in the early years of their Rule, the British cut away the thumbs of the Dacca Muslin-Weavers and of how the famous Muslin became a thing of the past. But by and large the handloom industry has survived not only the British Rulers of India, but also the onslaughts of the powerful textile industry. Even today, many millions of people depend on the handloom industry for their living.

The co-operative movement in India started towards the beginning of the twentieth century. It is more than eighty years old. In the early years of the 20th century, co-operatives were mainly organised as a defensive organisations for dealing with problems of rural indebtedness. In course of time, however, different types of co-operative institutions were formed. The introduction of the Co-operative Credit Societies Act in 1904 marked the beginning of the co-operative movement.

In 1912, the co-operative society Act was passed on the formation of societies for purposes other than the supply of credit. Further, by the Acts of 1919, 1929 and 1931 co-operation became a provincial important subject. In 1934, the International Co-operative Alliance (ICA) has formulated the principle of co-operation. In 1937, there were 8,10,000 co-operative societies of various types in 103 countries of the world. These societies had a membership of more than 143 million. Since 1937, the co-operative movement has grown by leaps and bounds throughout the world. After the Second World War, people realised the importance of co-operative movement.

After Independence, the co-operative movement has been making rapid progress in various directions. The All India Rural Credit Committee (1954), the Co-operative Planning Committee (1960) and the Vaikunthlal Mehta Committee (1964) have been formed to constitute co-operation. These committees pointed out that the main causes for limited progress of the co-operative movements in India were the 'laissez fair' policy of the state and the illiteracy of the people. Therefore, the Five Year Plans in India have concentrated much on co-operation.

It is during the plan period that the movement has taken the present shapes. In October 1952, the All India Handloom Board was established. It was entrusted with wide and comprehensive functions to advise the Government on the problems of the industry and to examine various schemes put forward by the states for the development and improvement of industry and to make recommendations for financial aid from the handloom fund.

The Khadi and other Handloom Industries Development (Additional Excise Duty on Cloth) Act was passed in 1953 and the Government desired to put a sum of Rs. 4 crore at the disposal of the Board for giving financial aid to the handloom industries during the year 1953-54. The Board decided to disburse this development expenditure through co-operatives.

The Khadi and Villages Industries Commission (KVIC) also introduced a special programme for organising co-operatives of workers in these industries; and extended assistance to them in various forms. Programmes for strengthening the societies, improving their technique and marketing their goods were introduced by the All India Handicrafts Board.

The Central Government set up the First Working Group on Industrial Co-operatives in 1957 which submitted its report in July 1958. Its recommendations were accepted by the Government with certain modifications in November 1959, and action on these recommendations was initiated towards the close of the second plan when greater attention began to be paid to the co-operatives in Handicrafts, small-scale and other industries.

The third plan made a reference to the Government of India Resolution of November, 1959 on Industrial Co-operatives, and expressed that these decisions, given the necessary climate and leadership, should facilitate the development of industrial co-operatives during this plan. In the fourth plan, efforts will be made to ensure a quicker pace of growth by co-operatives in the industrial sector keeping in view the estimates made by the working group, namely, 68,000 societies with a membership of 6.5 million. Special efforts were made in the Fourth Plan to revitalise inactive societies. About 50 per cent of the existing handlooms were in the co-operative sector.

The draft outline of the Fifth Five Year Plan (1974-80) stated that, co-operation is eminently suited to bring about desired socio-economic changes in the context of the existing conditions in the country. There is no other instrument as potentially powerful and full of social purpose as the co-operative movement.

The major strategy of the Sixth Five Year Plan (1980-85) is to strengthen the infrastructure for both agriculture and handloom co-operative sectors so as to create favourable conditions for an accelerated economic growth. In this plan, the total outlay earmarked for the implementation of various schemes of co-operation come to Rs. 914.23 crore. The textile policy (1981) stressed that special efforts would be made to ensure availability of adequate yarn so that the handloom sector will be enabled to achieve the production target alloted to it. The National Handloom Development Corporation assigned a key role for the handloom sector in the procurement and distribution of yarn at a reasonable price.

During the Seventh and Eighth Five Year Plan periods an expanding role is envisaged for the handloom sector that will include the production of the entire requirement of Janatha cloth. In spite of several schemes and policies implemented for the development of handloom industries in India, most of the handloom co-operative societies are facing, now, many problems for the continuous functioning of the societies.

A Study on Handlom Weavers Cooperative Society

Textiles, the single largest industry accounting for about 20 per cent of the total industrial output and employing about 15 million people, is also the single largest contributor to India's export earnings. Textiles, comprising garments, handlooms, cotton synthetic yarn, wool and woollen garments, are exported to almost all the countries, the major ones being European Economic Community member countries, U.S.A., Canada, Japan, Switzerland, Sweden and Australia.

Textiles earned foreign exchange worth Rs. 8,366 crore in 1990-91 as compared to Rs. 4,366 crore in 1988-89. It accounted for Rs. 5,918 crore during April and September 1991 registering an increase of 34.2 per cent over the corresponding period of previous year. This remarkable performance can, to some extent, be attributed to the various promotional measures taken by the Government to promote the textile exports.

In 1991, Tamilnadu had approximately 27 per cent of the handloom weavers in the country. Typically a household industry, handloom weaving accounted for around 45 per cent of employment in household industry in 1991, as against an all India average of 18 per cent. Manipur was the only other state with a higher proportion. In Tamilnadu, the heartland of the industry is the best running from Coimbatore in the west to Salem in the east through Periyar district. Secondary modes exist in the districts of Changalpattu and North Arcot, as well as in the Southern districts of Madurai, Ramanatha-puram, Trinelveli Kattabomman and V.O. Chidambaranar.

In Tamilnadu, today, a very large part of the weaver work force is in the co-operative sector. According to the most recent figures for 1990-91, around 60 per cent of the 5.56 lakh looms in the state, are in the co-operative system. There are currently about 1,600 societies in the state, with major concentrations is Ramanathapuram, Trinelveli and V.O. Chidambaranar districts. Most co-operatives cater to weavers who own looms.

The society supplies yarn and pays a piece wage when the product is returned. Weavers get this wage and also as share in the profits of the society, let., or co-optex - which co-ordinates yarn supply and marketing. Co-optex obtains yarn from the private sector and from co-operative spinning mills and routes it to the societies through a network of depots. It also lifts at least 50 per cent of the output of the societies, and markets them within or outside the state.

The handloom industries are facing two major types of problems i.e., from the powerloom sector and from the short-coming of the co-operative sector. The co-operative system is part of an overall framework of measures that have been taken to present the handloom sector from being wiped out by superior mill competition. In spite of progressive measures like reservation of some designs to handloom industries, coverage of looms under co-operative fold, incentives in the matter of wage, bonus, rebate and conditions of work under the co-operative fold, legislative measures in minimum wage and protection of weavers communities, the co-operative handloom societies do not yield the desired result.

It is also noted that there exists a controversial view over the impact of co-operation on handloom industry and its significance on the weavers socio-economic development process. The present study attempts to analyse the impact of the handloom weavers' co-operative societies on the economic development of the weavers in the Pudur block of V.O. Chidambaranar district of Tamilnadu.

The specific objectives of the study are:

(i) To study the functioning and performance of Handloom Weaver's Co-operative Societies in Pudur Block of V.O. Chidambaranar district during the period from 1990-91 to 1994-95.

(ii) To analyse the impact of the handloom societies on the economic status of the weavers in the study area;

(iii) To compare the socio-economic conditions of the

members of the Handloom co-operative society with the weavers of the Industrial co-operative societies;

(iv) To find out the various problems faced by the weavers of the co-operative societies in the study block; and

(v) To make the concrete suggestions for the promotion of co-operative societies and for the development of economic status of the co-operative weavers.

Methodology—Design of the Study

The most concentration of the co-operative societies are only in the Ramanathapuram, Trinelveli Kattabomman and V.O. Chidambaranar districts. The present study was conducted in the Pudur Block of V.O. Chidambaranar district. The handloom co-operative organisation in the V.O.C. district has four divisions, namely, Tuticorin division, Ayyan Bommaiyapuram division, Ettaiyapuram division and Paramankurichi division. The Ayyan Bommaiyapuram division are selected for the study on the basis of the criteria that the most of the industrial co-operative societies and co-operative weavers societies are actively functioning in this division. The study division includes the active functioning of 5 weavers co-operative societies.

After selecting the study district and the handloom textile division, the study block was selected for the interview purposes. There are 11 blocks in the V.O. Chidambaranar district. Pudur block was selected for the study and a sample of four co-operative societies were chosen. The four sample co-operative societies cover 2 weavers co-operative societies. The sample weavers co-operative societies are:

(i) 1,109 Nagalapuram Weavers Co-operative Society and

(ii) EE 82 Pudur Weavers Co-operative society.

The two sample Industrial Weavers Co-operative Societies are:

(i) TNH 90 Nagalapuram Industrial Weavers Co-operative Society and,

(ii) EE 370 Pudur Industrial Weavers Co-operative Society.

In order to find out the economic status of the weavers, 20 sample weavers were selected from each co-operative societies in the Pudur block. A total of 80 weavers were administered with a pretested questionnaire. The questionnaire includes the general particulars, employment and income level of the weavers, problems faced by the members of the society and their own suggestions for the development of handloom industries. Thus, primary data were collected from the sample respondents in the Pudur block of V.O. Chidambaranar district.

Secondary data were collected from the Directorate of Handloom and Textiles, Madras, Office Records of Assistant Director of Handloom and Textiles, Tuticorin, Regional Office, Co-optex, Madurai and V.O.C. District Central Co-operative Bank, Tuticorin. In addition to the office records, the annual reports of the co-operative societies in Pudur Block, various books, journals, newspapers and Government publications were referred for the present study.

The reference period of the present study is the co-operative year from 1990-91 to 1994-95. The primary data were collected during the period from January 1996 to March 1996 in the study area.

Concepts

The traditional household handloom industry has recently got three main types of organisations, namely, independent weaver, the master weaver and the co-operative society. The present study concentrates only on the weavers employing in the co-operative society. The two types of handloom co-operative societies are:

(i) Handloom Co-operative Weaver's Society; and
(ii) Industrial Handloom Co-operative Society.

Co-operative Weavers

The handloom weavers co-operative society supplies yarn to the weavers having own looms and pays a piece wage when the product is returned. The members of the society also get a share in the profit of the society. They are termed as "Co-operative Weavers" in this study.

Industrial Co-operative Weavers

Industrial co-operative society enroll members from among the loom-less weavers. The Industrial Co-operative Society, itself, is running a number of looms in a particular place and the members get the employment in the industrial estate. The weavers of the industrial co-operative society also get the piece wage rate. They are called as "Industrial Co-operative Weavers" in the present study.

Evaluation of Handloom Weavers' Co-operative Societies

The co-operative movement took a concrete shape in India for the first time in 1904, when the Co-operative Credit Societies Act was passed. Later in 1912, the Co-operative Societies Act paved way for registration of non-credit societies as well as federations of co-operatives. Since then, co-operative movement have made noticeable progress in stage by stage. Handloom co-operatives have been given due importance both in the national policy and in the Five Year Plans. This section deals with the evaluation of Handloom Weavers' Co-operative Societies in Tamilnadu, V.O. Chidambaranar district and Pudur block during the period from 1990-91 to 1994-95.

Registration of the Co-operative Society

A primary society means a registered society of an apex society or a central society. A primary weavers' co-operative society means a registered society which has its principal objective of the production of handloom cloth or fabrics or making production of cloth and marketing under co-operation of weaver members.

Any such co-operative society is registered under the Tamilnadu Co-operative Societies Act, 1961 (Tamilnadu Act 53 of 1961) on the basis of limited liability. Any weavers over eighteen years of age who is competent to contract, residing within the limited area referred by the co-operative bylaw may be eligible to become a member of a society.

For the formation and registration of a primary weavers' co-operative society, a minimum of 100 weaver members should join together and contribute Rs. 20 each and the remaining share of Rs. 80 for each shall be contributed by the Government to form the society.

Management Executives

The Government of India has always have the sponsor of the schemes under various Acts of cooperative movement to different states. By following its guidelines, different states including Tamilnadu appoints an Officer, Registrar to execute various schemes for all the co-operative societies within the state. The Registrar is the administrative head of all the co-operative departments of the State Government.

The co-operative departments provide five major types of assistance to the co-operative societies in the state.

They are:

(i) Participation in the share capital of the co-operative societies;

(ii) Grant of financial assistance by way of loans and subsidy to co-operative societies;

(iii) Provision of guarantee for repayment of deposits, investment and borrowing received by the co-operative societies;

(iv) Provision of services—Government staff to assist the co-operative societies; and

(v) Any other assistance.

In order to execute these assistance, Directors were appointed in each wing of the co-operatives such as Agriculture, Industry, Banks, etc. In this criterion, in Tamilnadu, Director of Handloom and Textiles is appointed to co-ordinate the activities of various co-operative and non-co-operative societies of the handloom and textile industry. The Director has Assistant Directors of Handloom and Textiles under his control to co-ordinate various works relating to the handloom and textile organisations in each district. The main responsibilities are as follows:

(a) Handloom and Powerloom Industry,

(b) Distribution of Raw Materials,

(c) Production of Yarn and Mill Cloth,

(*d*) Textile Industry,
(*e*) Enforcement of Various Textile Control Order,
(*f*) Statutory Control Over Mill Made Cloth,
(*g*) Tamilnadu Zari Union, and
(*h*) Co-operative Spinning Mills.

Among all the above cited works, the first and the foremost work of the Department of Assistant Director of Handloom and Textiles is to administrate the weavers' co-operative societies.

Organisational Structure of Co-operative Society

The organisational structure of a Handloom Weavers' Co-operative Society are depicted in Diagram 3.1.

Diagram 3.1

Organisational Structure of the Weavers' Co-operative Society

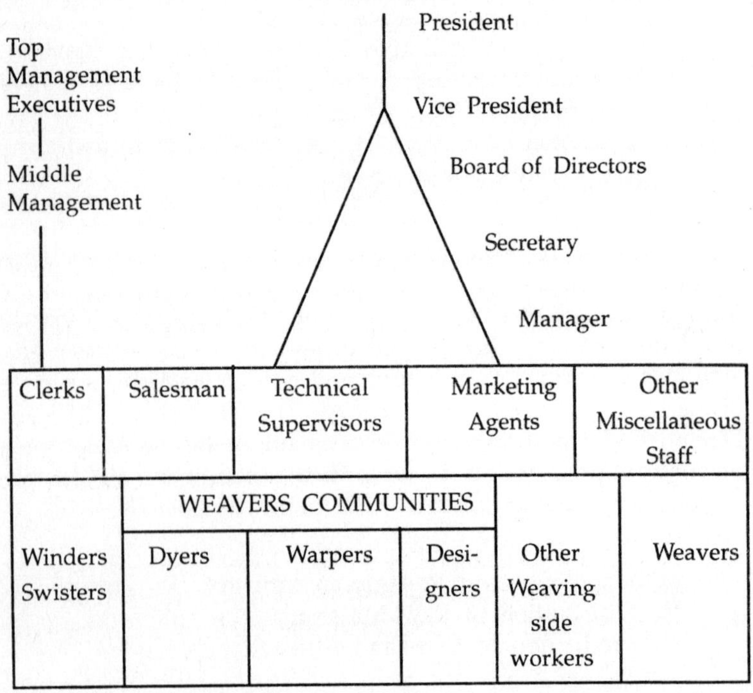

Board of Directors

The executive management of the affairs of the society shall rest on the Board of Directors. The Board of Directors shall consist of not more than 7 'A' class members of whom at least five shall be weaver members. When the Government has taken shares in the society, it may nominate a State Representative among the Board of Directors of the Society. The members of the Board of Directors shall be elected by the General Body for a period of three years as per the Rule 30 of the Tamilnadu Co-operative Rules, 1963. The Board of Directors shall frame suitable regulations defining the duties and responsibilities of the office-bearers and establishments.

President

After the members of the Board of Directors are selected by the General Body, the president and vice-president will be selected as per Rule 31 of the Tamilnadu Co-operative Rules, 1963. The president shall have a general control over all the affairs of the society.

Secretary

The secretary shall be responsible for the executive administration of the society subject to the control of the president. The Board shall appoint a full time paid Secretary and administrative staff. The paid secretary or Manager of the society shall have a custody of all the properties of the society.

General Body

The alternative authority in all matters relating to the administration of the society shall be the general body members who shall meet from time to time or at least once in a year to review the working of the society. The Board of Directors may at any time call a general body meeting of the society for the conduct of business. The quorum for a general body meeting of members on the list at the time whichever is less.

Characteristics of Weavers' Co-operative Society

The chief characteristics of a weavers' co-operative society as per its bylaws are:

- *(a)* It is an association of weavers.
- *(b)* It is an undertaking run by members themselves at their own risk.
- *(c)* It is a democratic organisation and every member of the society has only one vote.
- *(d)* It's keynote is service and not profit.
- *(e)* It has the basic principle of equality of all.
- *(f)* It is socio-economic movement.
- *(g)* It is a voluntary organisation.
- *(h)* It is not only to serve its members but also to serve the community as a whole.
- *(i)* It is a more equitable distribution of wealth.
- *(j)* It provides the means of social change without resorting to undesirable methods and violence.

Objectives of a Weavers' Co-operative Society

The bylaws of a weavers' co-operative society show the following objectives:

- *(i)* The objective of the society is the improvement of the handloom industry and of the economic condition of the weavers' residing in the area;
- *(ii)* To raise the money required for the society from weavers and others by issuing shares and borrowing by way of deposits or otherwise;
- *(iii)* To purchase raw materials and other appliance required to the society establishment;
- *(iv)* To give advance to the weaver members to purchase yarn and other materials to convert into finished goods and pay wages for the finished goods and to make regular employment and create good market;

(*v*) To act as an agent for the joint purchase of the domestic and other requirements for its members and sale of their finished goods; and

(*vi*) To obtain regular contracts for its goods from Government and public bodies with the help of the co-operative members.

Growth and Progress of Weavers' Co-operative Societies in Tamilnadu

The growth and progress of the weavers' co-operative societies in Tamilnadu is given in Table 3.1. It is clear from the table that there is a slow growth trend of number of societies, looms, weaver members, capital structure, production and sales. The number of co-operative societies has increased from 1,696 in 1990-91 to 1,974 in 1994-95. The weaver's membership under co-operative fold 3.68 lakh in the year 1990-91 has increased by 4.29 lakh in the year 1994-95. The weavers societies have utilised the 3.64 lakh active looms in the year 1990-91 and 4.24 lakh in 1994-95. Similarly the production and sales of the handlooms through co-operative societies in Tamilnadu was also raised. The value of the production was ranged from 1,390.3 lakh in 1990-91 to Rs. 1,618.2 lakh in 1994-95. The sales value was Rs. 1,295.2 lakh in 1990-91 and Rs. 1,507.5 lakh in 1994-95. These figures show the growth and progress of weavers' co-operative societies in Tamilnadu.

Weavers' Co-operative Societies in V.O. Chidambaranar District

The functioning of the weavers' co-operative societies in V.O. Chidambaranar district is divided into four divisions, for the purpose of administrative convenience. The performance of the co-operative societies of each division are analysed in this section.

Paramankurichi Division

Under this division, there are 12 weavers' co-operative societies which are actively functioning in the study district. The Paramankurichi division covers the Thathankulam,

Table 3.1

Growth and Progress of Weavers' Co-operative Societies in Tamilnadu

Sl. No.	*Particulars*	*1990-91*	*1991-92*	*1992-93*	*1993-94*	*1994-95*
1.	Number of co-operative societies	1,696	1,715	1,740	1,839	1,974
2.	Number of members (in lakhs)	3.68	3.73	3.78	3.99	4.29
3.	Number of looms (in lakhs)	3.64	3.68	3.74	3.95	4.24
4.	Paid up share capital (Rs. in lakhs)	752.50	760.93	772.02	815.95	875.85
5.	Working capital (Rs. in lakhs)	3,268.90	3,305.60	3,353.80	3,544.60	3,804.80
6.	Production in values (Rs. in lakhs)	1,390.30	1,405.90	1,426.40	1,507.50	1,618.20
7.	Sales in value (Rs. in lakhs)	1,295.20	1,309.70	1,328.90	1,404.40	1,507.50

Source: Office records, office of the Directorate of Handloom and Textiles, Government of Tamilnadu, Madras, 1990-91 to 1994-95.

Vijayapuram, Sayarpuram, Paramankurichi, Mukkani and Aral. The Paramankurichi division covers 2 Industrial weavers' co-operative societies (IWCS) and 10 weavers' co-operatives societies (WCS). The two IWC societies incur loss during the study period 1990-91 and 1994-95. The other 10 WC societies earn profit during the same period. But the progress and growth of the co-operative societies in the Paramankurichi division was in decreasing trend between the two period of times i.e., from 1990-91 to 1994-95. The growth trend shows the lower level in all aspects as number of members, number of looms, production, sales and profit. The value of production was increased from Rs. 71.66 lakh in 1990-91 to Rs. 76.26 lakh in 1994-95. Similarly, the value of sales was increased from Rs. 78.03 lakh in 1990-91 to Rs. 90.54 lakh in 1994-95 due to the inflationary pressure in the country.

Tuticorin Division

The Tuticorin Division of V.O.C. district consists of 9 weavers co-operative societies and one industrial weavers' co-operative society. The area covered by this division is Ettayapuram, Naduvirpatti, Silverpuram, Puthiyanputhur and Palayapuram. The growth and performance of weavers' co-operative societies in Tuticorin Division is exhibited in Table 3.2. The study found that the number of members of the 10 co-operative societies was decreased from 1,573 in 1990-91 to 1,474 in 1994-95 in Tuticorin division. But the active looms utilised by these societies were raised from 886 in 1990-91 at 941 in 1994-95. The production level was also decreased from 8,32,973 metres in 1990-91 to 7,62,807 metres in the year 1994-95. The value of production, sales level, value of the sales show the increasing trend during the study period in the Tuticorin division of V.O.C. district. Due to many reasons, the profit level was decreased from Rs. 12.39 lakh in 1990-91 to Rs. 11.89 lakh in 1994-95 in the Tuticorin division.

Ettayapuram Division

Under Ettayapuram division, there are 9 weavers' co-operative societies and 2 Industrial weavers' co-operative societies. The two industrial weavers' co-operative societies were incurring loss in study periods in the Ettayapuram division.

There was meager fall in the number of the society members and number of looms during the study period. The production level had fallen from 753 thousand metres in 1990-91 to 611.6 thousand metres in 1994-95. But the sales level was increased from 605.5 thousand metres in 1990-91 to 693.6 thousand metres in 1994-95. The total profit of the 11 weavers' co-operative societies was increased from Rs. 978.6 thousand in 1990-91 to 1,233.3 thousand in 1994-95.

Ayyan Bommaiyapuram Division

Table 3.2 reveals that the progress of co-operative societies was very slow in the Ayyan Bommaiyapuram division of V.O.C. district. The number of members of the societies were increased

Table 3.2

Growth and Progress of Weavers' Co-operative Societies in V.O. Chidambaranar District

Sl. No.	*Division*	*No. of Socie-ties*	*Number of Members*		*Number of Looms*		*Production* Metre (in thousand		*Production* Value (Rs. in lakhs)		*Sales* Metre (in thousand)		*Sales* Value (Rs. in lakhs)		*Profit Loss (Rs. in thousand)*	
1.	Tuticorin Division	10	1,573	1,474	886	941	833	763	89.88	101.77	760	870	86.27	118.12	1239.8	1,189.4
2.	Paraman-kurichi Division	12	1,131	1,091	652	577	643	573	71.66	76.26	614	580	78.03	90.54	410.7	404.6
3.	Ettayapuram Division	11	1,413	1,408	779	769	753	611	79.65	85.23	606	694	73.44	102.94	978.6	1,233.3
4.	Ayyan Bommaiyapuram Division	8	1,172	1,183	405	361	283	200	9.13	19.66	249	202	26.7	21.21	307.1	212.8
	V.O.C. District	41	5,289	5,156	2,722	2,648	2,512	2,147	250.32	282.92	2,229	2,283	264.44	332.81	2,936.2	3,040.1

Source: Computed from Administrative Report, Office of the Assistant Director of Handloom and Textiles, Tirunelveli.

meagerly from 1,172 in the year 1990-91 to 1,183 in the year 1994-95. But the active looms utilised was decreased from 405 in 1990-91 to 361 in 1994-95. the production level and the sales level also decreased during the study period.

The production level came down from 283 thousand metres in 1990-91 to 200 thousand metres in 1994-95. But the value of the production increased from Rs. 9.13 lakh in 1990-91 to Rs. 19.66 lakh in 1994-95. The sales level decrease from 249 thousand metres in 1990-91 to 202 thousand metres in 1994-95. The sales value as well as the profit level also decreased in the co-operative societies of the Ayyan Bommaiyapuram division of V.O.C. district during the study period.

V.O. Chidambaranar District

The progress and growth of weavers' co-operative societies in V.O.C. district during the period 1990-91 to 1994-95 is depicted in Table 3.2. It is clear that the number of members of the 41 weavers' co-operative societies had fallen from 5,289 in 1990-91 to 5,156 in 1994-95. The performance criteria, namely, number of active looms, production level, sales level show the decreasing trend in the co-operative societies in the V.O.C. district during the study period. On the whole, the profit increased from Rs. 2,936.2 lakh in 1990-91 to Rs. 3,040.1 lakh in 1994-95 in the V.O.C. district.

Weavers' Co-operative Societies in Pudur Block

The study covers 2 weavers' co-operative societies and 2 Industrial weavers' co-operative societies in Pudur Block of V.O.C. District. The selected handloom co-operative societies are:

(*i*) 01109 Nagalapuram Weavers' Co-operative Society;
(*ii*) EE82 Pudur Devangar Society;
(*iii*) EE370 Pudur Industrial Weavers' Co-operative Society; and
(*iv*) TNH 90 Nagalapuram Kumaran Industrial Weavers' Co-operative Society.

The performance at an average of the selected co-operative societies for the period from 1990-91 to 1994-95 are analysed in Table 3.3. The study found that the industrial co-operative weavers' societies had performed in a better way compared with the other weavers' co-operative societies. The IWCS also earned the higher profit level than the WCS in the study blocks.

With regard to the production level, the annual production in the WCS was 1,004.79 metre per loom, at an average, whereas the annual production was lower in the Industrial WCS 846.87 metre per loom, in the Pudur Block. The 238 members were involved in the 119 active looms in WCS and the 441 members had participated in the 114 active looms in IWCS in the study area. But the share capital of the members was low in the IWCS (61 thousand and 90 thousand) in performance criteria. There were 135 active members and 75 active looms in the Pudur society in the year 1994-95. The Government share capital for the society is 50 thousand and the member's share is 53 thousand in the same year. The performance result of Pudur Devangar Weavers' Co-operative Society during the period from 1990-91 to 1994-95 is depicted in Table 3.5. The production level (39,343 metre) at the value of Rs. 77 thousand in the year 1990-91 was increased to 1,07,003 metre at the value of Rs. 214 thousand in the year 1994-95. Similarly the sales value of 113 thousand in the year 1990-91 was raised to 238 thousand in the year 1994-95. The profit was also increased from Rs. 11 thousand 1990-91 to Rs. 34 thousand in 1994-95. The society earns, at an average, 21 thousand of profits by utilising the 74 active looms of the society.

Nagalapuram Kumaran Industrial Weavers' Co-operative Society

The TNH 90 Nagalapuram Kumaran Industrial Weavers' Co-operative Society was started on 20.4.81 at Nagalapuram of Pudur Block. The performance of the society during the period from 1990-91 to 1994-95 is given in Table 3.6. The study found that the performance of the society during the period from 1990-91 to 1993-94 was better than the year 1994-95. The society earns, at an average, the annual profit of Rs. 26 thousand during the study period. The society has produced

Table 3.3

Performance of Selected Weavers' Co-operative Societies in Study Area during 1990-91 to 1994-95 (Average in a Year)

Sl. No.	Name of the Selected Society	Number of Members	Number of Looms		Paid up				Production		Sales		Profit or Loss
						Share		Capital	Metre	Value	Metre	Value	
1.	0.1109 Nagalapuram Weavers' Co-operative Society	101	45	51	96	46	37	86	18,903	276	15,066	267	24
2.	EE82 Pudur Devangar Weavers' Co-operative Society	137	74	69	143	50	53	103	1,00,665	221	98,225	260	21
		238	119	120	239	99	90	189	1,19,568	497	1,13,291	527	45
3.	EE370 Pudur Industrial Weavers' Co-operative Society	339	42	14	56	98	27	125	50,354	1,002	52,717	1,032	103
4.	TNH90 Nagalapuram Kumaran Industrial Weavers' Co-operative Society	102	72	26	98	98	34	132	46,189	728	51,271	728	26
	Total of Industrial Weavers' Co-operatives	441	114	40	154	196	61	257	96,543	1,689	1,03,988	1,760	129

Source: Office Records, Weavers' Co-operative Society, Pudur.

Table 3.4

Progress of 0.1109 Nagalapuram Weavers' Co-operative Society during the Period from 1990-91 to 1994-95

(Rupees in thousands)

Year	Number of Members	Number of Looms			Paid up Share Capital			Production		Sales		Profit or Loss
		Active	Idle	Total	Govt.	Member	Total	Metre	Value	Metre	Value	
					Rs.	Rs.	Rs.		Rs.			Rs.
1990-91	104	56	63	119	49	35	84	31,260	314	21,326	242	32
1991-92	104	40	64	104	49	41	90	26,746	428	23,304	451	23
1992-93	103	45	58	103	49	36	85	19,546	309	17,861	374	22
1993-94	94	40	54	94	49	36	85	9,561	222	5,430	137	25
1994-95	101	45	51	96	49	35	84	7,402	107	7,411	132	17
	101	45	51	96	49	37	86	18,903	276	15,066	267	24

Source: Office Records, Nagalapuram Weavers' Co-operative Society.

Table 3.5

Progress of EE82 Pudur Devangar Weavers' Co-operative Society during the Period from 1990-91 to 1994-95

(Rupees in thousands)

Year	Number of Members	Number of Looms			Paid up Share Capital			Production		Sales		Profit or Loss
		Active	Idle	Total	Govt.	Member	Total	Metre	Value	Metre	Value	
					Rs.	Rs.	Rs.		Rs.			Rs.
1990-91	134	68	67	135	50	49	99	39,343	77	48,217	113	11
1991-92	134	75	68	143	50	53	103	1,17,401	271	1,05,928	315	22
1992-93	135	75	70	145	50	53	103	1,30,575	276	1,36,076	345	21
1993-94	146	75	70	145	50	54	104	1,09,003	265	99,953	291	17
1994-95	135	75	70	145	50	54	104	1,07,003	214	1,00,953	238	34
Average per year	137	74	69	143	50	53	103	1,00,665	221	98,225	260	21

Source: Office Records, Pudur Devangar Weavers' Co-operative Society.

46,189 metre of cloth by utilising the 72 active looms per year. The average sales value during the study period was 728 thousand in the society. The paid up share capital of the Government and members was Rs. 98 thousand and Rs. 34 thousand respectively.

Pudur Industrial Co-operative Society

EE370 Pudur Industrial Co-operative Society was started on 26.3.1964 at Pudur with 100 members and 20 active looms. The performance of the society during the study period is presented in Table 3.7. Table 3.7 reveals that the performance of the Pudur Industrial Co-operative Society was better in all years except the year 1994-95. The active looms were decreased from 43 in the year 1990-91 to 41 in the year 1994-95. The share capital of the Government and the members, at an average in a year, was 98 thousand and 27 thousand respectively. The average annual production of the society was 50,354 metre at the value of Rs. 1,002 thousand. The average annual sales of the society was also 52,717 metre at the value of Rs. 1,032 thousand. The industrial weavers society also earns an amount of 103 thousand as profit per year.

The details discussed, in this section, about the growth and performance of weavers' co-operative societies and Industrial weavers' co-operative societies in Tamilnadu, V.O.C. district and Pudur Block help to analyse the economic impact of the society on the weavers in the study area.

The Role of Co-operative Societies in Pudur Block

The various stages of production process of handloom textiles, functions of weavers' co-operative society and Industrial weavers' co-operative society, social economic status of the weavers in terms of caste, education, employment, income, expenditure, debt/savings etc. and the various problems faced by the weavers in their occupation are discussed in this section.

Stages of Production Process

There are serveral stages involved in the process of

Table 3.6

Progress of TNH90 Nagalapuram Kumaran Industrial Weavers' Co-operative Society during 1990-91 to 1994-95

(Rupees in thousands)

Year	Number of Members	Number of Looms			Paid up Share Capital			Production		Sales		Profit or Loss
		Active	Idle	Total	Govt.	Member	Total	Metre	Value	Metre	Value	
					Rs.	Rs.	Rs.		Rs.			Rs.
1990-91	100	65	32	97	98	33	131	60,875	727	72,169	742	29
1991-92	104	73	27	100	98	34	132	51,327	619	54,210	587	26
1992-93	103	71	25	96	98	34	132	52,124	628	63,114	648	28
1993-94	101	74	21	95	98	35	133	48,324	1108	47,629	1,254	31
1994-95	100	75	25	100	98	36	134	18,293	351	19,232	411	17
Average per year	102	72	26	98	98	34	132	46,189	687	51,271	728	26

Source: Office Records, Nagalapuram Kumaran Industrial Weavers' Co-operative Society.

Table 3.7

Progress of EE370 Pudur Industrial Co-operative Society during the Period from 1990-91 to 1994-95

(Rupees in thousands)

Year	*Number of Members*	*Number of Looms*			*Paid up Share Capital*			*Production*		*Sales*		*Profit or Loss*
		Active	*Idle*	*Total*	*Govt.*	*Member*	*Total*	*Metre*	*Value*	*Metre*	*Value*	
					Rs.	Rs.	Rs.		Rs.			Rs.
1990-91	339	43	13	56	98	24	122	52,875	1,061	58,139	1,108	110
1991-92	339	43	13	56	98	25	123	51,129	1,012	54,217	1,006	89
1992-93	339	42	14	56	98	26	124	49,675	876	50,319	984	108
1993-94	339	43	13	56	98	24	122	48,965	1,013	52,975	1,069	146
1994-95	340	41	15	56	98	36	134	49,127	1,046	17,936	992	62
Average per year	339	42	14	56	98	27	125	50,354	1,002	5,21,717	1,032	103

Source: Office Records, Pudur Industrial Co-operative Society.

production of handloom cloth starting from the stage of purchase of yarn. They are dyeing, loosening, twisting, winding, warping, dressing, sizing, piecing and fixing the warp with the loom for weaving.

(a) Purchase of Yarn

Yarn is usually purchased either from the local market or from the co-operative market or directly from the spinning mills. The co-operative societies in Pudur Block purchase yarn mostly from the co-operative market.

(b) Dyeing Process

If the yarn is undyed, it has to be dyed locally. Most of the co-operative societies make dyeing yarn either from co-operative dye houses or from government approved dye-houses. A few active co-operative societies have their own dye-houses. The dye process is based on a specific temperature. The industrial co-operative societies in Pudur block have their own dye houses. The other co-operative societies make dyeing process from the local dye-houses.

(c) Loosening, Twisting, Rewinding and Warping

Loosening and twisting are based on the courts of yarn; rewinding of yarn is done on reels and hands. Rewinding is done in the case of weft yarn or breathwise yarn. This is done with the help of charkha wheels by women and child workers. Wages are paid on piece rate basis and the rate of wage varies according to counts and weight of yarn. After rewinding, the yarn has to be warped. The warp yarn is usually warped on round wooden frame. The processes of loosening, twisting, rewinding and warping are usually done by the family members of the co-operative weavers in the study block of V.O.C district.

(d) Dressing and Sizing

Dressing and sizing are usually done at the time of dyeing and repeated after warping. These process of works are practiced in open space only to the fine varieties of sarees but in the case of coarse varieties, these processes are completed within the factory itself. The usual charges for these works are based on the various counts of yarn and the length of the warp.

(e) Piecing

Piecing refers to the joining of the thread ends of the old warp with the thread ends of the new warp. Each loom contains at least one set of reed and one set of heals. The numbers of reeds and heals depend upon the thickness of the cloth. The timer thread needs more reeds and heals and vice versa.

The new warp which joins with the old warp by means of piecing is again stretched in the street in the case of fine varieties. The wage rates of these work are usually fixed on the sizes of reeds, length of warp and design of the cloth.

(f) Fixing the Warp with the Loom and Weaving

After piecing, warp yarn is divided by many segments and is fixed into the loom. One end of it is fixed to the cloth beam and the other end to the warp beam. The distance of the cloth beam and the warp beam may depend upon the length of the cloth weaving.

The ordinary check and straight line designs are prepared by the segments of warp and weft yarn. In the case of flowers and designs, the handloom designers used jacquard punch card methods. The jacquard box includes design cards with hooks. The number of hooks differ from cloth design to design.

Turkey towels, half and full jacquard towels of the coarse varieties and putt border and petni designs on pure and art silk sarees of fine varieties are usually weaved by the jacquard looms. Wage will normally be more for these complex nature of weaving. The weavers are usually getting wage for their work on the basis of the variety and length of the cloth.

Functions of Weavers' Co-operative Society in Pudur Block

The functions of co-operative's society in Pudur Block are:

(i) Purchase of yarn from the market and supply the yarn to the members. The societies are also providing the charges to the preparatory works and weaving work done by the members.

(ii) The societies use the private dyeing houses for the dyeing works;

(iii) Selling the finished clothes to the co-optex and to the private traders.

(iv) The society also provides many other benefits to the members. They are pension scheme, health scheme, IRDP loan upto Rs. 6,000 and the bonus upto Rs. 400 per year.

Functions of Industrial Weavers' Co-operative Society in Pudur Block

The functions of the Industrial weavers' co-operative society in Pudur block are:

(i) Purchase of yarn from the market and use the yarn in their own industries by employing weavers for wages,

(ii) Dyeing process has been done in their own dyeing houses;

(iii) Selling the finished clothes to the co-optes and to the private traders; and

(iv) Housing facilities are provided by the Industrial co-operative societies in the Pudur Block.

Socio-Economic Status of Weaver-Member of the Co-operative Societies in Pudur Block

In order to compare the impact of co-operative societies of Pudur Block in V.O.C. district, 40 co-operative weavers and 40 Industrial co-operative weavers were administered in 4 societies of the Pudur Block. The findings of the survey are discussed in this section. The study gives the equal importance to the co-operative weavers' society and Industrial co-operative weavers' society in Pudur Block of V.O.C district. At present, there is no independent weavers and master weavers in the study blocks.

The study found that the female category dominated in the handloom weaving in the Pudur Block. The sample respondents consist of 67 female (83.75%) and 13 male (16.25%) weavers. Owing to the irregular work and insufficient wage earnings, the male weavers are not able to continue the weaving work in the study block.

The members of the co-operative societies in the age group of 25-35 years and 35-45 years have dominated in the weaving work. Only 13.75 per cent of the sample respondents are in the age group of below 25 years. It is clear that the involvement of the young weavers (below 25 years) are very low in the study area.

The most of the sample members of the co-operative society are belonging to the Sengundar Community (47.5%) and the Devangar Community (26.35%) in the study area. Only 13.75 per cent of the sample respondents are belonging to the Saliar community.

The 45 per cent of the sample respondents got the education from VI standard to XII standard in the school level. Only 13.75 per cent (11 respondents) got the above school level education at colleges, polytechnics and other higher institutions. The nine respondents (11.25%) are illiterate member of the co-operative society and 30 per cent had studied upto V standard in the study area.

Family Size

Table 5.6 reveals that only 18.75 per cent (15 respondents) have the family size of below 3 members. The 3 to 5 member family are 34 (42.5%) in the study area. The 38.75 per cent (31 families) of the sample respondents have more than 5 members in a family. It is inferred that the family size of the members of the co-operative societies are large in the Pudur Block of V.O.C district.

Employment Level and Wage

The weavers are involved in weaving, dyeing Rewinding, sizing and piecing works with the assistance of the co-operative societies. The study found that the members of the co-operative society have done the weaving works in their own houses during their leisure time. The female members are doing the work, in addition to their household works, such as cooking, child-care, etc. But the members of the Industrial co-operative members are doing the weaving work in a routine or regular hours in the industrial estate. But both the co-operative societies and Industrial co-operative societies have followed the piece wage rate system. The wage rate during the period from 1991-92 to 1994-95 is given in Table 3.8.

Table 3.8

Wage Rate in Handloom Co-operatives in Pudur Block

Sl. No.	*Items*	*Wage Rate Per Piece in* 1991-92	1992-93	1993-94	1994-95
		Rs.	Rs.	Rs.	Rs.
1.	Lungi	5.70	6.10	6.10	7.50
2.	Towel	2.10	2.20	2.40	2.45
3.	Bed Sheet	15.00	16.50	18.00	19.65
4.	Kada Piece	3.00	3.25	3.40	3.50
5.	Poly Dhotthi	5.70	5.75	6.00	6.50
6.	Janatha Saree	18.00	18.00	18.70	19.80

Source: Office Records, Weavers Co-operative Society, Pudur.

It is clear that the piece wage rate for the handloom weavers has increased in a small margin during the study

Table 3.9

Employment Level of the Sample Respondents

Sl. No.	*Category*	*Average Number of Days Employed* Pudur	Nagalapuram	Total
1.	Co-operative weavers	189	201	195
2.	Industrial co-operative weavers	267	231	249
	All	228	216	222
	Differences	78	30	54

Source: Computed from primary data.

period in the study block. The employment level of the co-operative weavers and Industrial co-operative weavers in Pudur Block are compared in Table 3.9.

The study found that the members of the wearvers' co-operative society got the average annual employment of 195 days through the society. The members of the Industrial co-operative society got the employment opportunities for 249 days, at an average, in the industries. It is inferred that the industrial co-operative weavers got the higher employment of 54 days, at an average, in a year, that of the co-operative society weavers. The average annual earnings from weaving work is anslysed in Table 3.10.

Table 3.10

Average Annual Earnings of Weavers from Weaving in the Study Area

Sl. No.	*Category*	*Average Annual Earnings from Weaving*		
		Wages	*Others*	*Total*
		Rs.	Rs.	Rs.
1.	Co-operative weavers	4,871	1,032	5,903
2.	Industrial co-operative weavers	6,053	Nil	6,053
	All	5,462	516	5,978
	Different			150

Source: Computed from primary data.

It is clear from Table 3.10 that the industrial co-operative weavers got higher earnings of Rs. 150, at an average, from weaving per year. The co-operative society weavers got the average wage income of Rs. 4,871 per year and the other income of Rs. 1,032 per year. Under co-operative society system, the yarn is supplied to the weavers and got the finished product from the preparatory works such as sizing, rewinding etc. The weavers also got the additional benefit by selling the extra cloth in their own production. So, the other benefits are balance in the preparatory charges, excess cloth in the production and bonus from the society. There is no possibility for other benefits except wages, in the industrial co-operative societies. Even though the weavers of the industrial co-operative societies got the higher earnings through weaving in the Pudur Block.

Annual Household Income

The average annual household income of the members of the co-operative societies is analysed in Table 3.11. The table reveals that the average annual household income of the weavers in Pudur Block was Rs. 7,356. The annual income of the co-operative weavers and Industrial co-operative weavers were Rs. 6,247 and Rs. 8,471, an average, respectively. It is inferred that the annual household income was higher for the industrial co-operative weavers due to the regular employment in the industrial co-operatives.

Table 3.11

Average Annual Household Income of the Weavers in Pudur Block

Sl. No.	*Sample Village*	*Average Annual Income*		
		Co-operative Weavers	*Industrial Co-operative Weavers*	*All*
		Rs.	Rs.	Rs.
1.	Pudur	6,484	9,980	8,232
2.	Nagalapuram	5,998	6,962	6,480
	Pudur Block	6,241	8,471	7,356

Source: Computed from primary data.

Expenditure Pattern of the Weavers

The average annual expenditure of the members of the co-operatives was Rs. 9,025 in Pudur Block. The annual expenditure of the co-operative weavers and industrial co-operative weavers was Rs. 7,694 and Rs. 10,356 respectively. The study found the industrial co-operative weavers spent more money than the co-operative weavers.

The members of the co-operatives had spent 63.77 per cent of their income on food items and the remaining 35.23 per cent income on the non-food items. The industrial co-operative weavers, after completing the regular hours of works in the industries, spent their time and money on the entertainment and other unproductive activities. This would lead to the increase in the expenditure of the industrial co-operative weavers.

Savings of the Members of the Co-operatives

Only 22.5 per cent of co-operative weavers (9 respondents) and 32.5 per cent of the Industrial co-operative weavers (13 respondents) saved their excess income in banks, post offices, co-operatives private chit funds etc. The average amount of savings was Rs. 1,249 per household. Since, the industrial co-operative weavers got the regular employment and earnings, most of them could save their excess income.

The study found that more than 70 per cent of the sample respondents are indebted to the average amount of Rs. 4,356 per family. The indebtedness of the co-operative weavers and industrial co-operative weavers, at an average, was Rs. 4,742 and Rs. 3,970, respectively. The 43.94 per cent of the co-operative members got their loan from the co-operative societies. They got the loan for the purpose of housing, handloom weaving works etc.

So far discussed about the comparison of the socio-economic conditions of the industrial co-operative weavers and co-operative weavers revealed the real impact of the co-operative societies on the weavers in Pudur Block of V.O.C. district.

Problems of Weavers

The survey revealed the following problems faced by the members of the co-operative societies in Pudur block:

(*i*) The rising price level affect the supply of yarn to the weavers by the society and it would create the irregular employment for the weavers in the handloom sector.

(ii) The co-operative societies are doing the sales of the finished clothes to 'Co-optex'. The delay payment of the co-optex to the societies affect the regular work of weaving. The credit sales of the societies to the 'co-optex' without any interest may retard the development of the co-operative societies.

(iii) The Government of Tamilnadu has fixed a ceiling for the rebate sales of the societies. The ceiling is based on the last year sales volume. It is difficult to market the handloom product without rebate.

(iv) The co-operative weavers are doing the weaving work in their own loom at their residence. The looms occupied the large pace of the house and it would create pollution in the houses.

(v) The industrial co-operative societies depend on their profit for the settlement of old debt of the society at the beginning. So, the industrial co-operative weavers do not get any bonus from the society.

(vi) Due to irregular employment and low earnings in the societies, male weavers are shifting their work from weaving to other activities.

(vii) Only female weavers are participating in the regular weaving work. They don't get any maternity benefits from the society.

(viii) There is no research centre for the promotion of handloom products in Tamilnadu.

(ix) Uncertain monsoon, non-availability of standard cotton seeds and traditional method of agriculture are the reasons for the low production of cotton in India.

(x) Raising the export quota and low productivity would create the irregular supply of yarn to the co-operative societies in Tamilnadu.

(xi) Two per cent tax for citta yarn and no power subsidy for handloom sector would raise the cost of production in the co-operative societies.

Suggestions

In the light of the results obtained; certain suggestions of practical use have emerged.

1. In order to solve the financial constraints in the co-operative societies, the Government of India may establish a separate Co-operative Bank, exclusively for handloom sector and take necessary steps in reducing in the interest rate to loans given to the weavers and higher credit limit for the handlooms industries.
2. Government of India may set up a cereal handloom house corporation in Tamilnadu to procure the handloom products directly from the weavers and manufacturers for export.
3. In order to promote the handloom sector, a research centre may be established by the Government of India in Tamilnadu.
4. The co-optex may expand the sales through the mobile sales centres to all places.
5. Prices fixed by the traders most concentrate on the Minimum Wages Act, Government Dearness Allowances, looms and profit of the weavers.
6. The Government may provide the income tax exemption to the weavers' co-operative societies and marketing co-operative societies.
7. Government of Tamilnadu may compel the Government servants to purchase the handloom products at least one time in a year.
8. Government of India may restrict the maximum limit in exporting the yarn to other nations.
9. Free power supply to the handloom weavers may be provided by the Government of Tamilnadu, like Gujarat, in order to encourage the handloom weavers.
10. Tax exemption may be provided by the Government to producers of the citta yarn.
11. The pension scheme, health package scheme, and housing scheme for the co-operative weavers may be introduced effectively without any delay.
12. The rebate ceiling to the co-operative societies in marketing the products may be avoided in order to increase the sales.
13. Co-optex must pay the amount to the co-operative societies without delay for their products.

In conclusion, it may be said that there is a positive impact of the Industrial co-operative societies on the economic status of the weavers in Pudur Block. The handloom co-operative sector will get success, only if the Government take necessary provision for setting up of many industrial co-operative societies with low rate of credit facilities. Regular employment to the weavers through the industrial co-operatives will effectively influence the growth of handloom sector in Tamilnadu.

References

1. Amarjit Singh and A.N. Sadhu, *Agricultural Problems in India,* Himalaya Publishing House, Delhi, 1996.
2. Beebi, R.B., *History, Theory and Practice of Co-operation,* Loyal Book Department Publication, New Delhi, 1977.
3. David, L. Sills (ed.), *International Encyclopedia of the Social Sciences,* The Macmillan Co., New York, 1972.
4. Desai, *Economic Planning and Policy,* Emerald Publication, Madras, 1984.
5. Duncan Bythell, *The Handloom Weavers,* English Paper Book Education, London.
6. Fray, C.R., *The Law and Practice of Co-operation,* Macmillan, Delhi, 1973.
7. Gupta, S.P., *Statistical Methods,* Sultan Chand & Sons, Delhi, 1979.
8. Iyengar, A.S.K., *A Study in the Co-operative Movement in India,* Current Book House, Bombay, 1961.
9. John, D.K. Sundarsingh, *The Handloom Industry in Madurai City,* Madurai Kamaraj University, Madurai, 1980.
10. Kulkarni, M.R., *Industrial Development,* National Book Trust, India, 1971.
11. Mathru, B.S., *Co-operation in India,* Staliya Bhavan, Agra, 1982.
12. Memoria, C.B., *Agricultural Economics,* Deep and Deep Publication, New Delhi, 1980.
13. Nambiar, P.E., "Handicrafts and Artisans of Madras State Silk Weaving of Kanchipuram", *Census of India, 1961,* Madras, 1964.
14. Paul Lambert, *The Social Philosophy of Co-operation,* Allied Publishers, 1963.
15. Phillips, R., *Economics Nature of Co-operative Association,* Orient Longman, Bombay, 1979.
16. Sankaran, S., *Economic Development of India,* Progressive Co-

operative Private Ltd., Bombay.

17. Seetharaman, S.P. and N. Mohanan, *Framework of Studying Co-operative Organisation—The case study of NAFED*, Oxford and IBH, Delhi, 1986.
18. Singh, K., *Rural Sociology*, Prakash Kendra Publication, Meerut, 1986.
19. Srivastava, S.K., *et al.*, *Industrial Economics*, S. Chand & Co., New Delhi, 1967.
20. Suri, K.B. (ed.), *Small Scale Enterprises in Industrial Development: The Indian Experience*, Sage Publications, New Delhi, 1991.
21. Weeram, P.E., *Law and the Co-operations*, Allied Publishers, Madras, 1976.

Journals

22. Ansari, A.A., "Co-operative Marketing in India: Progress and Problems", *Khadi Gramodyog*, Vol. XXXXI, No. 2, November 1994.
23. Aswini Kumar Mishara, "Social Impact of Handloom Co-operatives on Weavers in Western Orissa: An Empirical Study", *Journal of Rural Development*, Vol. 13, No. 2, April-June, 1994.
24. Bhole, B.D. *et al.*, "Trend and Potential for Export of Cotton from India", *Indian Journal of Agricultural Economics*.
25. Brij Bhadu, "Promotion of Co-operatives in Meghalaya", *Yojana*, Vol. 38, No. 16, September.
26. Debdee Banerjiee, "Market and Non-Market Configurations in Rural West Bengal Local Organisation and Silk Weaving", *Economic and Political Weekly*, Vol. XXX, No. 47, November 25, 1995.
27. Krishnaswamy, O.R., "Evaluation of Co-operatives Scientific Approach", *Tamil Nadu Journal of Co-operation*, April, 1987.
28. Leelamma Devasia, "Co-operatives as a Strategy of Rural Social Development: A Study", *Kurukshetra*, Vol. XXXVI, No. 9, June, 1988.
29. Menubhai Patel, "Reformation of Village Industries Co-operatives", *Khadi Gramodyog*, Vol. XXXVIII, Nos. 11-12, August-September, 1992.
30. Nonbasha Abdul, "Handlooms in Distress", *Economic and Political Weekly*, Vol. XXXI, No. 23, June 8, 1996.
31. Parthasarathy, G. and R.M. Mohanan, "Democracy, Politician and Business Efficiency", *Tamil Nadu Journal of Co-operation*, January, 1984.
32. Parbhakar, M.V.R., "Relevance of Khadi and Village Industries",

Khadi Gramodyog, Vol. XXXVI, No. 10, September, 1990.

33. Rajagopal, "Fibre Co-operatives for Rural Women—An Analysis of Organisational and Management Aspects", *Journal of Rural Development*, Vol. 12, No. 6, November 1993.
34. Raju, D.S. and V. Ram Mohan, "Rural Upliftment through Co-operatives", *Indian Journal of Agricultural Economics*, Vol. XLVIII, No. 49, October-November, 1993.
35. Serajul Islam, M. *et al.*, "Handloom Weaving in Rural Bangladesh—A Supplementary Occupation for Small Farmers", *Journal of Rural Development*, Vol. 11, No. 4, July, 1992.
36. Seetharaman, S.P., "Organisational Effectiveness of Co-operatives", *Tamil Nadu Journal of Co-operation*, November, 1981.
37. Showeb, M., "Women Khadi Spinners—A Study in Economic Self-sufficiency of Rural Women", *Khadi Gramodyog*, Vol. XXVII, No. 11, August, 1991.
38. Subudhi, R.N. and S.K. Padhi, "Indian Women in Co-operatives Management", *Khadi Gramodyog*, Vol. XXXVII, No. 7, April, 1991.
39. Suresh, K.A., "Organisational Liability of Co-operatives: A Case Study of PACS in Kerala", *Journal of Rural Development*, Vol. 11, No. 4, July, 1992.
40. Subbiah, P., "Co-operatives in Tamil Nadu", *The Tamil Nadu Journal of Co-operation*, Vol. 88, No. 10, 1995.
41. Venkata Ratnam, C.S., "Unionisms and Union Management Relations in Co-operation Sector—A Study of Selected Units in Visakapatnam District", *The Indian Journal of Labour Economics*, Vol. XXX, Nos. 1-2, April & July, 1987.

Reports

42. Block Development Office, *Annual Reports*, Pudur Panchayat Union, Pudur, 1990-91 to 1994-95.
43. Collectorate of V.O.C. District, *General Statistics*, Collector of V.O.C. District, Government of Tamil Nadu, Tuticorin.
44. Government of India, *Draft Fifth Five Year Plan*, Planning Commission, Vol. II, 1976.
45. *Fourth Five Year Plan*—A Draft Outline.
46. *Census of India, 1991*, Series I, Part II B, Appendix, 1992.
47. *Report of the Working Group on Handloom*, Ministry of Commerce, New Delhi.
48. *District Census Handbook*, Directorate of Stationary and Printing, Madras, 1991, Vol. I.
49. Government of Tamil Nadu, *Administrative Report on the Working of Co-operative Societies Rule in Tamil Nadu, Parts I-III, Madras,*

1963 Sections 1-9, Assistant Director of Handloom and Textiles, Tirunelveli, 1991.

50. *Annual Reports, 1990-91 to 1994-95,* Directorate of Handloom and Textiles, Madras.
51. *Annual Reports of Assistant Director of Handloom and Textiles, 1990-91 to 1994-95,* Assistant Directorate of Handloom and Textiles, Tirunelveli.
52. Handloom Weavers' Co-operative Societies, *Annual Reports of Weavers' Co-operative Societies in Pudur Block,* 1990-91 to 1994-95.

4

Voluntary Organisations for Rural Entrepreneurship

In India, with five year plans, there has been a growing realisation at policy level that rural poverty and unemployment can not be mitigated with wage employment programmes like National Rural Employment Programme (NREP), Rural Landless Employment Guarantee Programme (RLEGP) and Jawahar Rozgar Yojana (JRY) and the rural development programmes like Integrated Rural Development Programme (IRDP) alone.

Lack of adequate attention to small and rural industries has led to large scale migration of population from the rural to urban areas in search of jobs. Concentration of industries in cities has, in turn, led to congestion and other problems, including pollution.

The mounting problem of employment has brought into focus the importance of small scale, agro and rural industries as well as development of entrepreneurship in the related fields. Preliminary studies of the Planning Commission have emphasised that the potentials of this sector should be adequately tapped. Investment per job in this sector would be very low compared to the organised sector. Further, development of this sector would help dispersal of industrial activity reducing inequality and poverty. Development of this sector normally involves acceleration of entrepreneurship movement.

As far as the entrepreneurship development is concerned it may be mentioned that there is no shortage of inherent entrepreneurial talent in the country. What is necessary is to draw out this inherent potential to make the latest talent patent and on galvanise the men, women and the youth to work towards a harmonious blend of personal, corporate and national objective.

Compared to Government Organisation like District Industries Centre (DIC) and District Rural Development Agency (DRDA), the role of voluntary organisation in developing entrepreneurial skill is highly appreciable on account of numerous factors which associate with them. To cater to the needs of entrepreneurial development programme, a great amount of co-ordination among various agencies at work is all the more necessary and this alone can steer rural youth to success in their venture.

The learners of the literacy campaign in Madurai District formed a women organisation and named as "Arivoli Mahalir Iyyakkam" (AMI) for the development of entrepreneurial activities in rural areas. The present study attempts to evaluate the role of the organisation in the rural enterprise development in Madurai district of Tamilnadu.

The specific objectives of the study are:

(i) To study the growth and performance of Arivoli Mahalir Iyyakkam in Madurai District;
(ii) To analyse the role of the Iyyakkam on the rural entrepreneurs development activities;
(iii) To evaluate the successful implementation of DWCRA scheme on fair price shops, canteen, cooking powders and washing powders, rearing milch animals etc; and
(iv) To suggest various concrete measures for the successful implementation of rural enterprise development in the district.

Based on the above objectives of the study, primary data as well as secondary data were collected in Madurai district. In order to find out the growth and performance of the "Arivoli Mahalir Iyyakkam" and achievements of the literacy campaign in the district, secondary data were collected from the "Madurai

District Arivoli Iyyakkam" office, Madurai and from the records of the Arivoli Mahalir Iyyakkam office.

Primary data relating the rural enterprise development activities and impact of DWCRA assistance were collected by interview method. A total of 30 women groups were interviewed with pretested questionnaire. The major activities of the women group such as cooking powder preparation, washing products, fair price shops and canteen were given more importance in the survey period. The findings of the study are presented as the case study in fair price shops, canteen, cooking powders, milk depots, and washing products.

The findings of the study are presented in four sections. They are:

1. Literacy campaign in Madurai district.
2. Growth and performance of Arivoli Mahalir Iyyakkam in Madurai district.
3. DWCRA Assistance for Arivoli Mahalir Iyyakkam, and
4. Case Studies on Rural Enterprise Development by Arivoli Mahalir Iyyakkam.

Literacy Campaign in Madurai District

The illiterates under the age group (15-35) in Tamilnadu accounts for 5.87 millions. Total literacy campaign projects are covering over 7.45 million illiterates. This includes learners above 35 years also. The campaigns have been implemented in 21 districts. Of the 21 districts, post-literacy campaign was completed in Kanyakumari, Kamarajar Pudukottai and Pasumpon Muthuramalingam District. Post-Literacy Campaign is in the process of having implemented in 10 districts namely, Madurai, North Arcot, Ramanathapuram, Tirunelveli, Dindigul Anna and Coimbatore Districts.

The Achievement of Madurai district in the total literacy phase is 76.38 per cent against the total ranges of 3.28 lakh. Nearly 3.07 lakh learners have been enrolled. Among them 2.50 lakh learners have completed the level III. The target-age group for the campaign is (15-35) as per the sanction by the Ministry.

In Madurai, Post-Literacy Project was sanctioned in May 1993 to cover 1.80 lakh neo-literates. As much as 1.35 lakh neo-literates are reportedly enrolled. About 1.08 lakh learners attended PLC as on May 1994. The approved cost for post-literacy campaign is Rs. 1.46 crore of which Rs. 0.97 crore was sanctioned from National Literacy Mission and Rs. 0.49 crore from the State Government.

The PLC in Madurai district was launched with the main intention of facilitating a continuous approach for after becoming literate, an adult generally becomes motivated to learn more things and shows more interest in reading different types of books and other published materials. He/she wants to use and develop his reading, writing skills. In general, he wants to learn more and continues the process of education. It was felt that if suitable learning opportunities are not provided the neo-literates may lapse back to illiteracy.

The major objective of the post-literacy is to reinforce and consolidate the skills relating to literacy among the learners, and to equip the learners with better knowledge, perception, skills, attitude, understanding, awareness, functionality etc., of the surrounding society and the nation at large. So, they are equipped to remove the impediments coming in the way of leading a better, happier and more meaningful life that they become active members of the community and participate in the process of social reconstruction and national development.

In Madurai district, each Panchayat Union has one Block Project Co-ordinator (BPC), 2 Assistant Project Co-ordinators (APC) and one office assistant for the implementation of PLC at block level. There is a library in each panchayat maintained by the Panchayat Co-ordinator. The Panchayat Co-ordinator also co-ordinates and supervises the Centres (vattam) in the panchayat area. Generally each panchayat covers three to four centres which is guided by the Vatta Vazhikatti (Circle Guide). Based on these administrative and organisational background, the Vattam functions twice a week. The reading materials are supplied and circulated among neo-literates Vattams. Many self-help groups have been formulated in every Vattam of PLC in Madurai district.

Arivoli Mahalir Iyyakkam in Madurai District

Arivoli Mahalir Iyyakkam, Tamil name for the organisation of the women learners literacy campaign, was formed on 8.3.1995 by the neo-literates of post-literacy campaign in Madurai district. The office address for the organisation is 16, Old Ramanathapuram District Collector's Office, Madurai-625 020.

The Arivoli Mahalir Iyyakkam (AMI) was officially registered under the Societies Registration Act of 1860 (TN Act 27 of 1975) at Madurai on 15.5.1995. The office-bearers at the time of registration are as follows:

1. V.V.G. Ganeswari — President, Mellur
2. N. Vijayalakshmi — Vice President, Ellis Nagar
3. S. Navanitham — Secretary, E. Kottaipatti.
4. S. Vijayalakshmi — Assistant Secretary, Kallikudi
5. T. Thavamani Devi — Treasurer, Mellakkal
6. G. Mallika — Executive Member, Allinagaram
7. A. Puspham — Executive Member, Achampattu

The Neo-literates of the post-literacy campaign are enrolled as members of the organisation. The above 18 years girls are eligible to become the member of the society and they have to pay Rs. 2 as annual subscription. The specific aims of the society are:

(i) To organise various groups in all villages of the Madurai district in order to implement various women development programmes;

(ii) To help the members in maintaining the libraries, developing small savings, insurance and Government assistance for the women groups in Madurai district;

(iii) To implement the various schemes like Education For All, Health For All, Mother Child-care, Women Development, Waste Land Development, Water Resource Management, Environmental Protection etc.;

(iv) To provide training and assistance to develop the entrepreneurial skills of the women groups in villages to start the small scale industries;

(v) To identify the marking potentialities for the women entrepreneurs;

(vi) To generate employment opportunities for the members with non-profit enterprises; and

(vii) To develop the agro-based industries and to popularise the agricultural development schemes in the rural areas.

Under this AMI, at the initial stage, one women team was formed in each Panchayat. During the period of eight months (May 1995 to December 1995), nearly 240 women teams were organised in Madurai district. The 'Self-help' groups, at the beginning, start to save their excess income by opening an account in the nearby bank (Joint A/C of President and Treasurer of the women group). At the maximum of Rs. 10 to 20 per month, every member provide their savings. Each group consists of 10 to 15 Neo-literates of PLC in a village. After a few months, the saved money was invested in productive activities at a small scale level. The main productive activities are: Preparation of cooking powders, flouring of rice and wheat, cleaning powders, soap powders, blue drops, jam, juice, bathi, chips etc.,

Before getting the financial assistance from the Government, the AMI also involved in the productive activities

Table 4.1

Performance of Arivoli Mahalir Iyyakkam Before Getting Government Finance as on December 1995

Sl. No.	*Divisions*	*Number of Women Groups*	*Average Amount of Capital Invested Per Group*	*Activities Involved*
1.	Madurai Corporation	79	4,060	Sambar powder, phenyl, soap powders
2.	Madurai Division	76	3,055	Wheat, rice flour, sambar powder, phenyl
3.	Uslampatti Division	55	2,637	Liquid blue, cooking powders, soap powders, blue metal
4.	Periyakulam Division	30	2,984	Wire, basket, phenyl, ink.
	Total	240	3,281	

Note: All women groups are involved in small savings activity and the same capital was invested for the productive activities.

Source: Computed from the Office Records of Arivoli Mahalir Iyyakkam, Madurai.

with non-profit basis. The women neo-literates are participating during their leisure period. Some groups got training for tailoring, typewriting through the District Arivoli Iyyakkam. The performance of AMI in Madurai district, before getting the Government assistance is given in Table 4.1.

Table 4.1 reveals that during the period of 8 months, the AMI in Madurai district had mobilised the capital resource at an average of Rs. 3,281 per women group and they were involved mainly in producing the cooking powders, wheat and rice flours, preparation of phenyl, soap powders, blue liquid etc. The study found the following main features:

1. Before getting the DWCRA assistance, the production was in a small scale level and they earn a meagre profit.
2. With the limited finance, there was no continuous production and irregular employment opportunities.
3. The members of the group had equally distributed their produced commodities at the time of marketing problems.
4. The women neo-literates were involved only during the leisure period in production activities.

In order to rectify the above difficulties and problems, the AMI had approached the District Collector for the development of the Arivoli women groups in Madurai district.

DWCRA

A mid-term review of the implementation of Integrated Rural Development Programme (IRDP) revealed that flow of assistance to women members of target groups households or even women headed households had been very marginal. To subserve the overall objective of improving the quality of life of rural families living below the poverty line, a sharper focus on providing assistance to women as part of the IRDP strategy was considered essential. Development of Women and Children in rural Areas (DWCRA) was formulated as a sub-scheme of the IRDP within this framework.

DWCRA seeks to provide income generating activities to women and also provides an organisational support in terms of a receiving system for the assisted women so that they can become effective recipients of goods and services available in that areas. Women's income is known to have positive correlation with the nutritional and educational status of the family and in the building up of a positive attitude towards the status of women. Hence, the necessity of ensuring more income earning avenues for women.

While the target group of DWCRA is the same as IRDP i.e., families having an annual income of less than Rs. 6,400 (below poverty line). The methodology is through a group. The financial provisions under DWCRA are available only for the group. Individuals are financed on IRDP pattern from IRDP budget. The scheme envisages formation of a group of 15-20 women. The women are expected to come together for an activity of mutual interest to all. The entry point for the group may not be income generating activities but it must be an essential ingredient of the total gamut of activities in which the group is involved. The assistance available to a group is:

(a) Rs. 15,000 as one time grant contributed in equal measure by Government of India, State Government and UNICEF, which can be used as:

  (i) revolving fund for purchase of raw materials and marketing;

  (ii) honorarium to group organiser not exceeding Rs. 50 per month for a period of one year;

  (iii) infrastructure support (seed money) for income generating activities; and

  (iv) one time expenditure on child-care facilities.

(b) Traveling allowance at Rs. 200 for one year for the group organiser.

If the group is registered under the Registration of Societies Act, it can take loan from the bank as a group for economic activities. Individual women members will be entitled to subsidy as per IRDP norms and each member will be equally liable for repayment of the loan. In case the group is informal, it is not able to draw loan from the bank as a group and the composite loan may be disaggregated into individual loans and subsidies, with the group guaranteeing the total amount of loan.

Training of Rural Youth for Self Employment (TRYSEM) is expected to cater to fulfilling the skill requirements for beneficiaries of DWCRA also. The curricula, duration of training and rate of payment to trainers and trainees requiring the same should be in accordance with the norms of TRYSEM.

In Madurai district, the Arivoli Mahalir Iyyakkam, registered under the Registration of Societies Act, are eligible to get loan from the bank under DWCRA Assistance.

Arivoli Mahalir Iyyakkam after DWCRA Assistance

As on 1st June 1996, the total members of AMI are 10,840 and number of women groups are 770 in all villages of Madurai district. The details of members enrolment in AMI is given in Table 4.2. The table reveals that the 770 women groups were formed under AMI in Madurai district. Of the total women groups, a large number of groups (28.96%) were formed in Madurai division and lower number of groups (21.56%) were formed in Usilampatti division.

Table 4.2

Arivoli Women Groups as on 1st June 1996

Sl. No.	*Divisions*	*Number of Groups*	*Total Number of Members*
1.	Madurai Corporation	192 (24.94%)	2,812
2.	Madurai Division	223 (28.96%)	3,290
3.	Usilampatti	166 (21.56%)	2,298
4.	Periyakulam	189 (24.54%)	2,440
		770	10,840

Source: Computed from office records of AMI, Madurai.

For the administrative convenience, the Madurai District was divided into four divisions under total literacy and post-literacy campaign. The AMI got the DWCRA assistance in two stages. At the first stage, January 1996, 103 women groups got the assistance at the rate of Rs. 15,000 per group in Madurai district. During the period June 1996, another 113 women groups got the assistance under DWCRA at the rate of Rs. 25,000 per group. A total of 226 women groups got the assistance of Rs. 43.70 crore under DWCRA scheme.

The activities of AMI under DWCRA scheme are given in Table 4.3 It is clear from the table that the 216 self help groups, in addition with their savings and by using DWCRA assistance, have involved in the rural enterprise development such as preparation of cooking powders (18.06%) rearing milch animals (12.5%), running fair price shops (12.5%), providing domestic credit/household credit needs (10.19%), production of ink, shampoo, cleaning powders, Jam, pickle, bakery etc., (9.72%) in Madurai district. The above said activities were predominantly done by the groups.

Table 4.3

Rural Enterprise Activities of AMI with DWCRA Assistance

Sl. No.	*Activities*	*Number of Women Groups*	*Percentage*
1.	Cooking powders	39	18.06
2.	Tailoring, typewriting	19	8.79
3.	Milch animals	27	12.50
4.	Cooking vessels, canteens	14	6.48
5.	Weaving	4	1.85
6.	Fair price shops	27	12.50
7.	Blue liquid, phenyl	21	9.72
8.	Quarry and blue metal work	6	2.78
9.	Wire basket and bags	9	4.17
10.	Ink, Shampoo, cleaning powder	14	6.48
11.	Wheat, rice flour	14	6.48
12.	Domestic credit/household credit needs	22	10.19
	Total	216	100.00

Source: Office Records, AMI, Madurai.

A lower per cent of groups had involved in tailoring (8.79%) renting cooking vessels and ornaments for marriage purpose and running canteen in BDO Office, (6.48%), weaving (1.85%), blue liquid, phenyl production (9.72%) quarry and blue metal work (2.78%), wire basket and bags designing (4.17%), and preparation of wheat and rice flour (6.48%). It is inferred that most of the women groups had concentrated mainly on fair price shops, rearing milch animals and domestic credit activities.

Rural Enterprise Development by AMI—Few Case Studies

The performance and achievements of the Arivoli Mahalir Iyyakkam in Madurai district in employment and income generating activities through the rural enterprise development are discussed in this section. The research team had visited many villages (nearly 20 villages) and investigated the 30 women groups about the functioning of the women groups with the DWCRA assistance. The findings of the field visit are summarised below with a few case study analysis.

Fair Price Shops

The AMI in Madurai district had involved in running the 27 fair price shops in various villages. In addition to the DWCRA assistance, the Madurai District Co-operative Bank had provided the loan assistance to the women groups for running the ration shops. Nearly 200 card-holders got the benefits in each fair price shop of the women teams. The women groups are supplying the very essential commodities through the ration shops. The supplied commodities are rice, kerosene, sugar and wheat at reasonable rate with the correct weight measurement.

In Vachampatti, Keelavazhvu Panchayat Union of Madurai District, one AMI group under the president of Mrs. M. Thavamani is running the ration shop service to the public from September 1995 with the assistance of DWCRA and Madurai District Co-operative Bank. The experience gained from the fair price shops in Vachampatti are reviewed below:

(*i*) The fair price shops run by the AMI charged a lower price for all essential commodities than the shops run by the CMS Marketing Society. Both the AMI and CMS Marketing Society purchased the commodities from the Pandian Super Market, Madurai. But they charged the different prices. These findings are presented in Table 4.4

(ii) The AMI Groups had charged the profit of 13 per cent for rice, 14 per cent for wheat and 70 paise per kg. of sugar at the selling price, as per the Government norms. In addition to this profit, the used gunny bags are calculated as an additional income.

(iii) The gross profit includes the transport cost and salary to one sales girl and one assistant. Two women got the employment regularly in each ration shops. One sales girl got the salary of Rs. 250 per month and one assistant got Rs. 150 per month.

Table 4.4

Rates Charged by the AMI and CMS Marketing Society in Fair Price Shops in Vachampatti

Sl. No.	*Commodities*	*Rate Charged by CMS Marketing Society*	*AMI*	*Quantity Supplied per Month*
1.	Rice-I quality	4.00	3.75	20 kg.
2.	Sugar (1 kg.)	9.25	9.05	1/2 kg. per unit
3.	Wheat (1 kg.)	4.75	4.50	3 to 5 kgs.
4.	Kerosene (1 lit.)	3.25	3.00	3 litres

Source: Field visit at Vachampatti Village.

Mrs. Thavamani, President of the AMI in Vachampatti village revealed some difficulties and suggestions for the successful functioning of Fair Price shops by the AMI group in all villages. They are:

(i) Lack of accommodation for shops—Now in Vachampatti, the ration shop is conducted by the AMI in the community hall of the village. It lacks storage facilities, lighting facilities, etc., *(ii)* The AMI groups are purchasing the commodities from the Pandian Super Market at Government rate. But the Pandian Super Market is supplying the underweight bags of sugar and rice to the maximum of 2 to 3 kg. per quintal.

These are the main problems faced by AMI Group in running the ration shops in Vachampati. The president is very happy to say that the beneficiaries of the ration shop are satisfied with the ration shop run by the AMI because, they are receiving the essential commodities at lower price and with the correct weight measurement. The problems could be solved by providing the buildings, supply of goods at correct weight and in the sufficient level to the ration shops.

Production of Soap Powder, PTC

A team consisting of 15 members under the presidentship of Mrs. Panchavarnam (30 years old) is producing soap powder in large quantities before and after getting DWCRA assistance, in Achampattu. In the initial stages, each member invest Rs. 400 for the production of soap powder (surf powder). During their leisure period, they are preparing the powders for two hours per day. The team got the training for the preparation of soap powders from the Arivoli Mahalir Iyyakam at the central level.

A Book "Chine China Ettu Eaduthu" published by Bharat Gyan Vigyan Samiti (BGVS) Resource Centre, Madurai is useful for the production of soap powder and all other products. The required raw materials for producing the soap powder are washing soda (1 kg.) R.P. Soda (3/4 kg.) Sillary (250 ml.), D. Blue (10 gm.), Dinopal (10 gm.), Tri-sodium-phosphate (TSP) (30 gm.), STPP (20 gm.), and Scent (10 ml.). By using these materials, the team produces 2 kg. of soap powder every time. At an average, the team has produced 20 kg. of soap powder per month before getting DWCRA assistance.

After getting the DWCRA assistance, the team continues the production of soap powder and also involved in providing the domestic credit needs in the Achampattu village of Madurai district.

The Group sells the soap powder at the rate of Rs. 3.50 per 100 gram and earns the total sales revenue of Rs. 35 for 1 kg. production. The actual cost of production is only Rs. 21 and earns a profit of Rs. 14 per kg.

Mrs. Panchavarnam revealed some difficulties as follows:

(i) Without publicity and advertisement, it is difficult to market the product in the open market, even though, the products of AMI group is sold in the market at lower price than the established company product, for example, 'SURF'—Rs. 28 for 1/2 kg. and the AMI group products—Rs. 35 for 1 kg.

(ii) The produced soap powders are equally distributed among the members for avoiding the difficulties in marketing and the group also loses the profits from the production.

(iii) The group have to face the dangerous effects without using the hand gloves at the time of preparation.

If the AMI got the marketing facilities in the centre of the Madurai city by establishing a shop and make some advertisement of such products, the above said problems could be solved and the women entrepreneurs development in an unexpected level.

The research team had visited the phenyl production centre at A. Vellalapatti, Mellur Block. The group, consisting of 12 members, is headed by S. Indira. They are producing the phenyl as per the suggestion of the book "Chine, China Ettu Eaduthu" and training by the AMI of Madurai district.

The requirements for producing the phenyl are: Pine oil (500 ml.), soft soap (250 gm.), Rosanam (125 gm.), Jasmine Scent (10 ml.), by using these materials, the group has produced 15 bottles of phenyl. The cost of production was Rs. 4 per bottle. But the phenyl was sold at the rate of Rs. 9 per bottle.

In order to solve the marketing problem, the group approached the private clinics and Government Hospital in Mellur and sell the phenyl regularly to the hospitals. The Group earns a regular income through the production of phenyl. The group also sell the product at the lower rate than the market rate of the established products.

Canteen by Women Group at BDO Office

The Arivoli Mahalir Iyyakkam in Madurai district is running the seven canteens in panchayat union offices, namely, Usilampatti, Chellampatti, Sedappatti, T. Kallupatti, Thiruparankundram, Madurai West and Vadipatti. The Canteen is functioned in the DWCRA building in every panchayat union office. The women group is paying a rent of Rs. 150 per month. The experience gained from the Thirupparankundram canteen run by the women group are discussed in this section.

A women group, consisting of 10 members, under the presidentship of Mrs. Santha, Palaniammal (Secretary) and S. Padma (Treasurer) was formed on 30.10.1995. At the initial stage, the group involved in preparing the cooking and turmeric powders. Before getting the DWCRA assistance, the group earns Rs. 100 per member from the production of cooking powder etc. After getting the DWCRA assistance, the team involved in running the DWCRA canteen at Thirupparankundram Panchayat Union office. The team got the DWCRA assistance of Rs. 15,000 on January 26, 1996 and the canteen was started on the same date.

Of the total 10 members, 7 women are actually involved in the canteen work. Everyday, the canteen is functioning from 9 a.m. to 7 p.m., and the items supplied in the canteen are: tea, coffee, milk vadai and the variety rice, meals etc. The total sales, at an average, per day is Rs. 800. They earn 25 to 30 per cent of profit from the total sales. The seven women member working in the canteen got the salary of Rs. 25 per day. They got the employment for 5 days a week except Saturday and Sunday. In the meantime, the excess of unsold items are also used by the members. The group is also supplying the food items for bulk orders like marriage and the ceremonies. During the period of 8 months, the group repaying the DWCRA loan was Rs. 2,250. The only problem revealed by the women group (Mrs. Santha) is that the rent charged by the Panchayat Union Office for the canteen building. The research team find the speciality of the group, at the time of field visit, that all women members equally shared their work in the canteen and they got the equal salary of Rs. 25 per day per head.

Milk Depot

In Achampatti Panchayat, a women team was formed under AMI in the year 1995 with 16 scheduled caste members including 14 neo-literates and one volunteer Instructor of Post-Literacy campaign. The group started the savings as Rs. 10 per month. Before getting the DWCRA assistance, the members were involved in producing cooking powders, phenyl and blue drops. Most of the members are having one milch animal in their houses. The neglected scheduled caste people did not get the benefit of IRDP, so far, in this village. Only after forming the women group, the members get the DWCRA assistance through the AMI of Madurai district.

Mrs. Meenakshi is the Secretary for the group. She made some important observations about the running of milk depot with the assistance of Rs. 15,000 under DWCRA scheme. They are as follows:

(i) Of the total DWCRA assistance, Rs. 10,000 was distributed to the women member having a milch animal, as advance, for the regular supply of milk to the women group.

(ii) The remaining Rs. 5,000 were used to purchase 3 milch animals for the women group and handed over to 3 women members for rearing.

(iii) There are 3 women members involved in these activities as full time for account maintenance, procurement of milk and cleaning the vessels and supply of milk to the hotels in towns.

(iv) The milk turnover per day is 38 litres in the morning and 21 litres in the evening.

(v) The milk purchased at the rate of Rs. 6 per litre from the members and sold to the hotels and to the public at the rate of Rs. 8 per litre. But the actual market rate for the milk is Rs. 9 per litre.

(vi) After deducting the salary for the 3 women members (a total of Rs. 2,000 per month). The remaining profit was utilised for repayment of loan. The women group, so far, repaid the amount of Rs. 1,000 to the Bank.

The women group pointed out some difficulties and problems in rearing milch animals under DWCRA scheme. They are:

(i) There is no separate building for running the milk depot and for improving the enterprise.
(ii) The financial assistance of Rs. 15,000 is not enough to purchase the high breed variety of milch animals.
(iii) The members have to purchase the fodder for their milch animals from the town on credit due to the financial problem.

These problems could be solved by providing separate buildings, enhancing the DWCRA assistance to Rs. 30,000 per group and setting up of a store for milch animal fodder by the women group of AMI of Madruai district.

The AMI has also developed such type of milch animals programme in Ayyappanayakkanpatti, Vadipatti Block and in Alanganllur Panchayat Union.

In conclusion, empowering women through the employment and income generating activities under Arivoli Mahalir Iyyakkam of Madurai district is successful in reducing the gender gap and development of women after getting education through the Mass Literacy campaign. Such type of voluntary organisations could be encouraged by the Government and the Public for the Women's Movement.

5

Economic Reforms and Indian Textile Industry

The New Economic Policy (NEP) initiated by the Government of India since July 1991 envisaged a major shift from an over regulated and protected regime to a deregulated and market-oriented system. The policy is expected to encourage the Globalisation of Indian industries. The Liberalisation policy towards foreign technology and collaborations is enabling Indian companies to upgrade their production facilities or to, establish new facilities which help them to expand the foreign market. A number of companies have thus increased foreign business.

The economic reforms led to a favourable turn around in the performance of the external sector since the crisis of 1991. There was not only a strong and sustained export growth since 1993-94, but there was a marked rise in the ratio of exports to imports from the level prevailing at the turn of the decade. This ratio, for instance, rose from 75.3 per cent in 1990-91 to 87.5 per cent basket. Capital goods formed a major chunk of imports after reduction of import duty.

The Indian textile industry contributes about the fifth of our total industrial production, nearly one-third of total exports and provides employment to millions of people. In the post-liberalisation era, the textile industry has undergone several changes, mainly on account of technology developments and trends in fashion. With synthetic yarns replacing cotton, the industry has recorded a phenomenal growth over the last few years. An attempt has been made, in this paper, to analyse the level of growth and issues of textile industry in India after the introduction of liberalisation policy and to suggest suitable strategies for the globalisation of Indian textile industries.

Employment and Economic Reforms

Dr. Manmohan Singh, in his budget speech (1996) said that economic reforms had almost doubled the rate of creation of new jobs in the economy from 3.8 millions in 1991 to 7.2 millions in 1994-95 and predicted that the number of jobs created would even higher in 1996. There is even some statistical evidence that unemployment may not only have stopped growing but may have started coming down. The most reliable evidence come from the National Sample Survey.

Two successive quinquennial surveys in 1987 and 1992 showed that all the six indicators of rural unemployment, male and female casual, seasonal and permanent, have been coming down since the mid-eighties. The NSS data also show an overall decline in urban employment, between 1987 and 1992, but within this trend a rise in 1991 and 1992, the years of transition from the command to the market-guided economy.

One rough but reliable indicator of the impact of reforms on employment can be had from the number of job seekers registered with the live registers of the employment exchanges. During the period of transition from June 1991 to 1992, it went up dramatically by 1.7 million from 35.22 millions to 36.93 million. But thereafter it has declined fairly steadily to 36.31 million in June 1993, 36.10 million in June 1994, before rising against marginally to 36.41 million in June 1995.

The level of employment in public and private sector is given in Table 5.1 and Table 5.2.

It is clear that after implementation of New Economic Policy, the employment in the organised sector has been increased from 263.53 lakh persons in 1990 to 282.45 lakh persons in 1997. The changes in the private sector employment was 187.62 lakh persons in 1990 and 195.59 lakh persons in 1997. Similarly, the employment in public sector has increased

Table 5.1

Employment Level in India

(Lakh Persons)

	Employment in Private Sector			*Employment in Public Sector*		
	1981	*1990*	*1997*	*1981*	*1990*	*1997*
Agriculture	4.63	5.49	5.33	8.58	8.79	9.12
Mining & quarrying	8.18	9.66	9.78	1.30	0.99	0.92
Manufacturing	15.02	18.70	16.61	45.45	44.57	52.39
Electricity	6.83	8.97	9.56	0.35	0.40	0.41
Construction	10.89	11.34	11.34	0.72	0.68	0.54
Trade	1.17	1.50	1.64	2.77	2.91	3.17
Transport storage & Communication	27.09	30.23	30.92	0.60	0.52	0.63
Finance, Insurance and Real estate	7.48	11.54	12.94	1.96	2.39	3.22
Community, Social & personal service	73.55	90.19	97.47	12.22	14.60	16.44
Total	154.84	187.62	195.59	73.95	75.82	86.86

Source: Ministry of Labour (DGE + T).

Table 5.2

Estimate of Employment to Organised Public and Private Sectors

(Lakh Persons)

Year	*Public Sector*			*Private*			*Total*		
	Male	*Female*	*Total*	*Male*	*Female*	*Total*	*Male*	*Female*	*Total*
1990	165.22	22.5	187.72	61.88	13.94	75.82	227.09	36.44	263.53
1991	167.10	23.47	190.57	62.42	14.34	76.76	229.52	37.81	267.33
1992	167.81	24.29	192.10	63.67	14.79	78.46	231.48	39.08	270.56
1993	168.49	24.77	193.26	63.01	15.50	78.51	231.51	40.26	271.77
1994	168.80	25.65	194.45	63.41	15.89	79.30	232.97	42.28	275.75
1995	168.68	26.00	194.66	64.31	16.28	80.59	232.97	42.28	275.25
1996	167.94	26.35	194.29	67.20	17.92	85.12	235.14	44.26	279.41

Source: Ministry of Labour (DGE + T).

from 75.82 lakh persons in 1990 to 86.86 lakh persons in 1997. With regard to the manufacturing sectors, the employment in private sector has been decreased to 16.61 lakh persons in 1997 from 18.70 lakh persons in 1990. But in the public sector, 44.57 lakh persons were involved in manufacturing in 1990 and 52.39 lakh persons in 1997.

On the other hand the number of employment exchanges and the job-seekers level was also in increasing trend during post-reforms period. Table 5.3 shows that the number of employment exchange was 851 in 1990 and the number increased to 891 in 1995. The job-seekers (educated job-seekers and unskilled labours) in India was 34.6 million in 1990 and the number increased to 36.7 millions in 1995. But the growth rate of job-seekers level was comparatively lower during the post-reforms period than before.

Table 5.3

Job-Seekers in India

Year	*Number of Employment Exchanges*	*Number of Job-Seekers (in million)*
1961	325	1.8
1970	429	4.1
1980	638	16.2
1990	851	34.6
1995	891	36.7

Source: The Hindu (Madurai), 1.9.1997.

Global Trade in Clothing

The world trade level in clothing is presented in Table 5.4.

It is clear that the world trade in clothing grew by four per cent in 1996 and was valued at $ 163 billion. This constitutes about 3.2 per cent of world merchandise trade. During the six year period between 1990 and 1996, clothing trade in India rose every year on an average by seven per cent except for a small drop in 1993.

Table 5.4

World Trade in Clothing (1990-1996)

Year	*Clothing Trade Value (in billion $)*
1990	108
1991	117
1992	132
1993	129
1994	140
1995	157
1996	163

Source: World Trade Organisatioon, Annual Report, 1997, Vol. II.

Table 5.5

Imports and Exports of Clothing by Selected Countries (1996)

Country	*Export Value (billion $)*	*Merchandise Share (%)*	*Export Value (billion $)*	*Merchandise Share (%)*
China	25.0	16.6	1.0	0.7
Hong Kong	21.9	12.1	13.6	6.8
Italy	16.1	6.4	4.9	2.4
U.S.	7.5	1.2	43.3	5.3
Germany	7.4	1.4	24.1	5.3
France	5.5	1.9	10.9	4.0
U.K.	5.2	2.0	9.7	3.4
South Korea	4.2	3.3	1.5	1.0
India	4.1	13.4	Nil	Nil
Netherlands	3.1	1.5	5.4	3.0
Luxembourg	2.9	1.7	4.3	2.8
Mexico	2.7	3.4	1.9	2.6
Malaysia	2.4	3.0	0.1	0.2
Spain	1.3	1.3	2.9	2.4
Canada	1.2	0.6	1.0	1.5
Japan	0.5	0.1	19.7	5.6

Source: World Trade Organisation, Annual Report, 1997. Vol. II.

For the first time since the Nineties, Asias' clothing exports declined in value terms in 1996. Western Europe and North America, the two large net importing regions, expanded their trade for the third year in succession with their exports growing faster than imports. The WTO reports show that China, Hong Kong and Italy are the three leading exporters which account for 40 per cent of the total trade in clothing. The United States, Germany and Japan are the largest importers, together buying more than 50 per cent of global exports.

Among the countries listed in Table 5.5, Japan is the smallest exporter with global sales of a meager half a billion dollars. France, whose clothing industry was overtaken by Italy and others at fashions cutting edge, imports more apparel than it sells. India was placed at the 11th position of exporters, among the selected countries (based on 1995 data) but is absent in the importers's list. Clothing accounts for about 17 per cent of China's merchandise exports and a mere 0.7 per cent of its merchandise imports. India's share of clothing in its merchandise exports is 13.4 per cent.

Cloth Production in India

The cloth production in India by the mill sector and the decentralised sector (handloom and powerloom) during the

Table 5.6

Cloth Production in India (1996-97)

(in million sq. metres)

Sector	*1990-91*	*1991-92*	*1992-93*	*1993-94*	*1994-95*	*1995-96*	*1996-97*
Mill	2,589 (12.80)	2,376	2,000	1,990	2,271	2,019	1,957 (6.80)
Handloom	3,418 (16.90)	4,005	5,219	5,851	6,180	7,202	7,456 (25.92)
Powerloom	14,216 (70.30)	14,827	14,644	15,994	15,976	17,201	19,352 (67.28)
Total	20,223	22,208	21,863	23,835	24,427	26,422	28,765

Source: Handbook of Statistics of Cotton Textile Industry, New Delhi, 1996 and *The Hindu*, Survey of Indian Industry, 1998.

period from 1990-91 (pre-liberalisation) to 1996-97 (post-liberalisation) is exhibited in Table 5.6.

It is evident from Table 5.6 that the output of all sectors—mill, powerloom and handloom, was higher at 28,765 million square meters (MSM) in 1996-97 against 20,223 msm in 1990-91. The increase in cloth production has been mainly on account of the powerloom sector which raised its share to 19,352 msm in 1996-97 from 14,216 msm in 1990-91. The handloom sector also has participated in the rise with its share at 7,456 msm in 1996-97 against 34,188 msm in 1990-91 comparably. The mill sector, on the other hand, witnessed a drop in production to 1957 msm in 1996-97 from 2,589 msm in 1990-91. It is inferred that closing down and suspension of operation of mills, not functioning of yarn spindles and rotors affect the cloth production in the mill sector, after introduction of NEP in India.

The share of powerloom sectors in cloth production was 70.3 per cent in 1990-91 and it had decreased to 67.28 per cent during post-liberalisation period due to the adverse activities of the Pollution Control Board. But the share of handloom sectors had increased from 16.9 per cent in 1990-91 to 25.92 per cent in 1996-97, the handloom sector has also been specialising in furnishings, and other items and speciality products particularly have been well received in overseas markets.

Physical Developments of Indian Textiles

According to the Indian Cotton Mills Federation, New Delhi, (1996) , the number of mills in India had increased from 1062 in 1990-91 to 1569 in 1995-96. Similarly, the installed spindles and numbers of rotors were also increased after the implementation of NEP. These figures are presented in Table 5.7.

It is inferred that the installed capacity of spindlage, yarn production and cloth output has increased over the years. The installed capacity of rotors has also increased due to the tendency to set up 100 per cent export-oriented units. However, the installed capacity of looms has continued to decline from 177.81 thousand in 1990-91 to 132.18 in 1995-96.

Table 5.7

Development of Indian Textile Industry

Year	*Number of Mills*	*Workers on Roll (thousands)*	*Installed Spindles (million)*	*No. of Rotors (thousand)*	*Installed Looms (thousands)*
1990-91	1,062	1,108	26.67	66.92	177.81
1991-92	1,117	1,087	27.82	112.99	172.84
1992-93	1,142	1,112	28.09	126.68	162.49
1993-94	1,175	989	28.60	139.30	149.92
1994-95	1,416	1,023	30.70	185.89	139.45
1995-96	1,569	1,029	31.75	226.03	132.18

Source: Handbook of Statistics on Cotton Textile Industry, 1996.

Table 5.8

Itemwise Exports of Textiles (1990-91 to 1995-96).

(Rs. in Crores)

Item	*1990-91*	*1991-92*	*1992-93*	*1993-94*	*1994-95*	*1995-96*
Cotton	5,475.84 (66.11)	8,213.41	11,337.68	14,866.98	18,513.15	20,744.37 (70.07)
Rayon/ Synthetics	636.09 (7.68)	1,106.07	1,436.32	1,846.84	2,485.88	3,122.67 (10.55)
Woollen	92.33 (1.11)	166.72	312.45	448.40	359.95	438.86 (1.48)
Non-Cotton Garments	1,643.13 (19.84)	1,900.85	2,365.17	2,842.65	4,159.05	4,452.06 (15.04)
Silk	435.94 (5.26)	675.57	720.0	789.10	934.54	846.08 (2.86)
Total	8,283.33	12,062.62	16,171.61	20,793.97	26,455.57	29,604.04
Foreign Exchange Earnings	5,475.84	8,213.41	11,337.68	14,867.98	18,513.15	20,744.37

Note: Figures within parenthesis denote percentages.

Source: Handbook of Statistics on Cotton Textile Industry, 1996.

Exports and Foreign Exchange Earnings

The cotton textile industry has been growing in importance in recent years because of its valuable contribution to foreign exchange earnings through exports of yarn, fabrics, garments and hosiery products. The detail of exports and foreign exchange earnings during the period from 1990-91 to 1995-96 is given in Table 5.8.

Table 5.8 reveals that the total value exports of textiles from India had increased from Rs. 8,283.33 crore in 1990-91 to Rs. 29,604.04 crore in 1995-96. After the implementation of liberalisation policy, only cotton rayon/synthetic and woollen items occupied a major share in the export of Indian textile goods. The foreign exchange earnings had also increased from Rs. 5,475.84 crore in 1990-91 to Rs. 20,744.37 crore in 1995-96.

Issues in Globalisation of Textile Industry

1. The recent modification in the Exim Policy for 1997-2000 on import of raw silk paved the way for import of mulberry raw silk 2A grade and above by main six agencies without import license. The notification may help in raising fabrics export and put into peril the livelihood of two economically weaker sections—farmers and reelers of the society.
2. Another issue was lack of demand for Indian cotton in foreign countries. Out of the cotton export quota of 17 lakh bales for the year 1997-98 less than 2 lakh bales had been exported to other nations.
3. The cost of credit with interest rates at around 10 per cent, was one of the major hurdles in the way of competitiveness of India's textile industries.
4. The textile mill management in India, spent crores of rupees for modernising their equipments but they are not ready to spend a few lakhs in training the workers who would be manning the new machines.
5. Shipment delays could deal a blow to the exporters as foreign buyers insist on timely delivery.
6. In Tamilnadu, over 600 dyeing units were ordered and by the Tamil Nadu Pollution Control Board

(TNPCB) to close the units as per the directives of Green Bench of the High Court on grounds of causing pollution to the environment. The closure of dyeing and bleaching units has started hitting the flourishing export trade.

7. The mills are now confronted with the problem of "plenty" both in terms of installed capacity and production level. During the boom period which started in 1987-88 and continued till 1994, there was a phenomenal growth in capacity addition of textile mills. The liberalisation policy too has spurred others pursuing different covations to venture into the textile sector. Thus many units, mostly small scale had come up in far-flung areas. However, excess capacity has now turned out to be a bane.
8. The problems in powerloom sector relating to the use of dyes have been responsible for a reduction in imports by developing countries like Germany as the consumers were insisting that only fabric processed with vegetable based dyes were acceptable to them.
9. The sharp rise in the power tariff has also added to the woes of the mills, as their recurring expenditure would increase. The present tariff of 50 paise increase a unit amounts to Rs. 5 lakh a month for an unit of 25,000 spindles. A decade ago, the power charges were 75 per cent of the wage while it is 250 per cent now.

Suggestion and Conclusion

1. To protect the domestic industry, a higher import duty on imported raw silk should be imposed.
2. The Government may reduce the electricity tariff or extend subsidy facility to the mills.
3. The present rate of four per cent sales tax on cone yarn should be reduced to two per cent and there should be no tax on hank yarn which has a two per cent tag now.
4. Cotton cone yarn is at present reeling under the highest excise duty of 5 per cent and should be

reduced to 2 per cent. The export of hank yarn below 40 counts may also be allowed as there seems to be a great demand for such low count hank yarn. Hank yarn production in the country already exceeds the demand and hence the hank yarn obligation may be abolished immediately.

5. The Handloom Export Promotion Council (HEPC) also demanded that Shipping bill endorsement so far as cotton handloom fabrics, lunghis, real Madras handkerchiefs etc. should be transferred from Tex Procil to the HEPC to enable merchant exporters to claim duty drawback.
6. The investment limit in plant and machinery for a small scale sector may be fixed as Rs. 3 crore for the textile industry concerned. The limit should be retained not only for the readymade garment units but for all segments of the textile industries.
7. Unless the obsolete machinery used by various sectors of the textile industry was replaced, the industry would not be able to survive international competition both within the country and in the world markets. The Government must subsidise interest under the proposed Rs. 25,000 crore Textile Modernisation Fund to the extent of five per cent. The fund would be operated by financial institutions.
8. More participation in trade fairs such as contest India can be of invaluable help in preparation effort for raising the new demands in the international market.
9. The Government should direct the TNPCB to devise a simple and cost effective technology to treat effluents in the interest of small dyeing units.
10. It is suggested that in view of huge surplus capacity, non-viable and obsolete machinery should be allowed to be scrapped apart from reducing excise duties and allowing a higher debt-equity ratio with reasonable interest rates for working capital.

While concluding, the economic liberalisation is likely to increase considerably the demand for chapter unskilled labour. There is large scale retrenchment of workers. Schemes of voluntary retirement are being pushed in a quite large number of public sector undertakings because of the new policies. The private sector has also shown displeasure in the form of lockouts and closures. Quite a large number of agreements signed by the unions after lockouts, forced the unions to agree to retrenchment of workers. The Government of India has to take the alternative and suitable proposals for solving these problems under liberalisation policy in the labour surplus economy of India.

References

1. S.K. Umesh, "South's Silk Industry up in Arms Over New Policy—Farmer, Reelers See Big Threat in Chinese Imports", *The Indian Express,* (Madurai), December, 14, 1998, p. 7.
2. R. Ilangovan, "Spinners Struggle for Survival", *The Hindu,* (Madurai), August, 18, 1998, p. 9.
3. P.A.S, "Textile—Export Slump Induces Crisis", *The Hindu,* The Survey of Indian Industry, 1998, p. 369.
4. K.K. Modi, "Post Reform Challenges, *The Hindu,* the Survey of Indian Industry, 1998, p. 27.
5. *TICMF, Handbook of Statistics on Cotton Textile Industry,* The Indian Cotton Mills Federation, New Delhi, 1996, pp. 28-45.
6. Prem Shankar Jha, "Reforms and Employment", *The Hindu,* March, 19, 1996, p. 18.
7. M. Sundara Rao and M. Ramakrishna, "Impact of Economic Liberalisation on Employment and an Overview of the Eighth Plan Employment Strategy, *Economic Affairs,* Vol. 40, Qr. 2, April, June, 1995, pp. 73-78.
8. B.B. Bhattacharaya and Rup Mitra, "Employment and Structural Adjustment", *Economic and Political Weekly,* September, 18, 1993, Vol. XXVII, No. 35.
9. L. Deshpande, "Economic Liberalisation and Labour in India", *India Journal of Labour Economics,* Vol. 35, No. 14, 1992.

6

Bakery Industry

Bakery is named after the food-making process called baking. The other process of food-making are cooking, boiling, frying, roasting etc. The baking is done in hot air which facilitate to prepare hygienic product with less of nutrition. The backed products are easily digestible and has high palatability. It is a traditional food industry.

Bakery products like bread, Biscuits etc. are important sources of food value. They contains proteins, iron, calcium and several groups of 'B' vitamins. Further all bakery products can be easily fortified with additional proteins, minerals and vitamins to meet the special needs of the under-nourished. These possibilities have been used to be advantaged by some social welfare programme for people in the low and middle income groups as well as the midday school feeding programme in the country.

Our per capita consumption of bread and bakery products is the lowest in the world. This has been imparted due to the traditional food habits and impart due to the popular belief that bread is an easily digestible foodment for the sick and the invalid. However sociological changes primarily in the urban homes have resulted in a greater acceptance of bread and bakery products as nutritious food.

Being products with a short self-life the consumption and popularity of bakery products in the rural areas has been hindered by a dearth of distribution channels, which resulted in prohibitive prices, with a smaller area to clear to a bakery unit in a small town (or) a village can supply fresh products at a lower cost. Since the industry in the small scale sector is fully labour-intensive it offers employment to a number of semi-skilled and skilled workers. Hence to moffusil, towns, district headquarters and large villages, offer ample scope for the setting up of bread and biscuit manufacturing unit.

There is nothing sacrosanct about the size and shape of mass produced bakery products. Small scale units will have the added advantages of being able to experiment with variations to suit the palate and pockets of their customers. It is hoped that further modifications in the progress of manufacture and equipment design will result from the setting up and functioning of a large number of such units.

Cognizance has been taken of the bread for processed food of high nutritional value particulars in the rural area. The focus of this endeavours has been to aid and promote bread and biscuit manufacturing units in the small scale sector. It is in the light that an effect has been to enthuse entrepreneurs to set up bakery and biscuit manufacturing units in the small towns and villages.

The bakery units will go a long way to increase employment potential in our area and also give the much needed help to our programme to raise the nutritional standards particularly among our rural population.

In recent times food and food processing industries have gained increasing importance in comparison to other industries, originally conceived as small scale units. The units in these industries have gone medium and large scale units with the investment of sophisticated and the growing demand for ready to cat foods. The recent industries policy enunciated by the Government to combine bakery units to the small scale sector widens the scope for the setting up of a number of bakery units in urban as well as rural areas.

It can be able to play an important role in integrating the rural economy with urban economy with an agro-based country like India. In past years a huge amount of bread and biscuits go wasted due to poor harvesting, storage and transportation. Food industry has acquired added importance in recent times with the Government intention to give a thrust to agro-based and village industry. This will not only help indirect employment but also have a multiplier effect through forward and backward linkage. This industry is also placed by low capacity utilization, lack of raw materials, uneconomic operation size and a host of other problems. Demand of production of food has been considerably increasing the world over. In fact there is a vast scope of increasing of fast foods. The present study attempts to evaluate the growth and performance of bakery industry in Dindigul of Tamilnadu.

The specific objectives of the study are:

(i) To analyse the sales level of bakery products in Dindigul district.
(ii) To find out the growth of production technology in bakery industry in Dindigul.
(iii) To study the productwise differences between cost of raw materials and sales revenue.
(iv) To review the problems faced by the bakery entrepreneurs of the Dindigul district, and
(v) To suggest the suitable policy measures for the growth of bakery industries.

This is to some extent descriptive analytical study by observation and collecting information from the owners and entrepreneurs using a interview schedule. The investigator is able to collect the necessary information by observing the production process adopted in bakeries when he visit the above with a view to collect datas. This is the way with which necessary informations are collected and tabulated.

Dindigul District Bakery Owners Association is having a list of bakeries in this district. This is the only source from where one can get the list of bakeries functioning in the district. As most of the bakeries running on their own fund and they need not register the name in the above organisation. As per the list given by the above association, sample is taken at the rate of one or two bakeries. Total number of bakeries in the above district as per the list is 50 and the study was conducted only in 12 bakeries. The sample covers urban and rural areas.

Concepts

Yeast

Yeast is a microscopic one-called plant belonging to the

fungus order, which ordinarily multiplies by a process known as budding and which cause fermentation when placed under suitable conditions.

Fermentation

Fermentation is a general term which covers aerobic changes brought about by micro-organism and includes the production of carbon-dioxide gas, alcohol, acids and some other by-products.

Chemical Leavening Agent

Any process by which dough or batter is filled with holes which are retained upon baking is a leavening process. Any materials which brings this process is called leavening agent. Producing leavening action by use of chemicals as chemical leavening agent.

Dough

The function of dough make up is to transform the fermented bulk dough into properly sealed and moulded piece when baked after proofing, yield the desired finished products.

Flying Ferment

Take part of water (water should be minimum, four times the weight of yeast) which is lukewarm. Add little sugar and mix. Add dried yeast and let soak until all the yeast starch floating and the grain is left at the bottom (it might take 5 to 10 minutes time). If compressed yeast is used, just crumble yeast in water and mix thoroughly. Add enough flour to make a thick batter, beat the batter to incorporate some air and leave aside in a warm place (for 15 to 20 minutes) to allow it to rise. This mixture is known as flying ferment and purpose of invigorating the yeast activity in thinner medium which is congenial to yeast action before it is out in the stiffer dough.

Improver

They are strong oxidising compounds and four toughening action on the gluten. Also have stimulating effect on the yeast activity. Depending upon the baking process.

Baking

To transform unpalatable dough into a light porouts and readily digestible flavoured product. The duration of baking, humidity and temperature of the oven influence the quality of the product. The baking time depends on baking temperature; size and weight of product being baked. Baking temperature influences the bake loss and moisture in bread.

Bakery Industry in India

Production

Bakery industry in India has today come to occupy an important place in the industrial map of India. It is recognised as the larger among the processed food industries with an annual turnover of Rs. 7,000 crore. There are possibility over 60,000 bakery unit. Growth of production of bakery products in a decade (1980-1990) is given in Table 6.1.

Table 6.1

Production of Bakery Products in India

(in lakhs tonnes)

Sl. No.	*Particulars*	*Production 1980*	*(Lakh Tonnes) 1990*	*Growth Rate %*	*By 2000 AD App. Projected Production*
1.	Bread	5.1	16.2	217	35
2.	Biscuits	3.5	9.0	157	28
3.	Other items	1.9	5.8	210	16
	Total	10.5	31.0		79

Source: Rural Industries in India, 1999, p. 158.

Increased growth rate of all items of bakery products reveals that more and more people started consuming bakery products. Hence increased consumption of the above products will facilitates the growth of this industry in future.

Table 6.2 indicates the different size of bakery industry functioning in India as on 1990-91.

Table 6.2

Size of Bakery Industry

Type of Units	*Number of Unit*	%
DGTD sector—large-scale	54	0.1
Factory Units	4,133	7.6
Household Units	49,767	92.3
Total	53,954	100.00

Source: Rural Industries in India, 1999, p. 159.

More than 90 per cent of bakery units are household units, located in rural areas, meeting the needs of rural people. It also provides direct employment to both skilled and unskilled workers. Large-scale units are producing mainly bread and biscuits. Factory type units are concentrating on the production of biscuits. The Indian economic condition, as it requires less capital, more labour and with the use of simple machines. The production technology is also simple which can be handled by rural workers.

Marketing

The products are perishable and cannot be kept more than a week except biscuits and rusk. Some of the products like vegetable puffs, coconut etc. are to be sold over fresh or the day itself. Further, consumer wants oven fresh products. The day old product is suppose to be the old products or stale products. Effective steps are to be taken to market the bakery products.

The following avenues of sales are being adopted for selling bread, bull cake, puffs, cookies.

1. Direct sales through well furnished showroom attached to production centre.
2. Sales through vendors.
3. Mobile sales by tricyle, van etc.
4. Delivery to Tea shops, petty shops, hotels etc.
5. Supply to hotels, canteens, hospitals on order.

The channels of distributions suggested by management experts cannot be applied to bakery products as they are perishable in nature. Biscuits manufactured by factory type units, and to some extent, mechanised bread, can be sold through various marketing channels.

"Quality sells quantity and cleanliness fetch consumers from long distance to the bakery showrooms. Any thing exhibited properly in a proper place can be sold". The above are some of the suggestions to market the bakery products.

Peak season for market bakery products are June to March in a calander year, and off season is said to be only April, and May. This is also another advantage when compare to other industries, especially soft drinks which has only 7 months of peak season.

The statewise share of markets for the bakery products is exhibited in Table 6.3.

Rates of growth of consumption show that in selected urban centres, the demand for bread will increase much faster than the demand for biscuits. Further more, the share of selected urban centres in the total urban market for biscuits is only 37.2 per cent. The corresponding figure for bread is 82.8 per cent within the urban centres studies the market for bread in the five cities of Bombay, Calcutta, Madras Delhi and Bangalore constitutes 72.45 per cent of the market for bread in 32 cities. These data suggest that bread consumption is much more related to the cosmopolitan character of the population than the consumption much more widely than bread even though because of price factor in physical term is somewhat less than that of bread.

Statewise difference in level of consumption partly reflect the socio-economic status of each state and partly the eating habits of its people. States like Bihar, Madhaya Pradesh and Utter Pradesh with relatively low per capita consumption of

Table 6.3

Statewise Share in the Market for Bakery Products in India

States	*Rural Sector*		*Urban Sector*	
	Share in Population (%)	*Share in Bakery (%)*	*Share in Population (%)*	*Share in Bakery (%)*
1. Andhra Pradesh	7.9	3.6	7.6	3.4
2. Assam	3.2	7.4	1.4	3.3
3. Bihar	11.7	7.3	5.5	3.6
4. Gujarat	4.4	4.2	6.6	5.2
5. Haryana	1.9	2.4	1.7	20.0
6. J&K	0.8	3.1	6.7	4.7
7. Kerala	4.0	8.0	3.5	3.9
8. Madhya Pradesh	7.8	4.4	5.9	3.3
9. Tamilnadu	6.4	10.7	10.5	7.9
10. Maharashtra	7.8	4.4	5.9	3.3
11. Karnataka	5.0	4.5	6.5	2.9
12. Orissa	4.5	2.7	1.5	1.1
13. Punjab	2.5	3.1	3.4	2.8
14. Rajasthan	5.0	1.2	4.1	2.1
15. Uttar Pradesh	17.8	11.6	11.5	9.5
16. West Bengal	7.5	11.4	10.8	18.0
17. Union Territories	1.8	5.0	4.4	7.1

Source: Hand Book on Bakery Products—Small Industry Research Institute, New Delhi, pp. 25-27.

bakery products have also lower per capita income level in relation to the national average. Lower per capita consumption of bakery items in some states such as Andhra Pradesh and Karnataka may be due to food habits of the people. The higher per capita consumption of these products in Jammu and Kashmir is again because of a customary practice among a population whose food is rice to buy wheat-based bakery products from the Tandoors or bakeries rather than cool any wheat flour-based food at home.

Nutritional Value

Most of the bakeries are household bakeries and situated in rural area. As an industry it provided employment to both skilled and unskilled workers, especially rural women. In the process of selling bakery products, more gainful employment has been generated. As it is an agro-based industry it uses or process the agricultural products and thereby help the farmers in rural area.

Further, it helps to reduce or eradicate male nutrition in rural area by supplying products with more nutrition. The bakery products can easily be fortified with vitamins, minerals etc. As it has high palatability and acceptance, malnutrition can be eradicated from rural area easily. The nutritive value of some of the bakery products have been indicated below in Table 6.4.

Table 6.4

Nutritional Value for Bakery Products

Sl. No.	*Products*	*Calories Per 100 gm.*	*Protein %*	*Carbo-hydrates %*	*Fat %*	*Calcium mg. %*	*Iron mg. %*	*Phos-ous mg.%*
1.	Bread	275	8.1	50.0	4.7	26	4.8	217
2.	Palm cake	492	5.1	49.5	30.5	15	0.7	58
3.	Semolina cake	371	8.3	51.9	14.5	43	3.9	198
4.	Bun	281	5.0	45.9	8.7	91	2.1	139
5.	Milk biscuits	399	6.4	62.2	13.8	44	3.6	178
6.	Bread biscuits	482	4.4	70.1	20.4	9	0.4	37
7.	Sweet biscuits	349	6.8	58.1	10.1	21	3.9	177

Source: Bakery Industry in India, SIB, New Delhi.

Per Capita Consumption

Gone were the days when people treat the bread as the food for sick people. Changes in the socio-economic conditions, and employment structure, make the bread become the integral part of food-stuffs in the families of both rural and urban.

Particularly in the case of families where women going out for employment, bakery products must take place in their dining table. Urban population is reckoned around 25 per cent i.e., nearly 22 crore and the middle class population is 25 crore as per 1991 census and thus 47 crore of population have become regular customer of bakery products.

However, present statistics reveals that per capita consumption per annum is 1.8 kg. of bread and 1.2 kg. of biscuits. In developed countries it is 50-100 kg. of bread and 10-15 kg. of biscuits. The gap is thus wide there is ample score for increasing the production of bakery products in India manifold in the years to come.

It depends on the following factors:

(a) Development and growth of industries.
(b) Changes in the employment pattern.
(c) Increase in literacy etc.
(d) Awareness on hygienic food consumption
(e) Awareness on food nutrition.
(f) General consumer awareness on bakery products
(g) Changes in tax on biscuits.

Technology and Capital

Major raw material used in bakery is maida which is obtained by milling of wheat in flour mill. In India nearly 6 to 8 per cent of tool wheat is milled for maida, sooji, and atta, of which roughly 30 lakh of tonnes maida used in bakery industry for making bread, biscuits, etc. This is very meagre when compared to total production of wheat in India. The other raw materials are sugar, oil, vanaspathy, milk, egg, fruit, nuts, yeast, spices, etc., are from agricultural sector. Other chemicals like baking powder, ammonia are used at meagre percentage.

Thus most of the raw materials directly or indirectly come from agricultural sector. The growth of bakery industry will certainly help the growth of agriculture. Hence bakery is coming under Agro-based industry and as per KVIC specification it is coming under processing of cereals and pulses industry (PCPI). Bakery industry has been under the aid of

KVIC right from the inception of the commission as a sub-industry under PCPI.

Household bakery not using machine for flour mixing, cake mixing, bread slicing etc. However, now-a-days bakeries have work load of 50 kg. of maida for making bread, are owing flour mixing machine. It is advisable to own flour mixing and cake mixing machine. For baking brick oven is convenient as there is erratic power supply in India. In rural area firewood and other agro-waste are available at lower cost, which can be used as fuel for brick oven. This can be easily constructed by local mason, with locally available building materials. Maximum cost for 5' × 6' oven will not be more than Rs. 10,000 per cent. In India, 90 per cent of bakeries have only brick oven fuelled by firewood another agro-waste. Total cost of machines, oven work table, trays and their equipments will not be more than Rs. 75,000 per cent. This is for a tiny unit, which can produce products worth Rs. 5,000 per cent per day and earn a net profit of Rs. 600 per cent per day.

Time taken to convert raw materials into finished products is called production cycle. It varies from industry to industry depending upon the production process. The production cycle for some of the industries are given below.

(1) Leather processing	21 days (Chemical processing)
(2) Dhall processing	3 days
(3) Paddy	3 days
(4) Hand made paper	7 days
(5) Soap industry	5 days

In the case of bakery the production cycle is counted in hours and not in days. It varies from product to product, which are given below:

Production cycle for	Bread	—	8 hrs including cooling time
"	Cake	—	6 hrs including cooling time
"	Puffs	—	3 hrs "
"	Biscuits	—	4 hrs "

Shorter the production cycle less capital will be required for keeping inventory. Further the bakery products are perishable and is to be sold fresh, hence meagre capital will be locked up in keeping the finished goods.

The turnover of working capital is one-tenth of sale value provided there is easy availability of raw materials on credit.

Duration required to convert raw materials into cash, the period from payment of cash to purchase raw materials, stores, production charges, charges for keeping W.I.P in the pipeline and keep finished goods in the godown, and get bake cash after selling the goods. Cash to cash period is called cash cycle. In the case of bakery it is calculated only in days but in other industry it is calculated in months. Lower the cash cycle, less will be the requirement of working capital. Further, credit purchase of raw materials is available easily and this will reduce the amount of working capital needed. Hence cost of capital in bakery is less compared to other industries.

Cost of Production and Pricing Methods

Calculating the cost of production and fixing selling price in any business involves lot of intellectual exercise. In bakery industry price of products are fixed mostly on the basis of existing price in the market, the quality of the product and the reputation of the respective bakery industry. Prices are fixed by Government of India in the case of bread industry. Prices of other products like cake, cookies, etc. are varying from place to place, bakery to bakery depending upon the quality, size of the products. A study review that bakeries adopt a thump rule for fixing place. The cost of raw material is calculated and the same amount is added. The total amount will be divided by the number of kilos of products obtained. This can be explained with the following example:

Cost of raw materials	=	Rs. 200
Over head and Profit	=	Rs. 200
Total		Rs. 400
Products obtained—4 kg. of cake		
Selling price of 1 kg. of cake	=	Rs. 100

Cost of raw materials and fuel required for the production of the following fast moving bakery products are given below. This is calculated at the prevailing price in the 1998 year.

Bread

Maida	1 kg.	*	12.00	12.00
Sugar	200 grams	*	16.20	3.20
Yeast	3 grams	*	160.00	0.50
Oil	40 grams	**	45.00	0.75
Improved/preservations				0.50
Salt and other materials if any				0.50
Fuel				0.75
				20.00

Output: 1.600 kg. Bread (or) 400 gm. loaf 4 Nos.

Cost of raw materials for each	=	Rs. 5
Present selling price	=	Rs. 10

Vegetable Puffs

Maida	1 kg.	*	12	=	12.00
Fat	600 gm.	*	45	=	27.00
Egg	1 No.	*	1.50	=	1.50
Lemon	1/2	*	0.50	=	.50
Vegetable + Masala for fillings					25.00
Fuel					2.00
					68.00

Output:	=		50 puffs
Raw materials cost	=		68
	=	Rs.	1.33
Per puffs		Rs.	50

Prevailing price of puffs in the market ranges from Rs. 2 to 3.50

Sponge Cake with Icing

Maida	1.100 kg.	*	12	=	13.20
Sugar	1.100 kg.	*	15	=	16.50
Gel	80 kg.	*	250	=	20.00
Oil	600 gm.	*	1.50	=	33.20
Essence	10 m.			=	3.00
Baking powder	20 gm.			=	13.20
Fuel				=	5.00
					122.70

For Icing

Fat	250 gm.	*	45	=	11.25
Powder sugar	400 gm.	*	20	=	8.00
Essence and Colour					1.75
Grand Total			Rs. 143.70 or 145		
Output		=	80 pieces of cake		
Cost of raw materials for 1 piece					145.00 / 80.00
				=	1.75

Prevailing price in the Market ranges between minimum of Rs. 3 to 4.

The above calculation is given with a view to explain the profitability, economic viability and sustainability of bakery industry. For every rupee of sales the raw materials cost will not exceed 50 paise which include fuel also. The remaining 50 paise will certainly accommodate all other fixed cost, selling cost, establishment cost, office cost etc. Leaving at least 20 paise on sale of one rupee of products. But only problem is, products are to be sold very fastly as they are perishable in nature. The percentage cost of raw materials or sale value will be ranges between 40 to 50 per cent. Whereas in oil industry is 80 to 85. Dhall processing and paddy processing around 80 per cent lesser the percentage of raw materials cost on sale value more will be the economic viability of the industry. Hence it is needless to say that bakery is a economically viable industry.

Technological Growth in Bakery Industry

Produce Process

The bakery products can be grouped under two major heads:

1. Yeast raised products like bun, bread, rusk, pizza, etc.
2. Chemically leavened products like cake, biscuits, cookies etc., besides puff pastry.

The production process is very simple and require less skill and training.

Production Process of Yeast Raised Products

1. Mixing yeast, water and other ingredients with maida.
2. Allow to ferment.
3. Cut, weigh, mould and pen it.
4. Allow to ferment till it get full size.
5. Bake in the oven, cool, and slice it.

Production Process of Cake and Cookies

Cake

1. Yeast, sugar, egg, and gel.
2. Add essence and colour.
3. Add maida, baking powder and oil.
4. Bake, cool, add cream to decorate.

Cookies

1. Cream fat and sugar with essence.
2. Add maida and baking powder.
3. Make a sheet and cut with biscuit cutter.
4. Bake, cool it before serving.

Raw Materials

A variety of raw materials are used in bakery industry. Whereas raw material requirements for conventional bread and biscuits produced in mechanised units are well defined, a variety of raw materials in different mixes are used for a number of traditional bakery items such as cakes, pastries etc. depending upon the quality and taste requirements.

1. Wheat, atta, maida, leavening agents such as baker's yeast, barn and hops, fermented juice obtained from palm and lactic acid ferment, edible common salt and potable water.

2. Milk products such as condensed milk, in milk powder whey and curd, fat hydrogenated oil or refined edible oil of a suitable type or butter or ghee, margarine or their mixture, gluten, sugar and sugar products, honey, liquid glucose, malt products, edible starches such as potato starch, corn flour and tapioca flour, edible groundnut flour, vitamins, glycerine monostearate, lime water, fungal enzyme sorbitol and lysine etc.
3. Product improves such as ammonium persulphate, potassium bromate, calcium carbonate, calcium phosphate and mould inhabitors such as sodium or calcium propionate, acetic acid or lactic acid, sodium diacetate, acid calcium phosphate and acid sodium pyrophosphate.

These raw materials in the form of flour, yeast milk products, shortenings, sugars, eggs and other minor ingredients etc. are discussed in details in this book. Various bakery products grouped as yeast leavened foods, chemically leavened foods, air leavened bakery products and unleavened bakery foods are discussed under the heading of individual products like breads, biscuits, cakes, cookies, pie crust and sola crackers etc. The products especially dry products marketed by various companies under a variety of trade names.

Flour

It is the single most important and the basic ingredient in bread making. The flour used in bread-making is usually milled from aestivum wheat. The bread-making quality of flour depends to a great extent on the quality and quantity of proteins. The unique property of wheat protein to form gluten in the presence of water, enables it to be made use of in variety of bakery products. The bread dough made out of wheat flour, water, yeast and other ingredients is a complex coherent mass in which starch, yeast and other ingredients are embedded. Thus the gluten provides the framework for the retention of gas produced during the formulation.

Water

Water is an essential ingredient. It is involved in the hydration of flour and the formation of gluten. It acts as a dispersing medium for other ingredients such as salt, sugar, yeast foods, additives etc. The water is also involved in the leavening action due to formation of steam during the baking process. The inclusion of water should be at an optimum level. Excessive amounts of water make the dough sticky and difficult to handle.

Yeast

Like flour, yeast is also a basic ingredient. It is involved in the fermentation process of the bread dough. The yeast utilises the simple sugars already present in the flour and also produced during the fermentation by the combined action of diastatic enzymes of yeast such as a maltose convert the maltose in to the glucose, inversive acts on sucrose to convert it into monosaccharides and the enzymes acts in the simple sugars to produce alcohol, carbon dioxide, some organic acids and other flavour compounds. The carbon dioxide liberated during fermentation helps in leavening.

Sugar

The added sugar provide the requirement of yeast during the initial stages of fermentation. During fermentation, about 3 per cent of sugar is utilised by yeast. Generally the sugar is added at 2 per cent level in sponge doughs and at 3 per cent level in straight doughs. Higher levels averaging to around 6 to 8 per cent are commonly used to achieve crust colour, volume, flavour and keeping quality affects the gas-holding capacity of the dough. With very low levels of soft or without salt, the fermentation rate increases sharply, as a result becomes bread.

Milk

This is added to improve the nutritional quality. It

increases the acidity, the colour of the crust and the flavour. Milk also acts as a buffering agent and allows the pH to remain constant. Otherwise decrease in pH will affect the east activity. The milk should be sterilised before use to avoid the adverse effect on dough such as slacking and stickness and to prevent coarseness of grain and poor crumb texture.

Antimicrobial Agents

Some of the chemicals such as sodium of calcium salts of propionic acid and sodium diastases are commonly used to prevent mold growth. These chemicals act by forming a thin layer around the cell of the micro-organisms and prevent the uptake of nutrients from the medium (bread) or release of toxic wastes coming out of the cell. Also it is believed to increase the rate of fermentation. The sugar is almost instantly converted to dextrose and fructose by inverts of yeast and about 2/3rd is utilised by yeast.

Fat

Shortenings are the essential components of most bakery products. The type and level of shortenings and emulsifier in the formula affect both the handling/machining response of the dough and the quality of end-products. In yeast raised products such as bread and rolls, the inclusion of fat is more or less optional. The performance of plastic fats is much better than the oils.

Salt

Salt is addition to contributing flavour, increased palatability and appitising characteristics to the bread and also strengthens the gluten. It is added at 1.5 to 2 per cent level. Salt also controls the fermentation rate. Too much of salt affects the yeast activity and hence the rate of fermentation decreases, also it affects the gas-holding capacity of dough. With very low levels of salt to without salt, the fermentation rate increase sharply, as a result the bread becomes too acidic.

With regard to the use of raw materials all the 12 sample bakeries of Dindigul district are using essential raw materials like maida, yeast, sugar, fat, salt, water and optional ingredients like colour, essence, milk etc. As there is good demand for sponge cake 75 per cent of bakeries using gel which is coming under the category of raw materials (improver). The improver includes G.M.S., potasium permanganate besides gel. Most of the bakeries under study are small one. They need not keep the product for more than a day or two. Hence, the use of preservative like calcium proponate, acidic acid, lactic acid are very much restricted. The study also reveals that only 66 per cent of bakeries are using preservatives.

Preparation of Ingredients and Solutions

The flour is generally sieved before mixing the ingredients in order to *(a)* aerate, *(b)* remove coarse particles and impurities, and *(c)* make it more homogeneous. All the ingredients are weighed as per the formula. However, it is important to weigh the minor ingredients using a precision balance. Generally yeast is dispersed in a part of water and the remaining part of water is used to dissolve sugar, salt and other minor ingredients.

Sequence of Adding Ingredients to the Mixer

(A) Straight Dough Method

(i) Vertical Mixer

Part of dough water tempered to the temperature is used for suspending yeast. The balanced water is placed in the mixer and mixed with small ingredients, sugar, malt, yeast, foods and milk solids. As the mixing continues, first part of flour, yeast suspension and remaining flour are added. These are followed by shortening and finally salt at the cleaning stage. Depending on the speed of mixer the mixing time varies between eight to twelve minutes.

(ii) Horizontal Mixer

Dry ingredients are mixed first and then yeast solution

and the balance of the dough water. Half way through shortening and salt at the clearing stage are added. Delaying the salt addition until the dough begins to clear the mixer bowl appreciably reduces the mixing time. This procedure prevents splashing that occurs if liquid ingredients are placed first in the bowl.

B. Sponge and Dough Method

The sponge incorporates a major part of flour, yeast, yeast foods, enzymes and sufficient water. The dough is moderately stiff. The mixing procedure follows straight dough except that the time is about four minutes. If the dough stage the dry ingredients are added to the sponge. The liquid ingredients are then added and at about half way point shortening is added. Finally the salt is added. The dough is mixed to its optimum condition.

The study found that most of them do not know the importance of sieving the flour and all the bakeries are doing the above operation. Knowing the importance of flying ferment eight Bakeries are preparing flying ferment for mixing the yeast with maida. As most of the bakeries are small 50 per cent bakeries using only fresh yeast. This is because they are not in a position to buy refrigerator for keeping the yeast. Further the method of preparation of Bun and Bread followed by 75 per cent of bakeries are using the overnight sponge method.

Mixing

The major objectives of dough mixing process are *(a)* through and uniform dispersion of the ingredients to form a homogeneous mixture, and *(b)* to bring about the physical development of gluten in the dough into a uniform structure having optimum desired dough characteristics with respect to plasticity, elasticity and viscosity. The desired dough development in the mixer is achieved by the kneading action of the mixing elements. It is accomplished by blending, stretching, combining, pushing, compressing and holding the dough. The factor that governs the mixing is clearances between mixing elements themselves and also between them and mixer walls whether it is a vertical planetary mixer, horizontal bar mixer or developer head with impellers.

The study revealed that more than 83 per cent bakeries working physically for mixing the flour without adequate knowledge about the hygienic conditions to be maintained in bakeries, 75 per cent of them having only wooden tables which are to be replaced by marble. Store use of aluminum vessels and trays up of tin sheets are common in the bakeries studies.

Fermentation

Mixed dough should be allowed for fermentation for a suitable length of time for obtaining light aerated loaf of bread. During period, lot of changes both physical and chemical, take place in dough.

(i) Physical Changes

(a) Increase in volume due to production of CO2,
(b) Increase in temperature,
(c) Increase in the number of Yeast cells,
(d) Loss of moisture,
(e) Changes in the consistency of dough.

The dough becomes soft, elastic as well as extensible.

(ii) Chemical Changes

(a) Lowering of pH of dough comes down from 5.5 to 4.7 due to formation of acids like acetic acid from the bacterial as well as yeast activity.
(b) Formation of maltose sugar by diastatic enzymes, present in the flour by acting on starch.
(c) Development of dough due to the rupture of SS bonds and formation in new position which improve the gas retain property gluten.
(d) Conversion of starch into simple sugar which is then converted in to CO2 and alcohol by the following group of enzyme present in flour by yeast:

In Dindigul district workers either skilled or unskilled are directly involved in production activity are not undergone any formal training in bakery trade. They may not be in a position to know a scientific method of production of bread, Bun etc. It is clear that most of them do not know how to keep the dough for fermentation and prevent crust formation. The workers need formal training in the scientific process of bread-making which will enhance quality of bakery products.

Knock Back

Punching of the dough in between the fermentation periods increases gas retaining capacity of the dough.

The other effects of knock back are:

(i) Equalisation of temperature throughout the dough thereby assures more uniform fermentation.

(ii) Reduces the retarding effect of excessive accumulation of carbon dioxide within the dough by the removal of carbon dioxide.

(iii) Introduces atmospheric oxygen thereby stimulates effect of yeast activity and aids in the mechanical development of the gluten by the stretching and doling action.

The correct time for the first punch is usually determined by inserting the hand into the dough withdrawing quickly and observing the behaviour of the dough. If the dough reshapes itself, it is ready for the first punch. This point is generally reached when 60 per cent of the fermentation time is completed. The second punch if required is given in half the time required for the first punch. Fully nurtured flours take shorter fermentation time and less frequent punching than fresh flours.

The bakeries under study revealed that majority of the bakery owners don't aware about the process and followed their traditional method of operation.

Moulding and Planning

Scaling

The dough is divided into pieces of predetermined

uniform weight and size. The weight of the dough to be taken depends on the final weight of the bread required. Generally 12 per cent extra dough weight is taken to compensate the bake-loss. Dividing should be done within the shortest time in order to ensure the uniform weight as the doughs are scaled on a volumetric basis, longer times change the density of the dough due to production of carbon dioxide by yeast thereby changing the weight of the divided dough. If there is a delay in dividing corrective steps should be taken either by degassing the dough or increasing the size of the dough. The degasser are essentially dough pumps which feed the dough into the hopper and in the process remove most of the gas. The advantages of using degassers are:

(i) more uniform scaling;
(ii) uniform pan flows; and
(iii) uniform grain and texture.

Rounding

When the dough piece leaves the divider, it is irregular in shape with sticky cut surfaces from which the gas can readily use. The function of the rounder is to impart a new continuous surface skin that will maintain the gas as well as reduce the stickiness thereby increasing its handling umbrella type and bowl type.

Moulding

The moulder receives pieces of dough from the inter-nudity proof and shapes them into cylinders ready to be placed in the pans. Moulding involves three separate steps:

(i) Sheeting
(ii) Curling; and
(iii) Scaling.

Sheeter degasses the dough and sheeted dough can be easily manipulated in the later stages of moulding. Sheeting is accomplished by passing the dough through 2 or 3 seats of closely spaced rolls that progressively flatten and degas the dough. The first pair of rolls are spaced about 0.25" apart where the degassing takes place. The successive two rollers are spaced 0.125" and 0.06" apart for optimum grain and texture development in the finished products.

The sheeted dough piece now enters the curling section. The sheeted dough is carried by a belt conveyor under flexible oven mash chain that rolls into a cylindrical form. The rolling operation should produce a relatively tight curl that will avoid air entrapment.

The curled dough piece finally passes under a pressure board to eliminate any gas pockets within and to scale the same.

Panning

The moulded dough pieces are immediately placed in the baking pans. Panning should be carried out so that the sea of the dough is placed on the bottom of the pan. This will prevent subsequent opening of the seam during proofing and baking. Optimum pan temperature 90°F.

As the bakeries under study are small in size and operation, they have not any machineries for processing like sizing, moulding. The study reveals that most of them doing hand sizing and hand moulding. Trays and pans are cleaned with soda ash periodically and oiled before panning. This is done by more than 75 per cent of bakeries. This is appreciable in view of maintaining hygienic condition, as the bakeries employed less fixed capital.

Pan Proof

The purposes of pan proof are:

(i) to relax the dough from the stress received during moulding operation;

(ii) to facilitate production of gas in order to give volume to the bread; and

(iii) to change tough bucky gluten to good mellow extensible character;

Proofing is influenced by temperature humidity and time. Normal conditions are temperature 95°F and RH 85 per cent and proof time of 55 to 65 min. However, many bakeries proof at 105°F particularly for continuous mixed dough. Proof temperature depends on the variety of factors such as flour strength, dough formulation with respect to oxidants, dough conditioners, type of shortening, degree of fermentation, make up treatment, type of product desired.

Lower humidity gives rise to dry crust in the dough. Excessive humidity leads to condensation of moisture. Dough is generally to depends on the condition of the dough like under-mixed or over mixed, under-fermented or over-fermented. Its recipe contains proof to height as it compensates for variations in proof conditions resulting in uniform quality bread.

In Dindigul district, bakeries are not having separate room for keeping the dough for final proof. However the trays are arranged vertically and covered with cloths and gunny bags. The gunny bags and cloths become dirty in two to three days and need cleaning. The investigator while visiting the bakeries for collection of data observed that most of them using same old dirty black gunny bag and cloth. This practice should be given up immediately and hygienic arrangement is to be made for the process of final proof.

Baking

The purposes of baking are to transform unpalatable dough into a light porous and readily digestible flavoured product. The duration of baking humidity and temperature of the oven influences the quality of the product. The baking time depends on baking temperature, size and weight of product being baked. Baking temperature influences the bake loss and moisture in bread. There are two types of changes—physical and chemical—that are taking place during baking.

As there is lack of capital and non-availability of power supply in study area, more than 95 per cent are owning brick oven fueled by firewood is more convenient to them. The reasons are:

(*a*) It is economically cheaper;
(*b*) It will be constructed with local mason and materials available in local areas.

(c) This can be fueled by firewood which is also available at their doorstep. Further workers in the bakeries are not able to work with modern electric oven.

Cooling

Bread has to be cooled before slicing and wrapping to:

(i) facilitate slicing,
(ii) to prevent condensation of moisture in the wrapper.

Desirable temperature during slicing is 95° to 105°C. Cooling facilitates in redistribution of moisture. The migration from centre to the crust softens crust.

In order to avoid mold growth bun and bread are to be cool rack immediately after baling. Minimum two hours cooling is absolutely necessary for increasing the keeping quality of bread. The present study found that more than 58 per cent of bakery are not owning cooling rack and cooling is done on the table itself. This is improper and needs recepication.

Summary of Findings

This is, to some extent descriptive analytical study by observation and collecting information from the 12 bakery owners and entrepreneurs using the interview schedule. The summary of the findings are given below.

1. Production of bakery products in India—Increased growth rate of all items of bakery, reveals that more and more people started consuming bakery products.
2. Size of bakery industry—more than 90 per cent of bakery units are household units, located in rural areas, meeting the needs of rural people.
3. Statewise share in the market for bakery products in India—Rates of growth of consumption show that in selected urban centres, the demand for bread will increase much faster than the demand for biscuits.
4. Nutritional value for bakery products.
5. Use of raw materials—In sample bakeries of Dindigul district with record to the use of raw materials in all the 12 bakeries.

6. Preparation of ingredients in bakeries of Dindigul district—The practice adopted for pre-processing of bread-making i.e.., preparation of bread-making.
7. Process of mixing in bakeries of Dindigul district shows that more than 83 per cent of bakeries working physically for mixing the flour without adequate knowledge about the hygienic condition.
8. Process of fermentation bakery industries—Workers either skilled or unskilled are directly involved in production activity are not undergone any formal training in bakery trade.
9. Knock back method used for bakeries—As the bakeries under study show that majority of the bakery owners did not aware about the process.
10. Moulding and panning process in sample bakeries of Dindigul district—As the bakeries under study are small in size and operation.
11. Pan proof in sample industry—They are not having separate room for keeping the dough for final proof.
12. Baking process in bakeries—As there is lack of capital and non-availability of power supply more than 95 per cent.
13. Cooling process in bakeries—In order to avoid mold bun and bread are to be cool rack immediately after baking.
14. The location of the bakery units—Most of the bakeries are in the urban areas.
15. Size of the bakery units—The units classified into small size, medium size and large size.
16. Machinery and equipment used in bakery units—Dough kneader, bread slicing, cake mixer, electric oven etc.
17. Production methods—Manufacturing with use of modern techniques.
18. Cost of production—The total annual cost spent for raw materials, wages, interest on borrowing, depreciation.
19. Sales and review per year was Rs. 2,09,83,500 and Rs 1,91,44,000 respectively.

20. A composition of investments in bakery units required both for the working capital and fixed capital.
21. Most of the bakeries have lower level of expenses and high level income.
22. The various raw materials used maida, sugar and oils etc.
23. Varieties of production cake, bun, biscuit, puffs.

Problems

1. Non-availability of uniform quality of raw materials, especially maida. One type of maida is available from which all products are produced.
2. Non-availability of trained manpower for bakery industry, especially biscuits and cake, is said to be high and which retards its growth.
3. Exercise and Sales Tax levied on bakery industry, especially biscuits and cake, is said to be high and which retards its growth.
4. Non-availability of facility for quality testing laboratories accessible to bakeries for testing qualities of raw materials and finished products.

Suggestions

The study recommended the following measures for the sustainable growth of bakery industries in India.

There is no common forum to educate the people about the advantage of consuming bakery products instead of oil fried and other boiled products. This can be entrusted with food and Nutrition Board, Agriculture Universities, Foods Science Institutes etc. From the flour millers and that fund can be used for the Research and Development of bakery industry.

Further, availability of trained personnel, modern machineries, credit facility, technical guidance may take the bakery industry to 21st century flying colours.

The Government may supply the bakery products at cheapest price to the people through cooperative societies/ NGOs.

In order to encourage the development of bakery industry, wheat for maida, oil and sugar may be supplied to the household bakery industries at subsidised rate.

While concluding, it is suggested that the supply of raw materials to the household bakery industry at subsidised rate would solve the problems of unemployment, under nutrition status among rural masses, balanced buffer stock position of FCT, etc.

References

1. Soundarapandian, M., *Rural Industries in India,* Mohit Publication, New Delhi, 1999.
2. Sherlekar, S.A., Janardhanan C.P., *Essentials of Business Organisation and Management*, Himalaya Publishing House, New Delhi, 1992.
3. Dubey, S.C., "Basic Baking Science", *School of Baking,* Anand, Gujarat.
4. Kandhari, L.R., *Bakers Hand Book on Practical Baking,* 27, Barakhamba Road, New Delhi, 1980.
5. France, W.J., *The Student Technology of Bread Making and Flour Confectionery,* Rotledge and Kegan Paul Ltd., Store Street, London, 1947.
6. Pyer, E.J., *Baking Science and Technology,* Siebel Publishing Company, Chicago LL, 1573.
7. Albert, R. Danniel, *Bakery Material and Methods,* Maclaren and Sons Ltd., 1947, Stafford House, Norfolk Street, London.
8. E. Herisse, C., *Hermam Senn,* Ward Lock of O., Ltd., 6 Chancery Land, London.
9. Neil Lyall, *Some Savoury Food Products,* Food Trade Press Ltd., 7, Garrick Street, London.
10. Smith, W.H., *Biscuit, Cookies,* (Vol. I), Technology, Production Management, 1972, Applied Science.
11. *The Indian Baker,* Quarterly Journal, Society of Indian Bakers, New Delhi.
12. *Food Industry,* Quarterly Journal, Food Scientists Association, CFTRI, Mysore.

7

Poultry Industry

Poultry farming today has become one of the fastest growing industries in India (Taneja, 1998). Poultry farming is interesting because it gives pleasure as well as profit to persons of both sexes, all ages, all walks of life in all sections of the country. It is useful alike in the farm and in the city backyard in the cold north, in the sunny south, in the hill and mountain country, or on the plain. It may be conducted as an exclusive business or as a side line. It affords pleasure and profit for rich and poor alike. In fact, it is the universal agricultural industry (Louis M. Hurd, 1956).

The beauty of poultry farming is that the space and finance required for setting up a poultry farm is most elastic (Kulicrant, 1989). One can have it in big area of land and even as a Kitchen-garden and then the land and finance involved has no restriction. The National Commission of Agriculture (Rekhi, 1977) says that poultry farming has certain special features which favour its large-scale adoption by small and marginal farmers and agricultural labourers. Land required for poultry farming is very little, the capital investment for starting a poultry units is not very large and poultry farming can be started on a small scale and can be expanded gradually.

The main reasons for the poultry farm making tremendous stride is that poultry farming does not want heavy investment and the raw materials are easily available and short-term training facilities are available and even uneducated people could set up poultry farms. Finance is available from the financing agencies by way of institutional finance and veternary facilities are easily available in the state, which has veternary institution for every 5 to 10 kms.

Poultry does give good returns for the amount invested, time and energy spent and labour involved (Mantramurti, 1987). Some of the advantages of poultry-keeping are:

(i) Supplies nutritions food for the people.
(ii) Some effective medicines and tonics are obtained from poultry.
(iii) Serves as hobby and sport for some people.
(iv) Requires less capital to start a poultry unit and gives good and quick returns.
(v) Needs very little space.
(vi) Water requirement is less compared with crop cultivation or dairy farm.
(vii) Waste products like bran and substandard grains are profitably utilised and converted into valuable food for the people.
(viii) Eradicates garden pests such as caterpillars, insects and snails.
(ix) Give rich fertilizer for crop cultivation especially for vegetable gardens.
(x) Poultry feathers are useful in many ways.
(xi) It is a sideline to agriculture.
(xii) Gives income throughout the year.
(xiii) Not much labour is involved and generate self-employment.
(xiv) Support many ancillary units.
(xv) Easy to manage, even women and children can look after them.

At present the poultry industry has transformed itself in the fast growing sector of Indian animal husbandry. The poultry industry has converted the waste products of agriculture into efficient protein food. Even in this modern time the farmers breed some hens for satisfying their family needs. Poultry is an attractive and a home farm business. Investment made in poultry is relatively small compared with many other types of agricultural industries.

Profits are earned much sooner than any other farm

products. Poultry industry may be considered as soil breeding enterprises. Poultry manure has given nitrogen and phosphorous than the manure from other products.

In spite of many advantages of poultry industry at present, many factors, refers to the development of the industry. In Tamilnadu, Namakkal district is the leading place in developing the poultry industry. The present study attempts to analyse the economics of production of poultry in Mohanoor block of Namakkal district of Tamilnadu.

The specific objectives of the study are:

1. To analyse the egg production level of the poultry farm in Mohanoor Block of Namakkal district.
2. To study the average cost of production and profitability of a sample farms in egg production.
3. To find out employment and income generation level of the poultry farms in sample units and,
4. To identify the problems faced by the poultry farms and to suggest suitable remedial measures of the unemployment of the poultry industry.

A field survey was undertaken with a determined questionnaire. The poultry owners were interviewed with the help of interview schedule. The area of study is limited only to Mohanoor block in Namakkal district. It has been purposefully selected, because this block has large number of poultry units.

Tamilnadu is the second largest egg production state contributing to an average of one crore eggs per day to India's total egg supply. Namakkal district is the largest egg producing district, in Tamilnadu which contributed more than 75 per cent of the states egg supply. Mohanoor block of Namakkal district has purposively selected for the study. Since it produces a valuable percentage of eggs among the total egg production of the district.

The major reason for the phenomenal development of this sector here is because the dry climate, which does not make agriculture remunerative.

Mohanoor block has all facilities for farming, hatcheries and producing eggs. In this area there are a number of poultry feed industries, some of them are Ishwarya, Annam, Reena etc.

More than 20,000 people are depended upon this sphere and activity. The poorer sections of this block initially raised poultry, but now some educated people have joined in the race.

This Mohanoor block has very good road and rail facility to transport the eggs to other places of the country and abroad as export.

Here, there is one veternary science college which provides very essential assistance like creating awareness about the diseases for the chicks, how to maintain environment to the farmers. These things are done through conducting weekly classes, seminars and field demonstrations.

The price of the egg is decided by the National Egg Co-ordination Committee (NECC). This Committee meets once in a week to fix the price. This Committee fixes the price, after consulting the egg producers especially the small and cottage scale producers.

In this block there are some Government organisations like Tamil Nadu Poultry Development Corporation (TAPCO). This organisation has been set-up in the area to market eggs and improve the quality of eggs which one sent to other countries.

A complete list of farms in Mohanoor block was received from the Block Development Office. From the 217 farms of the population farms size, 10 farms were randomly selected as the sample. The unrestricted random sampling method was followed. The 10 farms were selected with the use of table of random numbers.

Both primary data and secondary data have been used for the study. Personal interview schedule were prepared and used to collect the primary data. Secondary data were collected from published and unpublished officials and non-official report. The owners of farms were helpful in giving all relevant data regarding the performance of their respective poultry farming. The data were edited for analysing an interpretation.

Poultry farming in India was largely a backward venture. Not much attention was paid to breeding, feeding, disease control and management of birds for commercial production and it has for long time remained largely a rural cottage enterprise (Ganamani, 1991). The poultry population was confined to desi-birds which are hardly but of low productivity. But bý the turn of this century some exotic birds of proven value and productivity were introduced in India by missionary organisations to help farmers. This supplement their income through poultry raising. Exotic breeds and improved chicks were distributed to the local farmers.

Poultry farming has emerged very fast as a commercial crop in India. Anti-poverty programmes rural areas has increasingly turned to poultry, resulting in adoption of intensive poultry farming by landers, marginal and small farmers.

Presently it is a well organised agro-industry where people with limited or adequate finances can start commercial poultry farming as a first choice due to its lack of social bare or communal taboo (Choudary, 1990).

"On the whole, within the community 6 to 8 year times, the poultry industry of the country is set for a total transformation putting India on the poultry map of a world as are of the advanced poultry nations" (Harbans Singh, 1982).

From 1955 onwards, poultry started receiving the recognition and encouragement due to an agro-industry. The first All India project on poultry development was launched in April 1956. Intensive poultry development programme was introduced in third Five Year Plan, to provide all the essential inputs and services to local farmers in the form of package deal. It covered the supply of chicks, feed, medicine, equipment etc. The computations of a modern and sophisticated poultry farming soon underscored the need for disease some imported with the exotic stock. As results, the leading agricultural universities in the country include poultry science in their curriculum. Some of these universities now offer Ph.D. in poultry science, Central Avian Research Institute, Izatnagar, near Bareilly (U.P) was established in 1979 to provide strong research support to the fast growing industry in public as well as private sector.

All the big hatcheries and poultry farms in the country are now thriving on these exotic stocks. Which lay almost four times more eggs than the desi birds. The broiler industry started taking shape in early seventies, but the real push come only in eighties when the eggs business did not remain very lucrative due to mushroom growth of local farms.

Egg Production

The egg production in India was only 1,780 million in 1960, jumped to 12,500 million in 1980, 25,200 million in 1990. The annual eggs production in India for the period 1992-96 is given in Table 7.1.

Table 7.1
Annual Egg Production in India

Year	*Egg Production (in Million)*
1992	22,740
1993	24,800
1994	26,290
1995	28,130
1996	30,000

Source: Financial Agriculture, 1997.

During the last three decades, annual output of eggs has gone up by over eight times to 22,740 million, making poultry the fastest growing sector of Indian agriculture. Poultry production in 1996 was projected to be 30,000 million hybrid and 73 million desi layers. Over 50 per cent of the egg come from just four out of 26 states. They are Andhra pradesh, Maharashtra, Punjab and Tamilnadu.

Per Capita Availability of Eggs

The per capita availability of egg (Table 7.2) can be calculated by dividing the total egg production in the total population in a year. The consumption level of egg in urban and rural areas in 1993 is depicted in Table 7.3.

The national per capita availability of egg average is 32. In the urban areas it is as high as 90 (in metro cities, almost 170 eggs) while in rural areas, barely 10. The potential for increasing egg consumption is enormous particularly in rural areas, where about 75 per cent of the population lives.

Table 7.2
Per Capita Availability of Egg

Year	*Per Capita Availability*
1992	21
1993	28
1994	29
1995	31
1996	32

Table 7.3
Consumption Level of Eggs in Urban and Rural Areas in India, 1993

	Egg Consumption Population Million	*Total (Million)*
URBAN		
Mega cities	70.6 (08%)	11,900 (48%)
Other cities	162.4 (18%)	6,700 (27%)
Total	233.0 (26%)	18,000 (75%)
RURAL		
Developed	215 (24%)	4,100 (17%)
Developing	430 (50%)	2,100 (08%)
Total	645 (74%)	6,200 (25%)
Grand Total	878 (100%)	24,800 (100%)

Source: Financial Agricultural, 1994.

Layers

A female chick above the egg of 150 days in case of light breed and 175 days in case of heavy breed kept for laying eggs.

Indian poultry industry was started during early 1960, when the Government imported 30,000 RIR and WLH baby chicks for breeding and production programmes in different

Table 7.4
Estimated Production and Availability of Eggs in Major States, 1993

State	*Area ('000 Sq km)*	*Population (Million)*	*Egg Production (Million)*	*Per Egg Availabilty /Year*
High Egg-Producing States				
Andhra Pradesh	275 (08%)	69 (08%)	6,420 (26%)	91
Haryana	44 (01%)	17 (02%)	1,110 (04%)	65
Punjab	50 (02%)	20 (02%)	1,959 (08%)	92
Tamilnadu	130 (04%)	58 (07%)	3,510 (14%)	60
Total	499 (15%)	164 (19%)	12,999 (52%)	78
Medium Egg-Producing States				
Karnataka	192 (06%)	46 (05%)	1,015 (05%)	21
Kerala	39 (01%)	31 (04%)	899 (04%)	29
Maharashtra	308 (09%)	82 (09%)	2,850 (11%)	34
Total	539 (16%)	159 (18%)	4,764 (19%)	29
Low Egg-Producing States				
Bihar	174 (05%)	90 (10%)	1,224 (05%)	13
Madhya Pradesh	196 (06%)	44 (05%)	608 (02%)	14
Orissa	156 (05%)	32 (04%)	580 (26%)	17
Rajasthan	342 (10%)	45 (05%)	581 (02%)	13
Uttar Pradesh	294 (09%)	144 (16%)	1,040 (04%)	7
West Bengal	89 (03%)	70 (08%)	1,261 (05%)	18
Total	1,251 (51%)	425 (56%)	5,294 (27%)	13
Grand Total	2,289 (82%)	748 (93%)	23,057 (98%)	30
All-India Total	3,290 (100%)	878 (100%)	24,800 (100%)	28

Note: Percentage of All-India total is shown in brackets.
Source: Financial Agriculture, 1994.

states during the second five year plan period. The source of exotic germplasm resulted in most state governments encouraging poultry farming in semi-intensive and intensive methods by providing incentives and subsidies.

Table 7.5

Growth of Poultry in India during Three Decades (Million)

Items	*1960*	*1980*	*1990*
Improved layers	1	56	120
Broilers	0	30	240
Egg production	1,780	12,500	25,200
Per capita egg consumption	4	21	30

Source: Poultry Adviser, Poultry Industry in India, Vol XXIII, No. 3, March 90, page 23.

As can be deduced from table, the poultry farms have helped to propagate the improved layers varieties in different regions of the country in the last three decades.

The private farms imported four grand parent stock to enter poultry business on commercial line. These highbrid chicks were hatched and marketed for commercial purpose in November 1962. The deep litter system was also advocated the same year in India by Mr. Mac Ardle. Two more hatcheries in 1969 in the private sector imported grand parents in the country. Venkateswara hatcheries also imported grand parent stocks during 1971 for their commercial operations. Thus commercialisation of poultry farming took rapid strides in the country on reasonable modern methods. Apart from the role played by private companies, the spectacular growth of this industry has been brought about by the introduction of modern intensive system of poultry rearing.

Indian Council of Agricultural Research (ICAR) started coordinated research project as poultry breeding for layers and broiler with 4 centres for each type in the country in 1970-71. A multi-disciplinary and coordinated approach was provided for carrying on the project.

There was a growing appreciation among the national planners, and the National Commission on Agriculture has pointed out in its reports that "poultry farming has certain special features which favour its large scale adopter by small and marginal farmers and agricultural labourers, land required for poultry farming is very little, the capital investment for starting a poultry unit is not very large and this farming can be started on a small scale and expanded gradually".

Indian egg production mostly comes from seven states, viz., Andhra Pradesh, West Bengal, Tamilnadu, Kerala, Maharastra, Punjab and Karnataka where 40 per cent of the country's population inhabit. The progress of this industry is currently 10 to 15 per cent per year to total.

Layer (1989) in the country was 15 per cent and 14.4 per cent in the southern, northern, western and both eastern and central regions, respectively. Egg production is derived from (countrywide).

* Intensive farming sector with 60,000 farms.
* Rural backyard and small units 200-250 birds. These units face marketing constraints which render them non-viable.

Table 7.6

Plan Outlay for Poultry

Sl. No.	*Plan/Year*	*Outlay for Poultry (Rs. in million)*
1.	Second Plan (1956-1961)	28
2.	Third Plan (1961-1966)	45.8
3.	Fourth Plan (1969-1974)	115
4.	Fifth Plan (1974-1979)	355.5
5.	Sixth Plan (1979-1985)	426.1
6.	Seventh Plan (1986-1990)	459.0
7.	Eighth Plan (1992-1997)	283.8

Source: Different years of five years plan documents.

The Government investment on poultry amounted to 28 million in second plan, when large scale efforts were made to put the poultry farms on scientific and commercial lines. This outlay rose to 115 million in the IVth Plan and 426.1 million in VIth Plan and 283.8 million in VIII Plan period. In the seventh plan (1984-86) Rs. 170.33 million was allotted and the value of poultry products produced was worth Rs. 11,300 million in 1989.

The organised investment on poultry through planning has a positive efforts on poultry development and egg production. It has brought the poultry farming on modern, scientific and commercial lines. The egg production per layer and availability per capita has increased due to creation of widespread infrastructural facilities.

Poultry Industry in Tamilnadu

In Tamilnadu the first poultry farm was established as a private enterprise. The Government of Tamilnadu established a special corporation in July 1974 for the development of poultry which is known as Tamil Nadu Poultry Development Corporation. From its origin this corporation assists the development of poultry by establishing various poultry research centres in various parts of the state, upto 1980 it had established 38 poultry extension centres, 3 chick hatcheries, 2 feed mixing units, 2 poultry production centres and 9 intensive poultry development blocks in Tamilnadu.

The TAPCO (Tamilnadu Poultry Development Corporation Ltd) was formed in July with a view to expand the poultry development activities in Tamilnadu. The TAPCO has plans to open a poultry estate in each district, on its inception it took over 38 poultry extension centres.

The TAPCO has three chick hatcheries, two feed mixing units, two poultry production centres and a intensive poultry development blocks. The corporation is engaged in commercial venture such as feed production, chick production, reading of layers and broilers chicks, marketing of eggs culled birds, supply of medicines and poultry equipment and after sales assistance to the farmers, credit facilities. The World Bank had granted loans through this corporation to poultry units amounting to 50 millions in 1985. The balanced poultry feeds produced at the units Nandanam (Chennai), Kottappathi (Tiruchy), are supplied to all poultry units in the public as well as in private sector during 1987-88, quantities of feed produced came to 5,337.7 tonnes in these units. The units at Chennai, Trichy, Madurai, Thirunelveli, Coimbatore and Salem produced 19,60,02,846 eggs and 38,559 kgs. of poultry meat during the year 1987-88. The ten extension centres maintained by the corporation are engaged in rearing the chick received from the hatcheries and selling the grown up pullets to the public panchayat unions SFDA and MFAL scheme.

Table 7.7

Poultry Production in Tamilnadu

No.	*Particular*	*1979*	*1981*	*1982*	*1983*
1.	Egg production in million	950	1,100	1,250	1,500
2.	Meat million	13,468	15,762	17,700	20,000
3.	Total number of poultry farm	740	810	1,320	2,200
4.	Per capita consumption	16	18	21	24
5.	Number of kinds of birds	5	7	9	12

Source: Financial Agriculture, 1984.

Findings of the Study

In order to study the economics of poultry farm, a study was undertaken by selecting some poultry farms in Mohanoor block of Namakkal district. On the basis of analysis of collected data following findings were made.

(i) Most of the poultry farms either small scale or cottage, it means total capital investment don't exceed more than 50 lakhs in all the cases.

(ii) Level of production is strictly in accordance with the daily requirement.

(iii) Most of the poultry farms using cage methods to produce the eggs.

(iv) Cottage scale poultry farms following the deep litter method to produce eggs instead of cage method.

(v) Use of traditional feed is completely dropped in all the poultry farms. This is due to the easy availability of high .quality nutritious feed.

(vi) In recent past thanks to easy availability of assistance from the feed producing industries, there is a mushroom growth of small and cottage scale poultry farms which supply high quality eggs to the export market.

(vii) In spite of availability of various hybrid chicks, it is found that all the poultry farms are having the traditional Babcock chicks. The reason stated was it yields more number of eggs and cost is less.

(viii) Purchase of feed and other requirements for egg production must be economical and made in time. There are different methods of purchase to keep proper quantity feed and other necessary things in order to have continuous production. All the poultry farms in Mohanoor block are making direct concurrent purchase of feed from the nearby feed industries.

(ix) Quality of the egg, good will and reputation of the farms are the favourable aspects for the farm owners to increase the price.

(x) In the case of marketing of the farm products 80 per cent of the farms making direct sales, other followed commission sales.

Most of the farms engage workers on weekly wages and monthly salary, and payment is made every last day of the week to the weakly wage workers, and last day of the month to the monthly salary workers.

Besides monthly salary and weekly wage payment some amount is given as bhatta to meet the personal expenditure for the workers. The intention is that the wage payment will go to their houses without any deduction.

Problems Identified in Poultry Industry

The poultry industry has grown along with many problems over the year. This has been revealed by an intensive problem on the growth of this industry. To put it, the problems (operational) of this industry are the result of "Poultry plenty" over the years. The problems identified are:

(i) It present the huge production of eggs depress the price of egg in the market.

(ii) This block does not have well equipped and modern specialities.

(iii) Namakkal farmers are progressive, it is unfortunate that proper sanitary methods have not been practiced and dead birds are not properly disposed of.

(iv) The IBD (Infections bursal disease) which eliminate so many birds is not an unknown phenomenon and it has been daunting this sector from the outset. The growth of birds population and poor hygiene, the virulence of the disease has also increased.

(v) Cost of feed is also equally depressing the production of birds and eggs. Because the cost of feed for bird raised to higher level, which could not meet out by the small and cottage scale farmers.

(vi) The price of the various vaccines also increased from Re. 1 per bird to Rs. 4 per bird. The price of other materials for putting of the cages has also gone up.

(vii) There is no modernised powder plant in this area which can be used to powder the damaged eggs. Now at present the damaged eggs are disposed of.

(viii) Cold storage facilities are not available in this district. To store the eggs, the farmers are taking their eggs to the distant cities like Coimbatore.

(ix) The fluctuation in the price of raw materials also increases the cost of production.

(x) The Government does not providing free or subsidised power to this industry.

(xi) There is no financial assistance from the state financial institutions like Tamilnadu Industrial Investment Corporation (TIIC)

(xii) The poultry farmers also facing problems in marketing the culled birds.

Suggestions

1. The farm-shed area may be kept clean and hygiene.

2. Workers may be given formal training at least for a fortnight to increase the skill and knowledge.
3. The farm should be provided with continuous water facility.
4. The power supply should be continuous without any interruption.
5. Modern equipment should be used to maintain the farm-shed and chicks.
6. The Government should establish one or more powder plant to avoid the dispose of damaged eggs.
7. The Government should construct one or more cold storage plants to store the eggs which are not marketed early after production.
8. The Government should provide financial assistance through nationalised banks and state level financial institutions with nominal subsidy.
9. The Government may give compensatory amount to the poultry farmers whenever the birds mortality is high due to some unexpected diseases and natural calamities.

References

1. *Indian Poultry Year Book,* 1994.
2. Pandey, N.K. and S.K. Tewari, "Economics of Commercial Poultry Enterprises", *Indian Journal of Poultry Science,* 20(4): 321-325, 1995.
3. Tameja, B.S., "Economics Importance of Poultry Industry in India", *Poultry Guide,* Vol. XXV, 1998, p. 17.
4. Kuklicarnt, V.R., "Poultry can Solve Rural Unemployment", *Poultry Adviser,* Vol. XXII, Feb. 1989, p. 49.
5. Marthramurti, I.D., *Rural Poultry Farming,* The Centre for Research on New International Economic Order, Chennai, 1987.
6. Choudary, M.R., "Poultry Industry in India", *Poultry Adviser,* Vol. XXII, No. 3, March 1990, p. 21.
7. Gananamani, R., *Modern Aspect of Commercial Poultry Keeping,* Hytone Publication, Madurai, 1991.
8. Harbans Singh, "Poultry Development in India", *Poultry Adviser,* Vol. XXV, Issue, 1992.
9. "Poultry Industry in India", *Poultry Adviser,* Vol. XXII, No. 3, March 1990, p. 23.
10. Rekhi, C.S., "Poultry for National Development—Past, Present and Future", *Poultry Guide,* Vol. XIV, No. 12, December 1977, p. 43.
11. Louis, M. Hurd, *Modern Poultry Farming,* The Macmillan Company, New York, 1956.

12. Raja, A., "Poultry Farming in Namakkal Taluk—A Bird's Eye View", *Poultry Guide,* 18(5): 53-54, 1981.
13. Ramachandra Reddy, K., "Bright Future for Poultry Farming", *Indian Poultry Review,* 11(6): 28-32, 1980.
14. Sexena, V.P. and S.C. Gupta, "Vital Problems of Poultry Farming in India", *Poultry Guide,* 7(3): 17-21, 1971.
15. K. Rajendran and R. Prabakaran, "Poultry Production in the Country", *Financial Agriculture,* July-September 1997, p. 15.
16. Ansari, M.A., "Training Needs and Poultry Farmers", *Poultry Adviser,* February 1990, 23(2), p. 29.
17 Rajan, S., "Poultry Farming as a Means of Increasing Productivity", *Poultry Guide,* April 1983, 20(4), p. 41.
18. Seculdev, A.K. and Balaraman, N., "Role of Poultry in National Economy", *Poultry Guide,* September 1978, 15(8), pp. 21-24.

APPENDIX—1

Monthly Average Layer Feed Price in Namakkal for the Past Six Accounting Year From 1991-92 to 1996-97

Month	*1991-92*	*1992-93*	*1993-94*	*1994-95*	*1995-96*	*1996-97*
April	262.00	347.00	327.00	395.00	475.00	500.00
May	268.00	347.00	309.00	405.00	475.00	515.48
June	288.00	350.00	300.00	415.00	475.00	533.00
July	302.00	357.00	319.00	435.00	490.00	547.42
Aug	302.00	357.00	319.00	435.00	490.00	554.19
Sep	302.00	350.00	331.00	435.00	480.00	577.19
Oct	296.00	350.00	331.00	410.00	480.00	576.13
Nov	316.00	340.00	342.00	430.00	487.00	560.48
Dec	323.00	330.00	342.00	450.00	499.00	554.52
Jan	332.00	330.00	342.00	458.00	500.00	557.50
Feb	338.00	315.00	361.00	480.00	500.00	569.35
March	338.00	323.00	375.00	467.00	500.00	569.00
Average	304.67	341.33	332.08	435.00	487.46	550.08
Index	100.00	112.03	109.00	142.64	160.00	180.55

Source: National Egg Co-ordination Committee Report, Namakkal, 1998.

APPENDIX—2

Monthly Average NECC Egg Rate in Namakkal None for the Past Six Years From 1991-92 to 1996-97

Month	*1991-92*	*1992-93*	*1993-94*	*1994-95*	*1995-96*	*1996-97*
1	2	3	4	5	6	7
April	58.33	63.06	78.13	78.72	88.83	87.50
May	73.19	81.51	80.77	93.90	89.74	104.65
June	69.80	86.96	89.70	107.93	105.80	124.50
July	79.87	88.74	86.19	102.19	112.74	130.19
Aug	72.54	79.58	81.93	89.16	92.26	114.77
Sep	68.40	88.66	83.03	94.54	98.60	101.80
Oct	66.55	86.03	78.45	86.13	100.00	104.35
Nov	77.30	97.23	86.63	107.83	110.50	130.00

(Contd.)

1	2	3	4	5	6	7
Dec	76.32	93.06	97.16	110.48	106.40	130.00
Jan	79.54	94.95	105.00	110.48	97.41	137.18
Feb	74.54	94.95	105.00	110.48	97.41	137.18
March	74.61	89.81	92.13	90.61	99.52	129.84
Year average	72.98	85.45	88.68	98.10	99.95	118.75
Index	100.00	117.09	121.01	134.42	136.96	162.72

Source: National Egg Coordination Committee Report, Namakkal, 1998.

APPENDIX—3

Monthly Average Daily Production of Eggs in Namakkal Zone for the Past Six Accounting Year From 1991-92 to 1996-97

Month	*1991-92*	*1992-93*	*1993-94*	*1994-95*	*1995-96*	*1996-97*
April	PNA	PNA	43.10	55.43	83.88	79.05
May	32.52	PNA	43.11	56.11	84.04	76.05
June	PNA	PNA	42.14	57.24	85.78	72.18
July	PNA	PNA	42.48	58.27	86.66	70.49
Aug	PNA	PNA	42.84	59.84	87.15	70.67
Sep	PNA	PNA	45.65	63.83	91.69	71.58
Oct	33.45	40.63	47.51	66.82	94.74	71.35
Nov	—	41.85	48.99	71.57	95.94	73.12
Dec	—	42.75	50.48	75.66	96.80	75.00
Jan	—	43.32	53.32	78.88	104.46	73.73
Feb	—	43.52	54.34	80.62	107.23	70.74
Mar	—	43.10	54.27	81.60	108.65	69.63
Year Avg.	32.94	42.53	47.26	67.17	93.89	72.80
Index	100.00	129.00	143.00	204.00	285.00	221.00

Source: National Egg Coordination Committee Report, Namakkal, 1998.

APPENDIX—4

Monthly Average Layer Bird Strength in Namakkal Zone for the Past Six Accounting Years From 1991-92 to 1996-97

Month	*1991-92*	*1992-93*	*1993-94*	*1994-95*	*1995-96*	*1996-97*
April	PNA	—	97.96	125.93	189.95	196.18
May	73.91	—	97.97	126.77	190.99	191.04
June	PNA	—	95.98	130.09	194.96	185.02
July	PNA	—	96.10	132.44	196.95	181.59
Aug	PNA	—	97.37	136.00	198.06	180.46
Sep	PNA	—	103.76	145.07	208.37	179.36
Oct	75.79	92.34	107.99	151.86	215.32	182.44
Nov	PNA	95.10	111.35	162.66	218.06	179.19
Dec	PNA	97.15	114.73	171.95	220.01	175.36
Jan	PNA	98.46	119.00	179.26	224.34	171.61
Feb	PNA	98.91	129.50	183.45	224.09	160.72
March	PNA	97.96	123.35	185.45	218.60	154.28
Aug	74.84	96.65	107.41	152.65	208.31	178.10
Index	100.00	129.12	143.50	203.94	278.30	237.94

Source: National Egg Coordination Committee Report, Namakkal, 1998.

8

Plastic Conversions Industry

The plastics industry today plays a significant role in most of the key sectors of the Indian economy which includes agriculture and water management, automobiles and transportation, building and construction, tele-communications and electronics. Besides a substantial increase in the contribution to those sectors, Defence and Aerospace, computers and power transmission are also expected to be significant and use sectors for plastics by 2000 A.D.

There is an adage which applies to plastics. It reads—'A scarce and deplating natural resource conserved is a resource generated: The role of plastics in this endeavour to conserve and effectively and efficiently manage the scarce resources has been important and significant, plastics have already started playing and would continue to play a very vital role in many application areas including some key sectors of the country's economy.

The use of plastics heavy duty width films in lining canals and reservoires can result in as high as 75 per cent saving of water which is otherwise lost through seepage and percolation. This result in availability of more water for irrigating a much larger area. Drip irrigation at the present level of technology seems to be the ultimate in irrigation efficiency compared to conventional irrigation, drip irrigation offers as much as 50 per cent increase in yield.

Polythene sachers used for unit packaging of milk in place of conventional glass bottles have brought about a substantial savings in terms of energy consumed (manufacturing and transportation) as well as investment cost.

The encouraging shift to multilayer composites and blow moulded bottles to replace tin containers for packaging of able oils would result in substantial savings in foreign exchange as imports of tin and tin plate can be avoided plastics have emerged as the most viable alternative packaging of fruits and vegetables. It is an effective step to conserve the forest wealth which has already dwindled from 22 per cent of forest cover to only 12 per cent of forest cover in course of the last few decades.

The increasing awareness for conservation of energy would also prosper the growth of plastics in many non-conventional applications, for example, the increased usage of plastics components in automobile manufactures has directly resulted in drastic reduction in the weight of the vehicle leading to a higher fuel efficiency. Moreover, with the use of plastic, it is possible to streamline the design of the exterior of an automobile resulting in reduced aerodynamic dray and reduced fuel consumption.

Presently, the plastic industry has a consumption base of about 5 lakh tonnes per annum of all types of plastics, resulting in an annual sales turnover of over Rs. 2,000 crore of finished plastic products. The relevance of the plastics industry to the Indian economy is evident from the contribution it makes to the national exchequer by way of excise and customs duties and other taxes. The magnitude of its contribution can be assessed from the latest available data given here, which is continuously on the increase. In 1986-87, out of total gross revenue of Rs. 25,770 crore from excise and customs duties, the plastics industry made a contribution of Rs. 823 crore, representing 3.2 per cent of the total contribution. This was substantially higher than the contribution made by traditional high volume groups like paper and paper products (1.5%), jute (0.1%), Aluminium (0.8%) and glass and glass wares (0.7%). Contributions were also favourable when compared to the giant sector—iron and steel (6.2%). The plastics raw materials sector contribution is approximately 60 per cent and that of processing units is approximately 40 per cent of the total contributions made by plastics industry by way of excise and customs duties.

The emergence of plastics as a viable substitute for a number of traditional materials of natural resources was visible just after the Second World War, when the limited availability of natural and conventional materials necessitated a search for alternatives. The plastics industry made an entry into this country in the fifties in the form of household items in a very small way. Today it has assumed a part of our everyday life. Its applications have become so extensive and natural that their presence and availability is taken for granted. In fact, it is difficult to think of any field where plastics are not used in one form or the other.

While the major manufacturers of plastics, raw materials processors who converts raw materials into finished products are mainly in the small scale and cottage industry sector. The plastics processing sector consists of small entrepreneurs, whose individual enterprises and ceaseless efforts have brought the industry to its present status. Low investment, more employment to capital ratio and utilisation of untrained labour has made the plastics processing industry ideally suited for India.

Plastics Processing

Plastic industry is one such field in which both large and small scale sectors of the industry have to develop in an integrated manner by the very nature of technology of processes involved. While raw materials of plastics are mainly produced in the large sector, owing to the requirement of high investment, the plastics processing units are more suitable for the development of the small scale sector. This sector has made significant achievements in the plastics processing industry and today constitutes a major segment of the plastics conversion industry in India.

Presently, there are around 14,000 processing units in the country, predominantly, in the small scale sector. Till recently, most of the machines used were of an indigenous origin, but of late, due to market compulsions, qualitative changes in this sector is being observed.

There has been a growing demand for sophisticated and hitch applications as also for larger and more intricate industrial mouldings. This demand is expected to grow further in future. Similarly, requirements in the field of packaging have undergone tremendous changes with the introduction of modern packaging media like co-extruded and high barrier films, form-fill-seal packs, aseptic packs, plastics corrugated cartons etc. which has drastically altered the packaging scenario. These market compulsions have led to a district, qualitative shift within the industry which has resulted in the emergence of medium and large scale units in the field of processing, equipped with some of the latest imported machines and modern technology.

This trend indicates that by the end of this century, the processing sector will be distinctly divided into three segments, namely:

- — Medium or large units to cater to sophisticated applications.
- — Small scale units to cater to non-critical low technology segments of the market.
- — Cottage/tiny units to service the rural/semi-urban markets.

The Government of India puts a lot of importance and takes timely necessary steps for the growth of the plastics processing industry. In the event of shortages of raw materials, the government of India extends its assistance to the processing units by making arrangements for importing the raw materials the apex committee for a perspective planning of petrochemical in Industry (1986-2000 A.D.) has projected the demand for plastics from the 1985-86 level of 0.5 million tonnes to 1.8 million tonnes by 1994-95 and 2.6 million tonnes by 2000 A.D. If this demand of raw materials is met, then down stream processing of plastics into consumable goods would involve an additional investment of Rs. 12,000 crore, taking an average investment of Rs. 13 lakh per unit. The committee has also recommended for the setting up of a Promotion and Development Authority. Plastics industry has come of age and has now attained national importance owing to its sheer growth and multifacet applications. Presently, the plastics raw materials sector is dominated by giant manufacturer like Indian Petrochemical Corporation Ltd., Polyolefins Industries Ltd., NOCIL, etc. On the other hand, the plastics processing sector is dominated by small scale units whose share is 85 per cent in number and 50 per cent in value of the products manufactured with an estimated investment of Rs. 2,500 crore in about Rs. 14,000 units.

The plastics processing sector today provides direct employment to about 6 lakh people in the country. Moreover, the raw materials sector plays an equally important role in the growth of plastics industry by producing the necessary raw materials for the processing industry as well as generating employment.

Although the employment potential of a basic petrochemical units is limited, the down stream industries are labour intensive and can create significant job opportunities. The plastics processing industries alone have an employment potential estimated at one technically-oriented job for every 10 of polymers. The total employment potentials, including non-technical personnel, could be four to five times that numbers. Thus by 2000 A.D. polymers could provide employment to over 3.5 lakh technically skilled persons and a total (technical and non technical) employment to nearly 1.4 million persons.

Since the downstream plastics industries are generally reserved for the small scale sector, growth in petrochemical complexes will act as a big stimulus to this segment of the industry. It is estimated that the number of small scale plastics processing units will increase from the present level of around 14,000 units to 30,000 units by 2000 A.D.

Demand for plastics goods touched 7 lakh tonnes in 1988 rising from a low of 13,000 tonnes in 1960-61 to 87,000 tonnes in 1970-71 and 4 lakhs tonnes in 1985. The rapid growth in the consumption of plastic goods is mainly attributed to its versatility as well as relative advantages in weight, processability, heat conductivity, non-toxic nature, energy conservation etc. In the current trend, of an average growth rate of 15 per cent is an indication, consumption of plastics in India is estimated at 25 lakh tonnes by the turn of the century, which would imply a per capita per annum consumption of 2.16 kg. The present per capita consumption of plastic in India is deplorably low at 0.67 kg. as against a world average per capita consumption of 14 kg.

Processing Technologies for Plastics

All plastics belong to one of the two families "Thermoplastics" or 'Thermosts' plastic from both of families softer when heated, so that they can be forced into a mould. When they cool, both harden and set. The difference is that thermoplastic can be softened again by re-heating, whereas the thermosets on the other hand, will have permanent set and will not soften again on re-heating.

Prospects of Processing Industry

Plastic processing industry in the country has undergone a phenomenal change during 1980-85, prior to this, availability of right grade of material was limited, which as one of the causes for the slow pace of growth in the processing sector. After the setting up of the Indian Petrochemical Corporation Ltd., at Baroda, various types of grades of raw materials in sufficient quantity were available. As a result, a large number of processing units were starked during 1980-85 for the manufacture of conventional as well as specialty products. Along with the availability of various grades of raw materials, the processing machinery manufacturing sector also contributed in the task of growth of plastics industry by developing the right type of processing plants indigenously. As a result of these development, there was a significant increase in the total installed capacity for processing of plastics in the country.

Table 8.1

Plastics Processing Industry Progressed during the Period from 1979-80 to 1985-86

Particulars	*1979-80*	*1980-81 to 85-86*	*as on 1985-86*
No. of units	6,500	3,500	10,000
No. of machines	21,500	22,900	44,000
Rated capacity (000 MT)	657	1,586	2,243
Real capacity (000 MT)	329	793	1,222
Investment in plant machinery (Rs. in lakhs)	7,642	34,194	41,836
Raw material consumption (MTA)	2,45,000	2,47,000	4,92,000

Presently, there are about 14,000 plastic processing units having an investment of around Rs. 2,500 crore, this trend obviously implies that plastic processing is fast expanding industry. It has now made its presence felt in almost all sectors of human and industrial activities. With rapid industrialisation and better standards of living, more and more plastics applications will find their way into areas such as electrical and electronics industries, household items, packaging, agricultural, industrial machinery etc.

It is a widely accepted phenomenon that plastics are fast replacing a large number of traditional materials like metal glass, paper etc. The pressing need for conservation of energy ecological balancing and depleting resources of natural materials would necessitate greater substitution and new applications of plastics rather than the supplemental role it has played so far.

The plastics industry is essentially linked to the growth of automobiles, electronics, telecommunications etc. As India is poised for a significant growth in all these. Industrial sectors, there is a tremendous all-round growth potential for plastics industry in the century.

Besides industrial and household applications, plastics play a very productive role in agricultural sector also. India being primarily an agriculture-based country, there is a good potential for plastics in the agricultural sector.

Prospects of the plastics processing industry is directly linked with the demand growth trend of various types of plastic products, which in turn is related to the demand of raw materials.

It has already been mentioned that there is a continuous rising trend in the demand of plastic raw materials. According to a study made by the Indian Plastics Institute, consumption of commodity plastics such as LDPE, HDPE, PVC PP etc. is expect to grow from a modest 4.92 lakh tonnes in 1985 to 24.5 lakh tones by the end of the century. The demand for engineering plastics products is also expected to rise from 35,000 tonnes in 1985 to 1.75 lakh tonnes by 2000 A.D. Engineering plastics are being increasingly used in automobiles and engineering industries.

Plastic have vitally conquered the packaging industry with their unique properties and enviable growth. It has totally revolutionised the field of packaging and renders appreciable improvements in all areas of protection, handling and design with economic advantages, both in flexible and rigid packaging.

By 2000 A.D. India will witness the emergence of the plastics industry as a vibrant.

The process of transforming softened plastic materials into finished plastic articles can be done with the help of differed processing technologies.

Finally, the hot plastics of desired shapes are solidified either through further polymerization called the cure stage in the case of mermosetting materials, or simply by silling in the case of thermoplastic matérials.

These processing techniques are either condineous or cyclic in nature. Selection of the processing technique largely depends on the end-products to be manufactured, type of polymer used etc.

Plastic Container Unit—A Case Study

A case study of the Khadi and V.I.P.C. Trust, Gandhigram has been producing the plastic container which is largely used for the sidha medicine produced by the trust. The unit received the grant from S.I.D.B.I under Mahila Vikas Nidhi Scheme. This chapter explains the performance of the plastic container unit of Khadhi and V.I.P.C. Trust Gandhigram .

Raw Materials

There are two very essential raw materials required to produce plastic container. The following are the two main raw materials.

1. High density polyethylene,
2. Low density polyethylene,

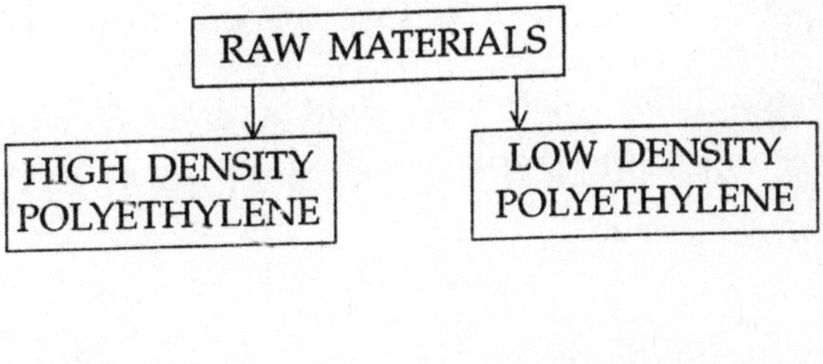

The above Raw Materials are Procured from the following industries

1. Madurai Meenakshi Plastics,
2. Madurai Dhivya Plastics,

Machineries and Equipments

There are two main important machineries and equipments required for container plastics. The following are the two main machineries.

1. Automatic blow
2. Hand injection moulding machine

(a) Automatic blow

Automatic blow is called as the heater. This type of automatic blow, to adopt 10 gram, 500 gram, and 1 litre containers (Dye) is required.

(b) Hand injection moulding machine:

It is called as manual and mechanical functioning.

Cap, and inner items are produced in this machine of hand injection moulding machine.

Processing of Raw Materials

Waste materials of plastics are reprocessing of this plastic unit. Again waste materials step by step reprocessing in this unit. It is rotating roll of reprocessing unit.

(a) Colour of containers:

Mostly, white colour is a very good colour of container, so, in every container, adopted colour is white.

If, we need colour, we could add many more colours like., Red, Blue, Yellow, Green, Black etc.,

Especially, the powdered colour is also added by this plastic container unit. It is the usual colour used for containers.

Now, here, only white containers are produced and in the field of local area, colour containers are not produced.

Accommodation

1. Type of building Rs. 2 lakhs (A 500 sq. ft)
2. Storage space Rs. 1 lakhs (2,500 sq. ft)

Manpower

(i) *Labours:-*5 members
Salary:- At the rate of piece level.
1 piece rate is—7 paise (bottle piece)
1 piece of cap rate inner rate—6 to 9 paise.
(ii) *Staff:-* Only one person
Salary:- Per month, Rs. 1,100
(iii) *Manager:-* Only one person
Salary:- Per month Rs. 2,500

Sales

Sales per month minimum Rs. 75,000
Sales per month maximum Rs. 75,000

The Sales Places are,

1. Chinnalapatti Siddha Ayurvedhic unit
2. Kashippalayam Siddha Ayurvedhic unit
—only sales for siddha Ayurvedhic unit.

Sales per year maximum and minimum Rs. 9.00.000

Profit

The average profit is 25 per cent from sales level Rs. 18,750.
Annual Income minimum Rs. 2,25,000 lakh
Annual Income maximum Rs. 7,00,000 lakh

Table 8.2
Cost of Production

S.No.	Particulars	Weight (kg.)	Rate (Rs.)
1.	Automatic blow	—	2,00,000
2.	Hand Injection moulding machine	—	1,00,000
3.	Raw materials:-		
	(i) High density	1 kg.	42
	(ii) Low density	1 kg.	53
4.	Electricity charges (per two months)	—	3,500

Quality Control

1. *Standard and Specifications*

Here, all the container plastics are standard under specification control system. In long period, these plastics are qualified.

2. *Keeping Quality Planning*

Keeping quality for long life. The planning is a properly motivated factors influencing method. So, the quality of the product is very good in nature.

3. *Scheme of Quality Control*

The Central Govt. and the States Governments approved the scheme of quality control for the plastic container produced under the Khadi & V.I.P.C. Trust of Gandhigram.

4. *Quality Audit*

The audit could be properly and regularly followed in this unit. This scheme also maintain good quality of audit.

Registers Maintained

The registers are maintained properly. In these units the registers used are: registers should be separate form of some other important registers. They are as follows:

(*i*) Purchase register
(*ii*) Stock register
(*iii*) Sales register

These are three separate registers to maintain audit in this container plastics unit.

Billing

There are two methods of billing adopted in the unit of plastic. The following are the important billing.

(*i*) Cash bill
(*ii*) Credit bill PA

Production

GANDHIGRAM KHADI AND V.I.P.C. TRUST G.G.M. PLASTIC UNIT

Table 8.3

Production of Plastic Container

Year	*Production Pieces*	*Amount*
1992-93	65,135	65,663
93-94	2,72,824	2,37,409
94-95	2,82,546	2,55,818
95-96	5,13,160	6,06,385
96-97	6,82,570	5,84,885
97-98	7,34,745	5,86,448
98-Jan	8,09,630	1,51,200

Table 8.4

Sales Level in the Plastic Container Unit

Year	*Sales Pieces*	*Amount (Rs)*
1992-93	43,052	49,709
93-94	1,83,835	2,23,543
94-95	2,08,285	2,37,914
95-96	8,53,975	6,80,113
96-97	6,31,708	5,60,502
97-98	7,42,929	5,88,753
98-Jan	8,35,330	1,14,943

Table 8.5

Employment Wage Level in the Plastic Container Unit

Year	*Workers*	*Wages*
1992-93	9	24,750
93-94	8	17,770
94-95	8	18,267
95-96	7	34,085
96-97	7	42,028
97-98	7	50,310
98-Jan	8	55,537

Plastic Pot Unit: A Case Study

In Dindigul district, there are plastic units producing the plastic parts. The present study attempts to analyse the three selected units processing the plastic pots. The selected units are, 1. Bharat plastic, 2. Rajani plastic, and 3. Sri Vijayalakshmi plastics. Each unit is analysed separately and the findings are summarized below.

Bharat Plastics

1. The Bharat plastic products, 177, Muniyappan, Theppakulam, Siluvattur Road, Dindigul was established during the year 1992 as a wholesale plastic unit at Dindigul.
2. The unit functioning in a rented building with one extrude moulding machine, the capacity of their machines are 75 tonnes of plastic products per year.
3. The production figures of the unit shows that the machines are underutilised. But the trend in production shows that there was steady increase during the period under study. The growth rate of production is satisfactory. The Bharat plastic produces only pots in this factoy.
4. The unit under study sell its products in Dindigul and surrounding areas. There is no wider market for its products.

5. The net profit ratio of the unit shows that the ratio is more or less constant during the period under study.
6. The employment aspect of the unit shows that there are 2 temporary workers and 3 permanent staff working in the factory. They are paid monthly.

Rajani Plastics

1. The Rajani plastic products, Mettupatty, Dindigul was established during the year 1993, a wholesales plastic products at Dindigul.
2. The unit is functioning in its own building with two extruder moulding machines, the capacity of their machines are 150 tonnes of plastic products per year.
3. The production figures of the unit shows that the machines are underutilised. But the trend in production shows that there was steady increase during the period under study. The growth rate of production is satisfactory. The Rajani plastic unit produces only pots in this factory.
4. The unit under study sell its products in Dindigul and surrounding areas. There is no wider market for its products.
5. The net profit ratio of the unit shows that the ratio is more or less constant during the period under study.
6. The employment aspects of the unit shows that there are 4 temporary workers and 5 permanent staff working in the factory. They are paid monthly.

Sri Vijayalaskshmi Plastics

1. The Sri Vijayalakshmi plastic products, Balakrishnapuram, Dindigul was established during the year 1993, as a wholesaler plastic products at Dingidul.
2. The unit functioning in a rented building with one extrude moulding machine, the capacity of their machines are 72 tonnes of plastic products per year.
3. The production figures of the unit shows that the machines are underutilised. But the trend in production shows that there was steady increase during the

period under study. The growth rate of production is satisfactory in Sri Vijayalakshmi plastic units.

4. The unit under study sell its products in Dindigul and surrounding areas.
5. The net profit ratio of the unit shows that the ratio is more or less constant during the period under study.
6. The employment aspects of the unit shows that there are 2 temporary workers and 3 permanent staff working in the factory.
7. The factory is following the Factory Acts of the government.

Suggestions and Conclusion

1. Bharat Plastics

1. The unit should achieve its fullest capacity in order to earn more profit.
2. At present the unit markets its products only in Dindigul district. A wider market coverage is very essential to improve its sales.
3. New innovation is required in production unit. It will help to develop the industry.
4. Plastics industry will die very soon because plastic products affect our environment, we should take an alternative arrangement.
5. Plastic industry is converted waste into wealth because plastics are re-cycling products.

2. Rajani Plastics

1. The present study suggests that proper training will be provided to the unskilled labour, it can be done with the help of various plastic training centres.
2. It is suggested that the plastic industries may install the power generators to face the problem of power failures.

3. Sri Vijayalakshmi Plastics

1. The unit is engaged only in the production of plastic

pots. It should diversify its produces. Different varieties of plastic products should be produced by this unit so that they can increase their production and sales.

2. The salary and wages of workers must be increased considering the increase in standard of living.
3. The modern techniques of sales promotions such as advertisement, display etc., should be followed by the unit in order to capture market.

There is a growing demand for plastic goods in our country. The plastic goods replaces so many traditional goods. The industry plays a very important role in economic development of our country. The investment required for starting plastic products manufacturing unit is very less. So an entrepreneur who is interested to start small scale industry can very well undertake this work.

9

Handmade Paper Industry

Paper is very essential for human being life, in modern days. Paper finds much use in many institutions, such as schools, colleges, courts, hospitals, industry, business etc. Paper is the purest form of cellulose. The paper is a substance manufactured from wood, fibres, rags, etc. The form of the paper sheets used for writing, printing drawing, wrapping, packing, marketing etc. Cellulose is the basic material of paper-making. Chemically, carbohydrate has an empirical formula of C_6H_{105}.

Cellulose is the main substance produced in the vegetable kingdom during its growth. It is the backborne or skeleton in cotton. It is always associated with pectins or gummy and mucilaginous materials, resins, oils, coloring matters, waxes, starchy material, etc. Such substances may be termed non-cellulose materials to distinguish them from cellulose.

Handmade paper refers to sheet of paper which has been manufactured by use of minimum number of machines, and or less sophisticated while it is also true that more labour hand is employed to produce a quality of handmade paper and to give employment opportunities. Handmade paper is an engine of economic development in these countries. The government realising the importance of the industry, has given it moral support by due recognition, financial and technical assistance.

The importance of handmade paper is as follows:

(i) Handmade paper is easy to start and most effective means resolving the shortage of paper.

(ii) Handmade paper depends upon indigenous sources of raw material and it utilises to the maximum extent possible. Raw material used are fibrous materials such as like waste paper for recycling, hosiery cuttings, tailor cuttings, old gunny bags, jute etc. These materials are easily available and can be put to economic use.

(iii) Mostly developing countries depend on agriculture as the backbone of their bagasse etc. are most profit. A substantial surplus has virtually been wasted and more worse cause a genuine disposal problem.

(iv) It requires a small amount of capital to start. Capital inadequency is a problem in developing countries.

(v) The industry provides employment opportunities to many people in India. As it is a labour-oriented scheme, it provides a large number of jobs either directly or indirectly. The industry is eligible for 15 per cent subsidy on projects cost. These are so long as prospective entrepreneurs start such industries in a country like India.

(vi) It provides a variety of quality paper products and a variety of beautiful products. Some set luxury items which are loved and appreciated. This industry would depend largely upon the consumption potential for its products within the country. This in term relies much on a country's population, literacy rates and economic progress, judged by this yardsticks. Hence the literacy rate is low and per capita consumption of paper is also very low.

In Tamil Nadu also funding institutions such as Nationalised Banks, National Small Industries Corporations, District Industrial Centre etc., give loans on normal rates of interest. This industry have provided a lot of employment opportunities in Tamilnadu.

Handmade paper industry needs better electricity and water facilities. Marketing and sales strategies, availability of skilled labours in the industry and availability of finance are the main problems in the handmade paper unit. The present study attempts to analyse the Mahendra Mangalam Handmade Paper unit with reference to production, quality and marketing.

Mahendra Mangalam handmade paper unit was the area of study. This unit was run under the control of Tamilnadu Khadi Village Industries Board. This unit is very suitable for collection of data. It is located in Musuri Taluk, Trichy district of Tamilnadu. The nearest town for this paper unit is Thottiam. This unit covers 2 acre and 72 cents land, on the Srinivasanallur Panchayat.

Earlier studies relating to handmade paper unit in various states are reviewed in this section. Mathur found that the developing economy of country is faced with many problems. Shortage of paper has been a cause of concern. Even for handmade paper, raw material constraint has come to fore. Here is an account of encouraging R and D results to utilise Arhar sticks for H.M.P. industry and the raw materials are abundantly available in all parts of the country.

A study of Bommaiah revealed that in the modern world paper consumption is considered to be a barometer for determining the advancement of civilization as it meets the cultural, educational, industrial and other human requirements. In the prevailing situation handmade paper because of the low capital investment, high employment potential and gestation period coupled with the increase in literacy rate, the demand of paper is growing day-by-day. So far the manufacture of handmade paper was confined to conventional raw materials like new/old cotton cuttings, press cuttings, and small amount of agricultural residues. But study conducted on the forest based raw material has found barks of shrubs/trees as a potential raw material for paper manufacture. Owing to its decentralised nature, handmade paper industry, can profitability use barks of scattered shrubs and trees in the production of a variety of papers that may ease the shortage of paper facing the country.

Handmade paper can definitely cash in on the fluctuating prices of mill made paper which is controlled by a few industrial houses by setting up mother pulp units as they will cater to the needs of small handmade paper units. There is also need to bring about the technological transformation to replace the traditional methods of handmade paper production which are not economical.

Another study of Kolase found that cardboard is prepared by using partherium and waste papers in different proportion as raw materials. Two treatments i.e. simple seeking and cooking with and without adhesives partherium and waste papers in 1:1 proportions the study reveals. Bringing to use a need that has so far been entirely useless but available every where in abundance is certainly welcome, especially in a developing nation like India.

Paper has been a very basic material with the advancement of education and the shortage has become one of the items of concern. Especially in developing countries, this problem is increasingly felt. It is therefore, imperative that the problem is examined in its totality and solutions found.

Compared to its growth in demand the production of paper and paperboard is far lagging behind. For various reasons, it has become difficult to bridge this gab. The world production of paper and paperboard in 1960 was 73 million tonnes and in 1997 it was of the order of 152 million tonnes, recording an annual growth rate of 44 per cent. According to the demand production prepared by FAO-UNO, this growth is likely to slow down to 3.5 per cent whereas the demand in 1985 has been projected to the order of 220 million tonnes, in 1990 somewhere between 250 and 275 million tonnes and in 2000 A.D. well over 350 million tonnes.

The findings of the study revealed that paper industry highly capital-intensive with long gestation period. The investment in a large integrated paper mill was marked out to Rs. 10,000 and for medium size Rs. 7,500 for each tonne of production per annum, some two years back. In this investment, 60 per cent accounts for plant and machinery. This estimate has further gone up because of price escalation. If the total investment in paper Industry, is computed on the existing installed capacity it will come to billions of rupees. But the industry has given employment to 75,000 people of all categories. Whereas employment potential for similar capacity of large integrated paper mills project which are under the stage of execution has fallen down to 35 persons for an investment of Rs. 10 million and 30 persons for 100 tonnes capacity per annum.

The handmade paper industry still lot of potential and scope for further development and the present production can be doubled within five years. However, this fact too cannot be over ruled that the said scope is limited. Therefore, looking at the employment potential of this industry in view of the Indian set-up economy, if development and rate of the growth of this industry has to be widened and speeded up the current varieties of the production need to be diversified. It is evident that the cultural paper is only 8 per cent of the total production of the paper and paperboard from the mills. Even then the country is not in a position to meet the demand as it has been pointed out earlier and the government has been thinking to strict the production only in 2-3 varities.

Doubts may be raised on the economic viability and life span of these units, which of course will be based on wrong assumptions and preconditioned mind. Raw materials of reasonable price, cheap labour, low investment, low overhead and managerial expenditure and cheap rural skill are all in its favour. The question is only of a proper organisation and the development of effective distribution system which could bring the benefits of the development plan and the work done in the laboratory to the foot steps of poor people.

The total production of paper and paperboard in the country consists of 60 per cent cultural paper, 18 per cent industrial paper, 19 per cent board and 4 per cent other miscellaneous varieties. Such units usually face marketing problem in the beginning. Certain varieties of indigenous demand may be reserved to these units, releasing the production of large scale units for export to developing countries. Certain varieties of speciality papers and boards which the present had made paper technology is fully capable to produce and some of which are imported viz. filter paper and board, electrical insulation paper etc., should be exclusively reserved for the handmade paper industry.

The percentages of different varities of handmade paper and board production in 1978-79 in quantitative terms were as under:

(1) board—48 per cent
(2) high grade—23 per cent

(3) cover and stationery—22 per cent

(4) cover writing, printing and blotting paper and others—8 per cent. In terms of value the respective shares in the total value were 19, 49, 21 and 10 per cent. The findings of the studies on handmade paper unit paves the way for the researches to undertake the present study in a popular manner.

Paper is the prest form of cellulose. The paper is a substance manufactured from wood fibres, rags etc. The form of the paper sheets are used for writing, printing, drawing, wrapping, packing, marketing etc.

The history of handmade paper industry can be traced back to 102 A.D. In India the All India Village Industries Association was established in 1935 under the guidance of Mahatma Gandhi. In the due course handmade paper industry flourished to the favourable surroundings in India.

As our Father of Nation Mahatma Gandhi remarked "Villages are the hearts of India" and if India has to develop, the villages has to be developed since 3/4th of Indian population is living in villages. In the Indian scenario in this particular structure handmade paper industry which is purely a village and small scale industry gain the momentum and it plays a prominent role in the Indian economy.

The handmade paper industry provides lot of employment opportunity to the villagers, especially the uneducated and skilled persons. It contributes to the main income as well as subsidiary income. Handmade paper industry provides, employment for both skilled and unskilled persons, based on their technical know how and ability. The persons who are involved in the production process gets direct employment from the industry and other persons like cultivators, tailors, etc., are also the other beneficiaries from this industry indirectly.

In this handmade paper industry we are using the by-products and waste products as raw materials. From these raw materials we can produce different types of papers by adding some essential chemicals and preservatives. Availability of raw materials for this industry is very high because they are only the waste products. So, we can say this is the only industry which makes wealth from waste.

To construct a handmade paper unit, there is no need to destroy the forest or other valuable things. It needs only 2 or 3 acre of land with sufficient water facility. No environmental imbalance is being created due to handmade industry.

We can use the affluent for irrigation. It does not affect the plants or crops which are irrigated by this affluent. We are using soft chemicals in the production of handmade paper. So, it does not affect the workers who are involved in the production process. Pollution by this industry is very mere comparatively to the other industries.

History of World Paper Making

The prediction of mankind to express itself by drawing or scratching on any suitable surface led to the development of paper. The discovery of paper in history has been wrapped in misery, but it is believed that paper was invented in China in C.05 by Te-Su-Iunn. However it is doubtful that he actually invented the process because silkfloos and cacoons were used in similar manner year before. Though they were deemed weak and expensive. Paper-making spread to Japan in C.160 and Samarkard in C.751 and it was introduced by the Arabs into Egypt in C.900 and by more into Spain (at Jativa) in C.1150. Mills were established in Itally in C.1276. In France C.1348, in Germany 1390 and England C.1495. Primitive bark paper has been used in Africa time immemorable, Mexico and Central Americas in Columbia times.

Paper was first introduced in American colonies in 1690 by William Ritten House at German town. Hand processes used by them in Europe and America, exemplify the fundamental processes of paper-making from vegetable fibre mixed with water is reduced to pulp into which a vatman dips a persons mould as he lifts out the mould holding the pulp, he shakes it to cross the fibres for strength. In Europe, early dipping mould were made of steps wire secured by widely spaced cross lines. The horizontal strips marked by the paper with so-called laid lines.

John Baskervile introduced in C.1757 the use of wire mesh so finely woven as to leave. Scarcely discernible marks on paper which became known as a woven paper. Water mark which was first used in Italy in C.1256, is produced by a design attached on the mould. A web of paper invented upon for commercial use by Henry and Society foundrinier of England.

Although paper remained a handmade product, expensive, and selectively used in Europe, it was not until early 19th century that the industrial revolution influenced it by introducing mechanisation. The paper-making industry came to India with the Muslim invaders and gained a firm footing especially in Kashmir & Punjab. From there the industry spread to the other parts of India with the establishment of Moghul rule. The Industry in these days was carried on mainly by Muslims who were called Kagadis.

They received support from the rulers in the form of supply of old records as raw material and the purchase of the finished paper. Paper, then, was mostly used by the rulers, sahukars and priests. The public had very little use for papers, as education was imparted by using slates, and writing on sand.

The All India Villages Industries Association was established in 1935 under the guidance of Mahatma Gandhi. He evinced great interest in handmade paper and efforts at the revival of this industry started. Samples for good hand-made papers were collected from various artisans, centers, and it was felt that there was ample scope for reviving this industry, a centre was started at Maganwadi Wardha. The traditional process of manufacturing paper was studied and efforts were made to improve it and to invent better types of tools.

Kagadis were called from artisan centres to work at Wardha, and to teach the art to others. In the beginning they felt that their occupation would be taken over by the educated and mainly trained artisans. Therefore they hesitated to reveal their art. Art after much trial, the centre attained a stage at which the traditional kagadis started manufacturing paper with their indigenous tools. Experiments were carried out to see if the quality of paper could be improved by using wastepaper as the only raw material.

Of course manufacturing paper from waste paper is no worthwhile industry except that the old material is converted into new. In the process the quality and strength of the paper deteriorated. In pulp from original materials such as rags, old gunny bags, tea, grass etc. was to be prepared by hand process, it took months. The quality was not of the approved standard and the cost of pulp was extra-ordinarily high. The late Shri. K.B. Joshi who conducted these experiments at Maganwadi requested Gandhiji to permit the use of power for converting the original raw materials into pulp and for certain other processes. Gandhiji examined the proposition and permitted the use of mechanical power in the handmade paper industry.

Market Information

Paper is a vehicle on which modern civilization moves. Its use in communication and information, industry and education, science and technology is well established. Per capita consumption of paper which is an index of educational, industrial and socio-economic development of a country is around 3 kg. Only in India as compared to 200 to 300 kg. in developed countries like U.S.A., Canada, Japan etc. with the growth in literacy and increase in industrialisation, per capita consumption of paperboard is bound to increase.

Products and their Uses

Handmade paper has the following unique characteristics.

(i) Handmade paper is having elegant and exquisite surface for writing.

(ii) It has indestructibility and super strength for permanence.

(iii) It has unmatched texture for drawings by artists and engineers.

(iv) It has scores of fancy varieties for decorative wraps.

(v) It has high tensile, bursting, tearing, and double fold strength as compared to mill-made paper and it does not turn brittle due to aging.

Handmade paper industry manufactures paper such as drawing for artwork, permanent document paper, dark coloured card sheets, deckle edged stationer, exclusive greetings, unique carry bags, watermark paper for certificates, filter paper, cultural grades like file covers duplicating paper, tissue paper etc. Among these unique items, product like declkle edged drawing paper and converted stationery, carry bags from natural fibres, account for over Rs. 60 million worth direct and indirect exports to developed countries. As per 1993-94 performance with the technological developments introduced in the industry in the recent years, handmade paper despite its glazing appearance is found to be ideally suited for four colours reproduction on offset machines. Therefore handmade paper is gradually, replacing mill products like cartridge paper, bank note and maplitho paper.

Saving of Forest-based Materials

Paper mills are using bamboo, eucalyptus and other forest-based paper mills require 2.5 tons of dry forest-based materials. Owing to heavy felling of Bamboo's, trees out forest, handmade paper sector. Jute waste, users non-woody raw materials, such as cotton tailor cuttings, hosiery cuttings, jute waste, waste paper, agro-waste etc. Thus handmade paper saves trees and help preservation of forests.

Infrastructure Required

In order to establish agreed handmade paper unit infrastructure facilities like soft water availability, 3 phase electric power supply and workshop facilities are required. The details of water and power supply required are furnished in the project profiles. The industry is fairly labour-intensive and therefore availability of labour on moderate wages is essential. Since various speciality grades of paper can be manufactured by the industry, it can afford to pay moderate ranging from Rs. 25 to Rs. 100 per day depending upon the skill of the workers. It provides employment to women to the extent of 40 per cent of the total work force.

The industry attracts the provision of the Factory Act and other labour laws and it can sustain payment of fringe benefit under these provision to the workers.

Market Potential for the Products

The industry today has diversified its products range with the growing demand for eco-friendly products both abroad and in domestic market. The industry is in a position to supply a major item of file covers required by various Government departments, Public sector undertakings besides industrial houses at competitive rates. The drawing paper produced by the industry has unique demand throughout the country and also abroad. Water mark papers for degree, share certificate etc., industrial pads have sustained demand in the open market. The bond paper for letter heads, envelopes etc., proposed to be made in the tiny units.

Export Potential

The industry has recorded significant growth in the export market during the last 3 years on account of eco-friendly nature of its products manufactured from non-woody fibres. Today goods worth about Rs. 6 crore per annum are being exported to mostly western countries. The market survey conducted under the aegis of UNDP, Handmade paper project indicated an untapped export potential, therefore there is necessity to promote growth of export-oriented handmade paper units to be set up by educated entrepreneurs in the years ahead throughout the country.

Availability of Machines and Equipments

The machines required for the industry are totally indigenous and are manufactured by over a dozen manufacturers throughout the country. Although KVIC had not efficiently recognised by these manufacturers, they have been supplying machines. Since long efforts are being made to evolve common specifications for all the machines as the specifications vary considerably from manufacturer to manufacturer.

As regards tools and equipments, most of them are got locally fabricated or procured under the guidance of technical personal/skilled workers. As such details are not furnished here. Prices of machines worked out in the project profiles are likely to increase from time to time and KVIC has no control over the same since they are manufactured wholly by private concerns.

Sources of Funding

As per the recommendation of high power committee constituted by Government of India, which have been largely accepted by KVIC, all the schemes under handmade paper industry have to be implemented under Bank finance with margin money ranging from 10 to 25 per cent as subsidy from KVIC. Since 70 per cent of the village industries programmes are implemented through state KVI Boards the margin money also may be released to the boards for assisting, implementing agencies of the programme.

Technical Support

The KVIC limited technical staff throughout the country and therefore it is not possible to extend full technical guidance for the growth of the industry. As such, the implementing agencies are advised to depute their suitable candidate for training both at Handmade Paper Institute, Pune and Kumarappa National Handmade Paper Institute, Sanganer, Jaipur to manage their units.

Steps to Establish Handmade Paper Units

The following actions are suggested for establishing the handmade paper units with a minimum possible gestation period.

(i) The implementing agencies may prepare detailed project report based on the model project profiles enclosed for the type of plant required by them with the help of professional consultants viz. Chartered Accountants and others. The project report may be furnished to their Bankers/KVIC, DVIBs for security and consideration.

(ii) On getting the Bank consent for funding the promoters may approach state KVIB or state office of KVIC for availing margin money as per rules.

(iii) Before construction of building, supply of soft water may be ensured by digging a bore-well or an open well at the site. Also letter of consent may be obtained from the nearby Electricity board authorities for power supply.

(iv) Provisional permission may be obtained from the regional water pollution control board for setting up the unit who will also issue permanent license after testing the affluent from the units.

(v) A few workers may be deputed for Artisan training before commencement of production activities.

From Table 9.1, it is clear that the working handmade paper units were increased from 84 in 1960-61 to 440 units in 1994-95. The value of production was also increased from Rs. 24.23 lakh in 1960-61 to Rs. 1,800 lakh in 1994-95. The employment opportunities provided by the units in India was 8,000 lakh persons. It is inferred that important rule in India for the economic development.

Table 9.1

Performance of Handmade Paper Industry in India

Year	*Working Units*	*Disbursement Grant*	*Loan*	*Production*	*Sales*	*Employment*	*Earnings*
1960-61	84	—	—	24.23	20.67	6,312	8.24
1965-66	149	—	—	38.68	35.97	4,754	14.43
1970-71	176	—	—	71.22	77.13	4,114	24.14
1975-76	188	—	—	138.00	145.00	4,144	44.63
1980-81	253	10.07	46.87	357.12	358.17	5,910	93.70
1985-86	275	1.40	45.21	439.00	463.00	5,500	131.00
1989-90	314	17.28	107.44	715.67	740.36	5,225	191.62
1990-91	329	16.15	192.62	782.97	842.99	5,829	237.65
1991-92	344	16.76	211.06	1,059.63	1,072.17	6,299	295.79
1992-93	394	15.54	400.49	1,243.48	1,278.18	6,102	340.05
1993-94	438	14.80	340.68	1,506.33	1,542.86	6,819	426.06
1994-95	440	—	—	1,800.00	1,900.00	8,000	510.00

Source: Project profile of handmade paper industry, Khadi Gramodyog, 1994.

Mahendra Mangalam Handmade Paper Unit: A Case Study

Production Process

In the handmade paper unit sector using different types of raw materials. Mostly agro-waste, textile waste, and other waste, which can't be used for commor. purpose.

Agro-waste	*Textile Waste*
1. Paddy straw	1. Cotton
2. Banana fibre	2. Hosiery cutting
3. Baggase	3. Gunny bags
4. Wheat Straw	4. Waste paper
5. Jute waste	5. Ropes
6. Bamboo	6. Fishing nets
7. Sunn-hemp	

There are 36 varieties of raw materials available in India. Some of them are the bark of the plant. Sometime the whole plant is used as the raw material. In Tamilnadu cotton waste, hosiery cutting, paddy straw, banana fibre waste, korai are mostly available. The textile waste are available regularly. This unit utilises some of the raw materials which listed below:

Table 9.2

List of Raw Materials

S.No.	*Raw Material*	*Rate* *Rs. tonne*	*Per Cent*
1.	Hosiery Cutting	8,000	52.02
2.	Tailoring Cutting	8,000	46.24
3.	Waste Paper	100	0.58
4.	Old gunny bags	100	0.58
5.	Fresh Cuttings	100	0.58
	Total	17,300	100.00

Source: Office Record in Mahendra Mangalam Handmade Unit.

In the handmade paper industry the essential raw materials which are used in producing handmade paper are hosiery cutting, tailoring etc. The main source for hosiery cutting is spinning mills which are located around Tripur and some other places. The cost of per ton hosiery cutting is Rs. 9,000. The another textile waste tailoring cutting is obtained from big and small tailoring shops. Garments manufacturing units etc., its cost is Rs. 8,000 per ton. The handmade paper industry gets the waste paper from general shops, the old gunny bags from gunny shops, and the fresh cuttings from this unit itself or from some other modern mills for paper. The cost of the above said raw materials are also used in the modern mills for producing paper. This is stated in the Table 9.2.

This handmade paper unit purchases the raw materials by tender method. It calls for open tender, in the tenders it specifies the type of the raw materials, quality of the raw material and quantity of raw material etc. After getting the quotations from all the sellers who asks tender, the authority selects one seller to purchase the raw material by analyzing all the quotations received.

Sorting and Dusting

This handmade paper unit has one sorting box for sorting the raw materials which is to be used in the production process. This unit dusting process is to find the unnecessary materials mixed in the raw material. For this purpose one dusting box is also available in this handmade paper unit. Sorting and dusting of raw materials is done by male labourers.

Cutting

The purpose of rag chopper machine is to cut or reduce the length of the raw material. With the help of this machine we can cut different type of raw materials for permanent iron stand length of 2.5 ft. and height of 2.5 ft. In the top of the iron bar there is a revolving type roller is fixed. In that roller, there are three knives in equal distance, these knives rotate parallel on top to a fixed based plate. There is a pushing roller which pushes the raw materials in equal distance or intervals. This pushing roller works with the help of a robe connected with cutting roller.

To reduce the length of the raw material, it is suitable for making pulp, otherwise the pulping time is to be increased and at the same time it could not get the quality pulp. So rag chopper is essential to cut the raw materials into small pieces. This handmade paper unit has one rag chopper machine for cutting process.

Soaking

The purpose of soaking raw materials is to remove dusts, non-cellulose materials, and to soften the raw material and cleaned and the hardness of the fibre is reduced. The effluent is not harm to soil or plants. Because very less percentage of chemicals is added at the time of soaking. This unit follows the above process for soaking the raw materials.

Pulp Making and Sizing

Pulp making is the important process in the production of handmade paper. In this process beater machine is used to convert the raw materials into pulp. We can set the pulp after grinding the raw materials in the beater machine. Unless the pulp is presized, the sheet is somewhat absorbent and is turned water leaf. The filter papers and blotting papers require absorbent. Resin is obtained as a by-product in the distillation of yellow resin turpentine. In this unit the sizing is done as a sub-process during the time of pulp making. For beater the sizing, will be done at the time when the raw material is in semi-pulp stage.

Lifting

This handmade unit is using dip vats. Eleven dip vats are used to produce hand-made paper. They also have two auto-vats. But these autovats are not used in the production process. The vat is filled three-fourths with water and the necessary amount of the pulp is poured in and the final volume of the linguised is made with more water. The man required are vat man who makes the sheet, the coucher who assist the vat man in spreading the cloth over the wet sheet on the frame and couches the sheet on the couching board and two assistants who press and dry the sheets.

Pressing

After lifting the wet sheet it is couched in wooden plant, this process is done continuously upto 200°C. That is placed for removal of water from the wet sheet. If the water is not removed from the wet sheet the paper is not suitable for calendering. So, the water has to be removed by uniform pressing. In olden days the water was removed by using of manpower. Due to the technological development, hydraulic press is used for squeezing the water from the wet sheet.

Drying

Drying is the next state of the production process. In this process the pressed wet papers are dried in the open place under the shed. For this purpose this unit have two sheds with asbestos roof. In these sheds there are number of ropes to dry the papers. Ropes are used to handle the wet sheets. After drying process is over the dry papers are sent to the calendering process.

Calendering

After drying the board the papers are come under the cleaning. While cleaning they sorts the papers according to the weights. In this handmade unit there are two polishing rooms. After drying, the surface is not suitable for paper and board, and is uneven. To make uniform surface this calendering machine is used. The calendering machine comprised two heavy weight iron rollers. The unpolished paper or board is arranged in between two g. 1. sheets then sheets are passed into the roller. When it pass in between the two rollers due to heavy pressure it make uniform surface on the board.

Cutting and Packing

Cutting is the final stage of the production process. Cutting is done by using cutting machine. This handmade paper unit has one cutting machine for this purpose. The paper is sized by the cutting machine according to the standard measurement specified by the T.N.K.I.B. If the buyers specify the measurement in his order, then the unit supplies the paper according to the size required by the buyer. After cutting process is finished the final paper is packed nicely by using polythene covers. Each pack contains 500 papers and it is technically called as a ream.

Table 9.3

Production Level in Mahendra Mangalam Unit

Year	*Quantity*	*Values* Rs.
1990-91	23,096	6,41,364
1991-92	29,800	7,68,640
1992-93	29,875	11,03,981
1993-94	18,700	7,56,937
1994-95	20,050	8,57,413

Source: Office records in Mahendra Mangalam Handmade Paper Unit.

From the above table we can get the information about the production of the unit which is taken for study. In production any unit cannot be taken as standard one, it depends only on the demand and sales of the particular product in the market. In the year 1990-91 this unit produced Rs. 6,41,364 worth of products and in the year 1992-93 this was increased to Rs. 11,03,981. This was a healthy improvement in the production of this unit. In 1994-95 it was slightly decreased to Rs. 8,57,413.

Quality Control

Though quality control facilities are available in most of the handmade paper units, they are seldom made use of. Even if the units are aware of the quality products produced and sold by them.

Quality Planning

Quality of the paper products was planned by Tamilnadu KVIB by considering the standards specified for all standards for each type of papers. This handmade paper unit produces various types of paper. The Table 9.4 gives the details about various types of paper and their standard quality specification. We can produce different types of paper in the handmade paper industry. Each type of paper has its own standard quality (G.S.M).

Table 9.4

Various Types of Paper

S.No.	*Types of Paper*	*Standard Quality (G.S.M.)*
1.	Wrapping paper	70 — 100
2.	Writing paper	70
3.	Bond paper	80 — 100
4.	Manifolding paper	30 — 40
5.	Impression paper	80 — 100
6.	Rags mottled paper	100 — 140

Source: Office Records of Mahendra Mangalam Handmade Paper Unit.

G.S.M. means gram per square meter. This varies from one type to another type of paper. Standard quality of each paper is formulated by handmade experts and scientiets and this was standardised by world level organisations. Every industry or unit in India or abroad should follow these specification for the types of papers to be produced. The Table 9.4 clearly explains the various types of papers and its standard quality (GSM).

Scheme of Quality Control

In this unit quality control is done at each stage of the

production process. At first, the supervisor checks the quality of the raw material which is obtained from various sources. During the sizing stage, sizing will be done according to the quality specified for the paper to be produced.

After getting the finished product the quality will be measured by various quality control schemes. Among those schemes, this handmade paper unit implements some simple schemes like checking the absorption of paper by pouring ink on the edges of the paper and taken one small bit as sample from the paper produced to measure the G.S.M. The size of the paper is maintained by setting the measurement constant for all the papers to be sized. This measurement will be specified by the consumer through Tamilnadu Khadi and Village Industries Board (TKVIB). The measurement will be checked periodically for every thousand papers by the person who sizes the paper with the help of cutting machines.

Implementation of Quality Control

Quality control can be done once in a month/once in a week/once in a day/continuous sequence in any industry. This unit quality control is done in continuous sequence throughout the day when the productions take place. To maintain the quality, this unit implements some simple schemes already discussed in the scheme of quality control paper. At present this unit uses only 18 kg. of raw material for production. So it doesn't need a separate quality control department. This quality control job is done by the supervisor itself.

Marketing

Market refers to the aggregate demand of the potential buyers for a product.

Marketing is also said that to refer the activities which effect transfer in ownership of goods and their physical distribution.

"Marketing is a total system of interacting business activities designed to plan price, promoted and distribute want satisfying products and services to present and potential customers"—Willam J. Stamtion.

Functions and Objectives of Marketing

I. Function of Exchange:
1. Buying and Assembling
2. Selling.

II. Physical Distribution:
1. Transportation.
2. Storage and Warehousing.

III. Facilitating Function:
1. Financing.
2. Risk taking, burglary, bad debts, decay, deterioration.
3. Standardisation.
4. Grading (Equality).

Objectives of Marketing

(i) To develop an intelligent appreciation of modern marketing practice.
(ii) To provide guidelining policies regarding the marketing procedures and their implementation.
(iii) To study marketing problems according to circumstances and to suggest solution.
(iv) To analyse the shortcoming in the existing pattern of marketing.

Sales

Marketing is the soul of any business without which survival and longing of any business will be questioned. Paper sales are in ream quantity. Each ream will have 500 sheets. Sales price is not a standard one, it varies from time to time according to the quality of paper or situation.

Sales can be classified into two types—cash sales and credit sales. Cash sales always said to be healthy in the case of any business. In actual practice major traders can't avoid credit sales in order to maintain the optimum turnover. No doubt that credit sales will create many problems of collection of dues and sometime this may lead to loss also.

The unit taken for study practices cash sales for private consumers and both cash sales and credit sales for government departments. This unit gives cash bill for the consumers who purchases the paper for cash and credit bill for the credit purchasers. It avoids credit sales for the private people, because there is lack of personnel to do jobs like collection dues, maintaining all records with regard to credit transaction.

Methods of Sales

In the handmade paper unit, different techniques are followed for selling different products through different ways. Most of the units follow only types of sales, for selling their products.

(a) Direct Sales

The final products are directly sold to the buyers by the seller is called direct sales. This method of sales followed by this unit for selling their product in the local market. Suppose the buyer resides in some other place which is more distant from the unit means he purchases the product through the orders. After getting the orders, this unit produces the product according to the quality and amount specified in the order. Then the produced goods are sent to the buyer through vehicles.

(b) Indirect Sales

Indirect sales means selling the goods to the buyer, with the help of middle man. This method is followed only for export market. This unit has no export market, so it doesn't need method of sales.

The Table 9.5 shows the total quantity of products sold and its money value for the past five years. This typically shows the market tendency for the particular unit. In the year 1990-91, the sales is 10,01,870, but this sales decreased to Rs. 6,86,831 in the year 1994-95. This shows the marketing inability of the unit.

Table 9.5
Sales Value of HMP

Year	*Quantity*	*Value* *Rs.*
1990-91	30,411	10,01,870
1991-92	20,662	7,71,012
1992-93	15,540	9,86,510
1993-94	10,983	7,84,763
1994-95	12,163	6,86,831

Source: Office record in Mahendra Mangalam Handmade Paper Unit.

Finance

Function is continued in Financial Management. Financial Management is the specialised branch of general management which is related to the procurement of finance and its efficient utilisation for the achievement of a common goods.

Financial Management function is divided into two parts. Such As: Executive finance function, Incidental Finance Function.

The above two functions of financial management take an important place in general management. Like functions are modification of data, analysis of data, formation business budget. Supervision of cash receipt, payment keeping, record credit, management.

Source of Finance

Source of finance are broadly divided into two types. One is short-term finance, another one is long-term finance.

(i) Short-term finance

The funds which are available for a period of one year or less is called short-term finance. In India, short-term finance are used to finance working capital.

(ii) Long-term Finance

The funds which are available for more than one year is called long-term finance. Long-term finance is used for purchasing the land, to construct the building, to install machines and for some permanent installations.

The long-term finance and short-term finance for this particular handmade paper unit is financed by TKVIB. In the year 1960 TKVIB sanctioned 1 lakh as long-term finance for this unit. Every year certain percentage of profit was paid to the TKVIB by this unit to refund the obtained long-term finance.

Annual profit is the only source of short-term finance for this unit. It utilises this profit to meet the working capital need. From no other source this unit obtains the short-term finance.

Personnel

Organization

Organization refers to the structure of relationship among position and jobs which is built up for the realisation of common objective.

Importance

(i) To facilitate administration.
(ii) It makes growth and diversification possible.
(iii) It provides for the optimum use of technological improvement.
(iv) It stimulates independent, creative thinking and initiative through well-defined areas of mark.

Organization Structure

Organizational structure is divided into two types. One is official, another one is non-official. Official means it is directly involved in the work and non-official means staff like accounts line. The Table 9.6 shows the employee status in the units.

Table 9.6
Staff and Workers

Sl. No.	*Designation*	*No. of Workers*	*Per Cent*	*Wages Rs.*	*Per Cent*
1.	Superintendent	1	2.08	3,000	27.87
2.	Lower Division Clerk	1	2.08	1,500	13.90
3.	Lifter	1	2.08	1,200	11.11
4.	Pulp Making Assistant	2	4.16	1,200	11.11
5.	Glazing Assistant	2	4.16	1,200	11.11
6.	Sevaks	2	4.16	1,200	11.11
7.	Watchman	1	2.08	900	8.23
8.	Labour on piece rate system	19	39.58	300	2.8
9.	Labour on daily wage system	19	39.58	300	2.8

Source: Office Record in Mahendra Mangalam Handmade Paper Unit.

Organization is an essential one for any business or industry. Without this any one cannot run business or industry smoothly in a positive manner.

From the Table 9.6 we can get information about the manpower consumption of this unit. In the table it is clearly stated by specifying the designation of workers, number of workers working under each designation and their salary and wage.

Organization of the Unit

This unit does not have efficient organisational structure. There is no top level management to manage the activities of this unit. The organisation of this unit is a vertical one. Superintendent is the superior authority of this unit. He is the only responsible person for all the activities of this handmade paper unit. There are 48 persons working in this unit at various levels under the control of superintendent. The wages and salary for the workers are sanctioned by the superintendent. To maintain the accounts and other official files, superintendent has one assistant. The designation of the assistant is lower division clerk. The other workers who are involved in the production, are skilled and unskilled workers.

The skilled workers are utilised in the production process and the unskilled workers are utilised to clean the premises, to dry the wet paper and to do some simple works.

Problems of Mahendra Mangalam Handmade Paper Unit

The Mahendra Mangalam handmade paper unit has some problems. They are as follows:

(i) This unit suffers due to lack of efficient management for the recent days.
(ii) The labourers working in this unit as daily wagers, want to regularise them as permanent workers.
(iii) The workers of this unit need some basic facilities like transport etc.
(iv) The unit does not have a efficient advisory committee to obtain advises in various fields like production, sales.
(v) This unit has some difficulties in getting the working capital assistance from government every year.
(vi) The workers are not getting their wages regularly.
(vii) This unit has no separate vehicle to transport their produced products.
(viii) The machines and equipments installed in this unit were very old, so the unit needs some amount frequently to maintain the machines.

Suggestions

The following suggestions are useful for the effective functioning of the Mahendra Mangalam Handmade Paper Unit.

(i) It is satisfactory that workers are getting normal wages in the Mahendra Mangalam Handmade Paper Unit. In view of the medium turnover of the unit, labour should be well remunerated, as this would dissolve in to better industrial relations and boost employees moral and output.
(ii) It is suggested that in places where agricultural waste is available in abundance should be linked and integrated with paper unit. Agencies can organise

such activities as the land development bank, KVIC which will enhance proper utilization on raw material resources thereby increasing the output.

(iii) The capacity of the utilization should be improved and well utilized viz., full utilization of existing installed capacity of the handmade paper unit should be ensured.

(iv) An increase in the sanitary facilities is necessary which considers the increase in the number of employees.

Conclusion

The conclusion from the foregoing case study, it is appropriate to say that handmade paper is an important unit with regard to the economic point of view. The unit contributes substantially towards economic development of the Musiri taluk of Trichy district. Its intermediate technology answers the vital socio-economic questions of the rural people and for rural development. It is appropriate to conclude that the unit utilizes scarce resources to the best extent possible based on environment friendly. Therefore in view of the unit tangible benefits to the economy of our country it can be viable project for the developing countries like India.

References

1. G.M., Mathur, "A Promising Hand Made Paper Raw Materials", *Khadi Gramodyog*, Volume XXXV, No. 8, May 1989.
2. M. Boommiah, "Utilisation of Forest Barks for Hand Made Paper", *Khadi Gramodyog*, Volume XXXVI, No. 10, July 1990, pp. 408-10.
3. Devendra, "Problems and Improvement in Hand Made Paper from Printers Point of View", *Khadi Gramodyog*, Volume XXXVII, No. 10, July, 1991, pp. 377-86.
4. M.N. Kolase, "Utilisation of Parthenium Weed for Card Board Making", *Khadi Gramodyog*, Volume XXXVIII, No. 1, Oct. 1991, pp. 534-36.
5. S.N. Singh, "Solution to Paper Shortage", *Khadi Gramodyog*, Volume XXVII, No. 11, Aug. 1981, pp. 578-82.
6. S.N. Singh, "Global Scene and the Third World", *Khadi Gramodyog*, Volume XXVII, No. 12, Sep. 1981, pp. 578-82.

7. S.N. Dhaundial, "The Capital Investment and Employment", *Khadi Gramodyog,* Volume XXXVI, No. 12, Sep. 1981, pp. 435-37.
8. N.B. Gore, "Future Possibilities", *Khadi Gramodyog,* Volume XXXVIII, No. 2, March 1991, pp. 40-44.
9. V.K. Kalmegh, "Economic Viability", *Khadi Gramodyog,* Volume XXXIV, No. 3, May, pp. 340-45.
10. B.D. Gupta, "Marketing and Reservation", *Khadi Gramodyog,* Volume XXXV, No. 7, July 1989, pp. 38-42.
11. N.P. Paritrakar, "Production Pattern and Standard", *Khadi Gramodyog,* Volume XXXIV, No. 1, Oct. 1990, pp. 44-52.

10

Village Oil Industry

The vegetable oils are essential ingredients of food needed for the growth and maintenance of human body. Crushing of oil-seeds to obtain edible oil for human consumption has been an age-old village industry in India. It provides nutritious oil with natural flavour and taste. Either they have been crushing oil-seeds procured by themselves or providing oil extraction service to oil-seed producers. Thus the *telis* have been an important component of the village society.

The village oil industry employed lakhs of artisans in rural areas. Therefore, it is an important sector in the industrial fabric of the country. The indisputable fact that this item of human diet, has to be supplied in its fresh, unadulterated and nutritive form, serves as the basis and justification for village oil industry.

In view of its indispensable position in the rural economy and with a view to restructuring this important but declining industry, the KVIC took up number of steps. These aimed at bringing the *telis* under some kind of organisational umbrella preferably a co-operative set-up, giving them improved equipment viz improved power-operated Ghani, with a view to improving the technological base of the industry and thereby enhancing their earnings, training them in the operation and manufacture of improved tools and equipment providing them financial assistance for stocking oil-seeds, conducting research and field trials to bring about improvements in the overall functioning of the Industry.

The industry has taken countries for its evolution from the *chappa* to bullock-driven *ghani*. Since 1972, the ghani has undergone a radical change from technological point of view from bullock-driven to overhead power-operated ghani and to portable mortar rotating power ghani and finally overhead power ghani. As such the introduction of power ghani has helped the operator in getting higher earnings. It has thus been a major technological breakthrough in the field of oil ghani industry. The introduction of protable power ghani has also minimised the gestation period since no foundation is required and it can be assembled, installed and operated in a few hours, provided, of course, the power is available.

This industry renders service to the society in two-ways—it supplies fresh, flavoured and nutritious oil to the consumers on the one hand, and provides employment to the traditional artisans and others unemployed, on the other.

The Sources of Availability of Edible Oil Seeds in India Are:

Mustard: U.P., Bihar, West Behgal, North Eastern States, Jammu and Kashmir, Punjab, Haryana, Himachal Pradesh and parts of Rajasthan

Groundnut: Tamilnadu, Maharashtra, Gujarat, Madhya Pradesh, Southern parts of Karnataka and Andhra Pradesh

Gingely: Rajasthan, Southern parts of Tamilnadu, Andhra Pradesh (coastal area) and Gujarat

Coconut: Goa, Kerala and coastal areas of Karnataka, Tamil Nadu

Safflower: (Kardi) Marathwada region of Maharashtra and parts of Karnataka

Linseed: Vidarba region of Maharashtra

A further discussion portrays that India is the world's largest producer of groundnut, seasamum and niger. The castor and safflower rank second, while rape seed-muscara, linseed and coconut rank third. The major edible oil-seed crops are groundnut, mustard, rapeseed, sesamum, soybean, sunflower, safflower nigerseed and coconut while castor seed and linseed are the important non-edible oil-seeds. The minor but non-conventional oil seeds viz. neem, sal, karanja, kokum, mango kernel, mahua and punnai also contribute substantially to the oil market of India. As a result of the larger scale plantations of oil palm in various parts of the country indigenous palm oil has been made available in small quantity in the recent period.

Sources of Commercial Fats and Oils

Oils and fats are essential constituents of all forms of plant and animal life, with differing characteristics which intact from the bases for the Industrial applications. The available sources of vegetable oil in the country can be categorised into

- *(a)* Seasonal oil seeds—such as groundnut, mustard/ rapeseed, sesamum, sunflower, safflower, niger, soyabean, castor and linseed.
- *(b)* Pernnial oilseeds—such as cocount and oil palm
- *(c)* Minor oil goods—such as dal, neem, karanja, mahua, piea etc.
- *(d)* crop by-products—such as rice bran and cotton seed, besides residue oil obtained from oil cakes.

Table 10.1

Area-Yield and Production of Edible Oil Seed Crop in India, During 1980-81—1992-93

Oil Seed Crop	*Year 1980-81*			*Year 1992-93*		
	A	*Y*	*P*	*A*	*Y*	*P*
Groundnut	6,802	736	5,005	8,351	1,060	8,854
Rape/mustard	4,113	487	2,002	6,305	773	3,872
Sunflower	119	555	66	2,093	566	1,185
Soyabean	61	728	44	3,626	856	3,106
Sesamum	2,172	180	446	2,364	361	853
Safflower	720	465	335	907	414	342
Niger	598	244	146	590	308	182

A=Area in 00'0 hec, Y=Yield in kg/ha, P=Production in '000' mt.

Source: Oil seeds in India, 1996.

The production of oil-seeds started showing trends of increase from 12.70 million tonnes (per hect 620 kg.) in 1987-88 to 22.37 millions tonnes (650 kg/hect) yield in 1995-96. The favourable price structure for oil-seeds did induce farmers to devote more area for oil-seeds. However even today our average yields compare very poorly with the average yields obtained elsewhere in the world. With regard to performance of major individual oil-seed crops, the situation is not altogether different.

Minor Oils

There are 200 different tree borne oil-seeds having 10 per cent oil content, only dozen species are being exploited for oil extraction to some extent. If all these oil-seeds are extracted, there will be surplus of oil after meeting the industrial requirement.

Vegetable Oils

In India, vegetable oils are marketed in various forms like filtered or unprocessed oils, refined vegetable oils, vanaspathi or partially hydrogenated oils, and industrial hardened oils. From the data, it is evident that groundnut oil and mustard/rape seed oils have dominated the market. They will be continued to do so because of consumer preferences. These two oils hold more than two-thirds of share of the market.

Vanaspathi

Vanaspathi is a partially hydrogenated fat. It is usually a blend of several partially hydrogenated oils. The major oils used for vanaspathi are oils extracted from cottonseed, soyabean, rice bran, sunflower, safflower, mustard, rapeseed, mahua, maizniger seed and sal. Almost 70 per cent of the available cottonseed oil and 80 per cent of the soyabean oil are utilised in the manufacture of vanaspathi. The use of non-conventional oils for the manufacture of vanaspathi has increased in recent years. Vanaspathi was quite popular until

1970s. However, after the mid-1970 the educated class people started shifting towards the consumption of refined oils as coronary atheroscierosis became a serious health concerned which is believed to be enhanced due to the consumption of vanaspathi.

Nutritional Importance of Oils and Fats

Oils and fats have been used by man in good preparations for many centuries now. Oils and fats are important sources of our energy requirements. For weight they furnish 2.25 times more energy than proteins and carbohydrates. Thus they help reduce the bulk of food we take. Oils and fats are excellent sources of fat soluble vitamins A, D, E & K. Oil provides the essential fatty acids, linolic acid, which is needed for human health.

Oil seeds are also rich in proteins and oil cake obtained after extraction of oils from seeds can be processed to product protein rich foods. Such foods are in the market and have helped solve the protein deficiency of vulnerable sections of our population such as infants, children and pregnant mothers.

Table 10.2

Recommended Scale for Balanced Diet Compared with Actual

Commodity	*g/head/day*		
Foodstuff	*Recommended*	*Available*	*Percentage*
Cereals	400	436	109.00
Pulses	85	38	44.71
Fats/oil	28	19	68.00
Sugar	57	38	67.00
Vegetables	280	120	42.86
Fruits	120	40	(33.3)

Source: Shathatala Manay, 1987.

The Indian Council of Medical Research has suggested the above scale for providing a balanced diet to an average adult Indian. Thus the average availability of food (especially fats and oils) to an Indian is less than the recommended level.

The annual per capita consumption of oil is estimated about 7.0 kg. as against recommended level of 18 kg. To fulfil the demand of edible oils, imports had to be initiated. It is evident from the data that our imports were as high as 3 lakh metric tonnes absorbing a foreign exchange of about Rs. 1,500 crore.

Table 10.3

Edible Oil Production and Per Cent Share of Imports in India

Year	*Production (in lakh tonnes)*	*Per Cent Import in Total Production*
1971-72	25.43	3
1980-81	25.60	32
1987-88	34.63	36
1993-94	53.97	2
1996-97	63.00	3

Source: Kisan World, 1998.

Status of Oil Processing Industry

There are several devices available for oil crushing such as ghanis, rotaries, expellers and solvent extraction plants. The country's production of edible oil-seeds was only 22 million tonnes during the year 1996-97 and it is far below than the

Table 10.4

Status of Oil Processing Industry

Sl. No.	*Processing Unit*	*Number*
1.	Village ghanis	4,00,000
2.	Oil mills	15,000
3.	Solvent extraction units	350
4.	Refineries	100
5.	Vanaspathi plants	90

Source: Kisan World, 1998.

actual requirement for fullest capacity utilisation of the above machines. The present status of processing industry is shown in the Table 10.4.

These industries put together has the in-built capacity to process over 30 million tonnes oil-seeds. However, capacity utilisation is not beyond 60 per cent in most of the cases.

Ghanies

One of the rural industries which have lived through the bright and dark days of our country is ghani oil industry. The ghani oils are being used to fulfil our fats requirements in our country since ages. The crushing was done by village oil man and fresh oil was supplied to the rural populations. People prefer the natural colour and flavour of the ghani pressed oils. Almost all varieties of oil-seeds can be crushed in ghanies. There are 4 lakh ghanis in India and they provide employment to the extent of 4 lakh artisans. However, it is understood that their capacities are not being fully utilised due to the shortfall in oil-seed supply.

The 4 lakh ghanis available in India have a crushing capacity of 30 lakh tonnes of oil-seeds. This is only 18 per cent of the total oil-seeds available for crushing. The remaining oil-seeds available in the country are crushed by mill sector. But mill sector provides employment only to 75 thousand peoples.

Oil processing is traditionally a village industry and was exclusively the province of the village *telis* till the last quarter of last century. Then oil mills entered the field.

These mills gained ground over a period of seven to eight decades and affected the village oil industry. To face competitions from mill sector, technological development needed for ghani sector.

Technological Developments in Ghanis

The bullock ghanies which existed till 1954 were about 500 years old. Except some minor changes in size or shape, the ghani has not undergone any change during this period. There productivity is not increased. These traditional bullock ghanis were owned by the *telis* (oil mongers) whose income was very low. So, technological development in ghanis felt needed to increase the production, yield rate, reduce drudgery and also to improve the earnings of the people engaged in this sector. With this objective in view the Research and Development Wing of Khadi and Village Industries Commission has taken so many experiments. They introduced appropriate technologies for the development of ghanis.

Introduction of Appropriate Technology for Ghanis

The appropriate technology should have the following characteristics.

1. The technology should reduce the drudgery
2. It should enable the users to earn more wages.
3. It should improve the productivity and quality.
4. It should help to utilise the local raw materials.
5. It should also help to diversify the product.
6. The technology should be labour-oriented and not capital intensive.

The ghani has mainly four components viz:

(a) Ghani drum, (fatcher)
(b) a rotating wooden pestle (lat)
(c) a mechanism for providing pressure
(d) a motive power for rotation of pestle.

The technological development were taken place in the above mentioned components.

Traditional Ghanis

The main features of traditional ghanis are as follows.

1. The mortar is made out of stone or wood
2. The pestle is made out of wood
3. The pressure is applied by a connecting tie to load beam and the pestle in a triangular way; some heavy weight is put at the end of the load beam which applies the pressure, and
4. The motive power is bullock or camel.

The traditional ghanis are not fitted with any drudgery removing mechanisms. There were no drainages in the ghani to drain out the oil. It requires 3 to 4 hours to complete a charge. The recovery rates were very low. The area required for operation was also high. So these ghanis were economical.

Improved Ghanis

In this ghani the length of the pestle was reduced (5 feet). The tie-rod of the load is replaced with arms made out of stander mild steel plates. The pestle cap is made with a separate piece of wood and fitted with two taper roller bearings and connected with arms. These ghanis were run with single bullock. The area required for functioning of this ghani was only 100 sq. ft. Whereas it is 400 sq. ft in the case of traditional ghani. The crushing time also considerably reduced.

Concept of Power Ghani

Even after making all the improvements is the traditional ghani evolving standardised and improved ghanis. The ghani oil industry could not pull on well. Since,

(i) the bullocks consumed practically all the income earned by the artisan.
(ii) with the gradual mechanisation of the agricultural sector, use of animal power exclusively for running the ghanis became an uneconomic proposition,
(iii) during the late sixties establishment of the high capacity extraction units in country made not only ghani units but even small expeller units also uneconomical and the traditional and improved ghanis could not sustain competition.

Technical experts committee constituted by khadi commission recommended for the introduction of power ghani during 1968. Subsequently the Jamnalal Bajaj Central Research Institute, Ward designed and fabricated a power ghani during the year 1969 which was modified by KVIC with the help of the technical committee in the year 1970. They designed a power ghani with overhead drive mechanism which has two distinct characteristics. On the one hand it did not disturb the basic design of the improved ghani because the ghani drum though made out of iron was fitted with wooden fatcher and the Epestle too was made of wood and in the other hand the overhead drive could be fitted in any improved or standardised ghani. These ghanis were accepted by artisans in all parts of the country. The drawback in this ghani is that it requires a sizable quantity of timber to construct the overhead.

The artisan found it difficult to arrange timber for the construction of overhead power ghani. This problem has given serious thoughts and researches were conducted in order to find out a ghani which does not require cement and timber. This ghani has distinct features that

- *(i)* it can be assembled and commissioned within a few hours,
- *(ii)* it is an appropriate technology to reduce drudgery of straticans with increased productivity,
- *(iii)* it is very much compact in structure,
- *(iv)* occupies less floor space, and
- *(v)* does not require any cement for foundation and timber for structure.

The technical data of improved bullock driven ghani overhead power ghani and portable power ghani are given in Table 10.5.

The Table 10.5 clearly indicates that the portable power ghani is the best among all types of ghanis. The yield rate is higher in these ghanis when compared to traditional and improved ghanis.

The ghani oil faces the following problems:

1. The problems of irregular supply of seeds due to heavy competition from mills sector.
2. Shortage of fund for purchase and stocking of oil-seeds in time.
3. Low yield rate which leads to high cost of production.
4. The facility for testing the quality of oil-seed, oil and cake is remote in ghani sector.
5. Inadequate facility for oil-seed decortication.

Table 10.5

Performance Compression of Ghanis

Sl. No.	*Particulars*	*Improved Ghani Bullock Driven*	*Overhead Power Ghani*	*Portable Power Ghani*
1.	Capacity per charge (kg.)	6 to 10	12 to 15	12 to 15
2.	Daily crushing capacity	60 to 80	100	115
3.	Crushing time per charge (mts.) Groundnut/gingelly	90	60	50
4.	Cost on motive power Rs. (8 hours) Groundnut/gingelly	30	15	18
5.	Floor space required (sq. ft)	400	80	36
6.	Cost of machine Rs.	20,000	30,000	35,000
7.	Increase in yield rate when compared to traditional ghanis	1%	2%	2%

Source: Khadi Gramodyog, November, 1985.

Importance of Ghani Oil Industry

(i) The ghani oil is good for health since it is consumed in its pure and natural flavour/form

(ii) Ghani sector helps in solving the problem of rural employment because it possesses potentiality to generate employment

(iii) The ghani industry strengthens rural economy as the local raw materials are processed locally.

(iv) Since the level of production is small in Ghani. The chances of adulteration are less.

(v) It does not pollute the environment.

(vi) It does not create any urban problem involving congestion, housing, transport, water supply etc.

(vii) Ghani, pressed oils, being cold drawn ground 60°C retain natural nutrients, natural characteristics, aroma tase, pungoncy, colour and vitamins whereas the machine pressed oils lack these properties due to high temperture generated during processing of the seeds as the crushing takes place between metal parts.

Ghani Oil Industry in India

The oil-seeds occupy pivotal position in the agricultural economy of india. They happen to be the second largest category of crops produced after foodgrains. The cultivation of major oil-seeds covers an area of about 27 million hectares. This consitute about 10 per cent of the total agricultural production in value terms and are next only to foodgrains. India is second largest country in terms of area allotted to oil-seeds accounting for about 10 per cent of the world oil-seeds. On the production front, India stands fourth in the world next only to USA, China and Brazil.

Table 10.6

Production, Sales, Employment Productivity Per Capita Earnings, Performance for the Last Five Years Under Ghani Oil Industry

Year	*Production Rs.*	*Sales*	*Employment FT nos.*	*Employment PT nos.*	*Productivity Rs.*	*Per Capita Earnings*
1990-91	39,436.35	32,980.81	51,390	45,871	31,294	3,439
1991-92	32,006.67	34,648.30	47,354	44,867	34,706	8,594
1992-93	33,218.43	36,616.12	45,505	47,287	35,798	3,576
1993-94	32,518.22	35,615.88	44,256	43,879	37,752	4,193
1994-95	35,843.72	35,972.38	46,256	45,879	37,479	3,848

Source: Annual Reports, KVIC, Mumbai, 1990-91 to 1995-96.

Working and Maintenance Guideline

1. Before starting the ghani it should be seen whether all the three pilot lamps are burning i.e whether there is proper flow of current in all the three phases.
2. All the seeds should not be put into ghani at a time. In the beginning it should be slowly fed. It is better if very little quantity of seed is put in the pit at the time of starting and the rest is accumulated on the tray and slowly fed.
3. Another important thing that is necessary for proper pressing is reduction in addition of water as compared

to bullock ghani. This is necessary because the pressure exerted on the cake is much higher. Similarly the oil drain is opened after about 10 minutes of working and in case of oil-seed with higher percentage of oil or soft in nature the drain may be kept open even from the beginning. If the pestle shows the tendency to come out the material of the lower champer is removed through dunka hole as well as from the top.

The pressure may also be reduced to some extent. Feeding the ghani can be distributed in 2 to 3 stages in first 10 to 15 minutes after watching the disintegration process. This may help proper disintegration and the tendency of lot coming up is reduced.

4. In the beginning the pressure nut should be loosened to release pressure from the spring but the spring should not be allowed to come out the guide collar on its side. The pressure will automatically increase as the seed is fed into the ghani and layer of material increases in thickness.

   The pressure of the spring is gradually increased for proper pressing. The cake thickness may give the required judgement for proper pressing. The cake thickness should be uniformly maintained, undue pressure will give unnecessary pressure on the ghani and the structure. The process of the pressing remains otherwise unchanged.
5. Pressure on the seed meal can be increased or decreased as per the flynut. However such variation in the pressure should be made gradually to get better results.
6. The ghani should be stopped when taking out the cake or when rectifying any defect in processing.
7. Sometimes the pestle gets pushed up by the collection of meal or oil cake underneath the pestle. It may be due to the following reasons:
   - *(a)* Due to dry seeds being fed with lesser amount of water
   - *(b)* Due to adding more quantity of water thereby blocking drain hole

(*c*) When the angle between the pressure screw and the pestle is below 90 degrees

This may be avoided when fully understood and detected. However no risk should be taken when pestle has been pushed sufficiently out of its proper position. At that time pressure should be released, drain should be opened and if necessary pestle should be taken out and the seed meal or cake in the lower part of pit should be completely removed and again the pestle be fited. If the pestle comes up often it may mean that the pestle is worn out and need replacement.

8. During operation if any unusual sound is heard it should be properly checked and defects should be rectified by stopping the ghani if necessary. Carelessness may cause damage to the equipment.
9. Ammeter: when the reading on Ammeter exceeds 3.5 amperes the machine should not be operated.
10. Voltmeter: The power ghani should not be operated

Table 10.7

Greasing/Oiling the Ghani Oil Industry

Sl. No.	*Items*	*Frequency of Greasing/Oiling*
1.	Ball bearing connected with counter shaft	Greasing once in a month
2.	Taper roller bearing No. 32211	Greasing once in a week
3.	Bearing no. 6218	Greasing once in a month, with grease pump through the hole provided
4.	Roller (a) Inside	Greasing once in a week
	(b) Outside (ring) of the drum	Daily oiling
5.	Pressure screw	Daily greasing

N.B. 1. Bearing grease is to be used for greasing.
2. Heavy duty oil is to be used for oiling.

when volt meter reading is below 360 volts or above 500 volts.

11. Pilot lamps: Ghani should not be operated if any of the three pilot lamps are not glowing.
12. Greasing/oiling:

Technical Data

Important technical data of portable power ghani are indicated below:

1.	Use	: For crushing oil seeds
2.	Power supply	: 440 volts; 3 phase 50 cycles
3.	Motor specification	: 2 HP 3 phase 1,440 RPM; I.S.I. marking with 'B' class Insulation
4.	Starter	: D.G.L. starter with single phasing prevention device
5.	Volt meter	: Range 0-500
6.	Ammeter	: Ramge 0-10
7.	Pilot lamp	: 3 numbers
8.	R.P.M. of drum	: 11
9.	Machine size (outer)	: Length, breadth, Height 4 ft 3ft 9 inch 5 ft
10.	Facher and pestle	: Wooden replaceable pit and wooden pestle
11.	Capacity	: 12 to 15 kg. of seed per charge
12.	Total weight of the machine including pestle and facher	: 530 kgs. (approximate)
13.	Painting	: On metal portation Base coat with red oxide by brush on all sides followed by enamel paint (Hammer stone I.S.I. standard) One bursh coat and final spary coat starer box : French polish
14.	No. of operator	: One for each unit of two ghanis
15.	Space required for operation	: 6 ft x 6 ft
16.	Average earning of worker a day (8 hrs)	: Rs. 30 to Rs. 40

17. Percentage of yield

(a) Groundnut	: 40 to 47 per cent
(b) Sesamum	: 40 to 45 per cent
(c) Coconut	: 60 to 63 per cent
(d) Mustard	: 25 to 33 per cent
(e) Safflower	: 48 to 50 per cent (on kernel)
18. Crushing time per charge	: 50 Minutes to 75 minutes (depending on variety and quality of seed)
19. Special feature	: Does not require any foundation or super-structure and can be commissioned almost instantly (within a day). It can be shifted from place to place.

Production Process

Groundnut crushing by power ghani

Capacity per chare	- 15 kg.
Oil extraction	- 33 per cent; cake 67 per cent
First water	- 200 ml (pulverisation stage)
Second water	- After 20 minutes 500 ml (cooking stage)
Third water	- After 40 minutes (100 ml before cake to be ducked out)

Total time taken for crushing 45 minute

Practical

To crush 15 kgs. of groundnut kernal in power ghani

Raw Material

1. Groundnut
2. Water

Apparatus

Power ghani
Enamal mug
Water container

Procedure

1. Put 15 kg. of groundnut kernal and operate the ghani
2. Sprinkle 200 ml of water in kernal
3. After 20 minutes add 500 ml of water in the power kernal
4. Apply more pressure to get the pulverisation kernel cook and to expect the oil
5. After 40 minutes sprinkle 100 ml water and open the oil outlet hole (Ruska hole and collect oil)
6. After 45 minutes extraction cake is removed
7. Both the cake and oil is taken and weighted

Result: Obtained 5 kg. of groundnut oil and 10 kgs. of cake.

A basic knowledge about the composition of oil-seed is of considerable help in evolving proper process for extracting oil.

Co-operative Society and Oil Industry: A Case Study

A case study has been conducted at KVI. 71 Batlagundu Oil Producers Cooperative Cottage Industrial Society Ltd., Nilakottai Taluk, Dindigul District.

Details of Batlagundu Oil Society

1. Society Name	: K.V.I. 71 Batlagundu Oil Producers Cooperative Cottage Industrial Society Ltd. Nilakottai Taluk, Dindigul District
2. Registration Date	: 2.2.1962
3. Society Starting Date	: 3.2.1964
4. Number of Members	: 164
5. Share Capital	: 3,055
6. Employers	: 4 Members

Value of Investment at the Year 1976

Electrical Oil Machines

Land Cost	: 40,000
Building Cost	: 75,000

Machine Estimation details:

Date of bought - 20.10.1976	Power ghani - No. 4 -	Rs. 13,022.00
Date of bought - 19.03.1976	Motor + foundation -	Rs. 950.00
Date of bought - 28.03.1977	Value of wood -	Rs. 761.00
Date of bought - 15.07.1977	Value of stone -	Rs. 600.00
Total cost for complete estimation		Rs. 15,333.00
Total investment,		Rs. 30,333.00

PERFORMANCE OF BATLAGUNDU COOPERATIVE POWER GHANI OIL SOCIETY

Evolution of the Society

Table 10.8

Share Capital in the Batlagundu Cooperative Society

Year	*No. of Members*	*Share Capital*	*Percentage Change in Share Capital*
1990-91	153	2,946	
1992-93	153	2,946	
1993-94	153	2,946	No change
1994-95	153	2,946	
1995-96	153	2,946	

Source: Office Records, Cooperative Society, 1991 to 1997.

The Table 10.8 reviews that the number of members and share capital of the society has not increased for the past five years from 1991-92 to 1995-96. The number of members are only 153 and share capital is Rs. 2,946 in the society. It is inferred that the society is earning the normal profit. So the members ever are constant for the past five years.

Working Capital

The working capital is a very important fund in any production unit. Lack of sufficient working capital will lead to shortage of raw material. Since raw material is the life line for production these items will lead to unemployment, stoppage of production which will further increase the loss in the production unit. So efficient working capital management is a very important task of the company's continuous flow of fund towards working capital is very essential. The working capital position of the society under study is given in the Table 10.9.

Table 10.9

Working Capital in the Society (Rs.)

Year	*Beginning of*	*End of the Year*	*Change*
1991-92	60,946.50	59,133.85	1,812.65
1992-93	59,133.85	56,340.75	2,793.10
1993-94	56,340.75	54,853.50	1,487.25
1994-95	54,853.50	50,625.50	4,228.00
1995-96	50,625.50	50,625.50	—

Source: Office Records, Cooperative Society, 1991 to 1996.

From Table 10.9 it is clear that the working capital was decreased from Rs. 60,946 to Rs. 59,133 and next year the working capital was decreased from Rs. 59,133 to Rs. 56,340. In 1993-94 the capital decreased from Rs. 56,340 to 54,883 and next year from Rs. 54,853 to 50,625 and next year the working capital is stable. During the study period 1991-92 to 1995-96 the working capital was decreased from Rs. 60,946 to 50,625.

Table 10.10

Raw Material Purchase

S.No.	*Year*	*Gingelly*	*Coconut*	*Groundnut*	*Palm Gur*
1.	1991-92	56,589.55	7,908.15	3,06,646.85	2,146.30
2.	1992-93	42,708.65	10,637.30	4,00,512.90	1,938.80
3.	1993-94	60,211.90	4,899.25	3,39,747.15	3,853.50
4.	1994-95	27,384.85	5,580.00	4,15,446.75	2,680.20
5.	1995-96	41,863.60	4,793.75	3,21,934.25	2,009.20

Source: Office Records, Coopertive Society, 1991 to 1996.

The Table 10.10 reveals that all raw materials show diminising trend during the study period. The value of groundnut, purchased in the society, was decreased from Rs. 43,60,646.85 in 1991-92 to 3,21,934.25 in 1995-96.

The table reveals that the next value of coconut purchased in society was decreased from Rs. 7,908.15 in 1991-1992 to Rs. 4,793.75 in 1995-96. The above table reveals that all raw materials shown diminising trend during the study period. The value of groundnut purchased in the society was decreased from Rs. 3,60,646 in 1991-92 to Rs. 3,21,934 in the year 1995-96.

Production

The produced oil and cake are sold in the market without handling the storage in the society so the production and sales value are same in the all items that is groundnut, ginelly and coconut oil and cake in the cooperative society.

Production of Groundnut

The production and sales of groundnut oil and cake are given in the Table 10.11.

Table 10.11

Production of Groundnut Oil (Value in Rs.)

S.No.	*Year*	*Oil*	*Cake*	*Total*
1.	1991-92	2,91,031.95	76,728.00	3,67,759.95
2.	1992-93	3,30,142.70	1,13,002.20	4,43,144.90
3.	1993-94	2,69,796.99	1,01,391.55	3,71,188.50
4.	1994-95	3,09,171.65	1,25,217.05	4,34,389.70
5.	1995-96	2,43,116.85	1,05,988.20	3,49,105.05

Source: Office Records, Cooperative Society, 1991 to 1996.

The total value of production of groundnut oil and cake was Rs. 2,91,031.95 in the year 1991-92 and it was decreased to Rs. 2,43,116.85 in the year 1995-96. It is inferred that the production value of cake of groundnut was increased from Rs. 76,728 in 1991-92 to Rs. 1,05,988 in 1995-96. The value of cake dominated in the groundnut section to previously four ghani were functioned but at present only two are functioning due to the low demand for the societies's product so that production level has been decreased in recent years.

Production of Gingelly

The production and sales of gingelly oil and cake is given in Table 10.12.

Table 10.12

Production of Gingelly (Value in Rs.)

S.No.	Year	Oil	Cake	Total
1.	1991-92	56,968.90	10,802.10	67,771.00
2.	1992-93	47,321.00	11,425.45	58,746.45
3.	1993-94	55,202.40	12,605.05	67,807.45
4.	1994-95	39,142.60	8,988.85	48,131.45
5.	1995-96	38,580.30	8,981.75	47,562.05

Source: Office Records, Cooperative Society, 1991 to 1996.

The total value of production of gingelly oil and cake was Rs. 56,968.90 in the year 1991-1992 and it was decreased to Rs. 38,580.30 in the year 1995-96. It is inferred that the production value of cake of gingelly was decreased from Rs. 10,802.10 in the year 1991-92 to Rs. 8,981.75 in the year 1995-96 the value of cake dominated in the gingelly section.

The Production of Coconut Oil

The production and sales of coconut oil and cake is given in the Table 10.13.

Table 10.13

Production of Coconut Oil (Value in Rs.)

S.No.	Year	Oil	Cake	Total
1.	1991-92	9,025.10	475.30	9,500.40
2.	1992-93	9,882.00	750.25	10,632.25
3.	1993-94	9,189.50	706.90	9,896.40
4.	1994-95	7,922.75	691.50	8,614.25
5.	1995-96	6,327.75	737.70	7,065.45

Source: Office Records, Cooperative Society, 1991 to 1996.

Table 10.14

Total Production in the Society During the Study Period

Year	Oil			Total	Cake			Total
	Groundnut	*Gingelly*	*Coconut*		*Groundnut*	*Gingelly*	*Coconut*	
1991-92	2,91,031.95	56,958.90	9,025.10	3,57,025.95	76,728.00	10,802.10	475.30	4,45,031.35
1992-93	3,30,142.70	47,321.00	9,882.00	3,87,345.70	1,13,002.20	11,425.45	750.25	5,12,523.60
1993-94	2,69,796.95	55,202.40	9,189.50	3,34,188.85	1,01,391.55	12,605.05	706.90	4,48,892.35
1994-95	3,09,171.65	39,142.60	7,922.75	3,56,237.00	1,25,217.05	89,88.85	691.50	4,91,134.40
1995-96	2,43,116.85	38,580.30	6,327.75	2,88,024.90	1,05,988.20	89,81.75	737.70	4,03,732.55

Source: Office Records, Cooperative Society, 1991 to 1996.

the quality of products, most of the people consider the low price product. So marketing is one of the serious problem of the co-operative society.

(*b*) The private ghani oil mill owners purchase the raw materials at low rate during the season and store at huge level in order to compensate the higher price for the raw materials during the non-season period, the procedure followed in the co-operative society is procurement of raw materials are very weak in the society has to purchase the raw materials at higher prices

(*c*) At present out of four power ghanis, only two are functioning in this co-operative society. The machineries are used on the basis of the demand for oil and cake. Due to the heavy competition in the market with the private ghani oil dealers the demand for oil and cake produced in the society is very low. So the fuller utilisation of the available machineries in the society are not possible. This is another serious problem.

(*d*) In an oil producers co-operative society there are two major items of production involved. They are oil and oil cake. The society under study produces three varieties of oil such as groundnut, gingelly and coconut. Since groundnut oil is mostly used for domestic use in Tamilnadu, its production is the highest.

(*e*) Even industry should calculate the cost of production of the product produced by the unit, for this purpose the industrial unit usually keep a cost chart. The cost chart will show the actual expenses, such as raw material cost, wages, electricity charges etc., which incurred for the production of the definite quantity of a particular product. The situation of price can be effected considering the cost of production. The cost of production does not include the overhead expenditure and marketing expenses and the profit margin. The manufacturer should add these items of expenditure with the cost of production when the sales price is fixed. Some commodities may have a uniform sales price in the market, for example, the non-edible oil soap produced by khadi and village industries sector follows a uniform price policy in Tamilnadu. In such cases the Industrial unit cannot fix a higher price than the price fixed by the uniform price commodities. But they can assess their profitability by knowing the cost of production. If the cost of production does not permit to include the above expenditure and really making a loss. Then the industrial unit must try to rectify the defect. They should analyse how the cost of production increases, what measures should be taken to reduce the cost of production. The cost of production can be minimised and the profit margin can be kept intact. So maintaining cost chart is very essential to understand where the industrial unit stand at a particular period.

(*f*) In the oil market there is no uniformity in price of different oils. The prices are fixed by each producers according to their own considerations. There will be even 20 per cent variations in the price of some variety from producer to producer. The quality depends upon the oil-seeds and also the processing method. So higher price fixation can be done by an oil producer if he is able to market the product.

Suggestions

1. The share capital of the society is very meagre. The society should raise the share capital in order to generate more fund towards working capital.
2. The society under study has not included all the overhead expenditure except depreciation. There must be provision to include all expenditure in the cost of production.
3. The price is not fixed correctly. A margin of 10 per cent is added along with cost of production which will not cover all the expenses. So naturally the unit under study will incur losses. In order to avoid the loss the overhead expenditure must be included with

cost of production and also a profit margin of 10 per cent should be added so that the society can avoid loss. But if there is high variation between the price fixed by the society and prevailing market price, the sales will be effected. In such cases concentration should be given to purchase suitable quality of raw materials at lower rate.

4. The society should make sets to increase its membership position.
5. An oil producers cooperative society which is functioning with two ghanis is not economical. It should increase the number of power ghanis. There must be minimum of 10 ghanis in the society.
6. An efficient marketing system should be avoided in order to sell more oil. Thereby the society can produce more for this purpose. The society should have some marketing links with Madurai city.

Conclusion

Edible oil is an essential item in human diet because it contains fat which is very essential for the human body. An average Indian is expected to consume about 50 gms. of oil every day. But the consumption is very low. It is about 20 gms. in a day. The very low consumption is due to shortage in the supply of oil. The country faces oil shortage for the past three decades. In order to increase the production of oil, all sources of equipments must be utilised. Since ghani is a simple machine which need low capital and small quantity of raw materials, it must be encouraged. There is always a possibility of cheating village oil manager by merchants. To overcome this cheating, formation of industrial cooperative is very essential. There are number of oil producers co-operative societies in Tamilnadu. But performance of many societies is not satisfactory.

References

1. J.L. Chandani, and K. Selvaraj, "Technological Development in Ghani Oil Industry", *Khadi Gramodyog*, Vol. XXXII, October,

November, 1985, Khadi and Village Industries Commission, Bombay.

2. *Annual Report of KVIC, 1995-96,* Khadi and Village Industries Commission, Bombay-56.
3. P.V. Shrikanta, *A Study of Village Oil Industry in India*—Appropriate Technology Development Association, Lucknow.
4. *Oil Seeds in India,* The Quantity of Economic and Market Research, New Delhi, 1996.
5. Satyabrava Maiti, *et al., Handbook of Annual Oil Seed Crops,* Sultan Chand & Sons, Delhi, 1988.
6. N. Shakuntala Manay and M.S. Shadaskharaswamy, *Foods, Facts and Principles,* Mohinder Singh Sejwal for Wiley Eastern Ltd., New Delhi, 1987.
7. The Editor, *Kisan World,* February, 1998, Guindy, Chennai.

Index